There's More To Life
Than Surface

There's More To Life Than Surface

Kate Turkington

PENGUIN BOOKS

PENGUIN BOOKS

Published by the Penguin Group
27 Wrights Lane, London W8 5TZ, England
Viking Penguin, a division of Penguin Books USA Inc, 375 Hudson
Street, New York, New York 10014, USA
Penguin Books Australia Ltd, Ringwood, Victoria, Australia
Penguin Books Canada Ltd, 10 Alcorn Avenue, Toronto, Ontario, Canada
M4V 3B2
Penguin Books (NZ) Ltd, 182-190 Wairau Road, Auckland 10, New Zealand
Penguin Books (South Africa) (Pty) Ltd, 1A Eton Road, Parktown,
South Africa 2193

Penguin Books (South Africa) (Pty) Ltd, Registered Offices:
1A Eton Road, Parktown, South Africa 2193

First published by Penguin Books (South Africa) (Pty) Ltd 1998
Reprinted 1998 (twice)

ISBN 0 140 26754 9

Typeset in 11 on 13.5 pt Aldine
Printed and bound by Interpak, Natal
Cover design by Aliza Bender
Illustration on page 262 by Ulla Blake
Author's photograph by Paul Gordon

To my mother, who taught me that anything is possible

Also to Malcolm and Alan
and our children Simon, Sarah, Tara and Tiffany

And to fellow pilgrims everywhere

Contents

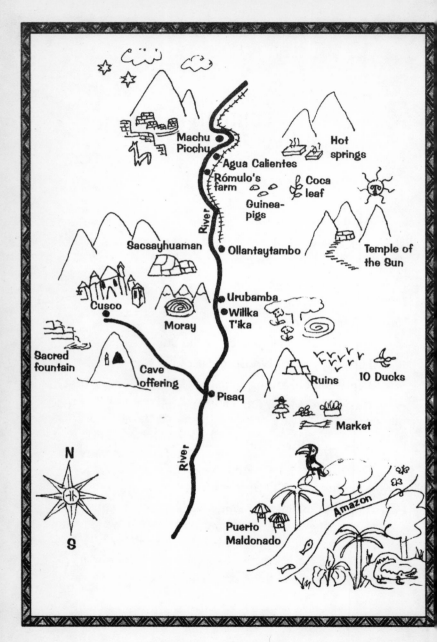

A Magical Journey

Author's Foreword

I sat down at my computer one morning in early September and typed 'The Beginning' at the top of the empty page.

Exactly one month later I had finished the manuscript of *There's More To Life Than Surface*.

I can't claim that I was 'channelled' by some spiritual being, had gone into a trance-like state, or had sat feverishly pouring out 'automatic' writing in the manner of the wife of W B Yeats – an activity no doubt presided over by the Great Poet himself. Certainly the extensive research for the book had been done over the last few years, perhaps had been going on all my life.

What I *can* claim is that during those few weeks I possessed an extraordinary energy. It seemed as if the positive spiritual forces that had entered my soul on the top of Ayers Rock – Uluru – in the Red Centre of Australia, at ancient Anasazi sites in America's Southwest, and in the high temples of the cold, pure air of the Andes, were pushing me on in a whirlwind of creativity. The stories of the memorable people who had been part of my own spiritual journey coalesced and warmed me. Each of us in our own way had found our own spiritual path.

Now it is up to you to find yours.

Caminante, no hay camino
Se hace camino al andar.

Traveller, there is no path,
Paths are made by walking.

Antonio Machado

All the people in this book are real and all the stories are true.

ONE

The Beginning

I suppose it's always best to begin at the beginning.
Except in this case there is no beginning. Not a proper
one anyway. No point where I can say exactly *this* is where it
all began.

My friend Blind Dan, poet, artist, philosopher, prophet
and mystic, would tell me that it was all meant to be, pre-
ordained if you like, but that doesn't really help when you're
looking for an exact point of departure.

Maybe it all began for me deep in the Amazon jungle. Or
on top of mile-high Ayers Rock – Uluru – in the Red Heart
of Australia, the most sacred of all Aboriginal sacred places.
Maybe it began when I was standing in the very end of a
rainbow in County Donegal in Ireland, where the colours of
the rainbow enfolded me as they simultaneously sank into
and rose up from the green turf. Maybe it began at the
Hitching Post of the Sun at the top of the grey-walled ruined
city of Machu Picchu in Peru, or in the Valley of the
Sangomas in Southern Africa where a score of shamans,

traditional healers and wise ones practise their ancient craft. Maybe it all began as I awoke from a deep sleep on a road journey from the west of England, to see the great rough-hewn pillars of Stonehenge looming up in the early morning mist on the edge of Salisbury Plain. Or in Paradise Bay in Antarctica, where it is like the dawn of the world – untouched, unspoiled, perfect.

But it doesn't really matter where it all began. Or where it is going to end. What matters is the journey.

And that you come with me on the journey.

*

I've been a writer, editor and broadcaster for many, many years. When I was with BBC Television in the UK in the Sixties, I interviewed everybody and everything from a talking dog and an American professor of music who had written a Symphony for the Hosepipe, to The Beatles, The Burtons, the Prime Minister of England, and a very young Anthony Hopkins. I covered royal events for the BBC World Service and met most of The Royals. I once attended a banquet given by the Worshipful Company of Goldsmiths at London's Guildhall, where we ate off huge plates of beaten gold.

As the years went by I chatted with boxers, athletic stars, footballers, racing drivers, tennis, cricket and rugby players. I wrote radio and television documentaries on alcoholics, adoptions, drug addicts and child abusers. I became head of a university department, wrote several academic books, worked at the New York Film School, did a stint at a PBS television station in Austin, Texas, and gave courses in communications at several Australian universities. And although I come from a long line of unsuccessful English witches (unsuccessful because most were burnt at the stake or drowned by dunking in the local village duck pond), none of my past experience really led me to undertake a spiritual journey. That I finally did, not on my own behalf but as a kind of interested observer, is what this book is about.

I'm sure you've often wondered what makes one person choose a certain spiritual path over another. Why do some people find spiritual contentment and fulfilment early in life, others late in life, on their deathbed, or not at all? Why do some people rejoice in the restraints and comfort zone of an organised religion whilst others seek a more unconventional path? Why are some people happy with what they find in their own hearts, whilst others seek a guru or spiritual mentor? Why will one person go into a sweat lodge, another into a confessional box? Why will one person pray and fast, whilst another will read tea-leaves or follow the progression of the stars and planets? Why will one person worship alone, another with hundreds or thousands?

Is there a Divine Plan, Predestination or Free Will, Fate, Karma, Reincarnation, Heaven and Hell, or Nothing? Or just surface – what you see is what you get.

Certainly the world is filled with evidence that man, from the beginning of his time on earth, has been obsessed with a potential other world – a spiritual dimension beyond the merely physical. Sometimes this obsession has focused on the sky, the stars, the universe. Ruins of ancient civilisations like those of the Mayans, the Incas, the Egyptians, the builders of the European stone circles, the Native Americans, the ancient cities of the East, reveal observatories, calendars and measuring instruments used to make sense of the things that

3

man desperately wants to understand. In some faiths the Creation Story is taught as the answer to all our questions – God created the world in six days and on the seventh day he rested. Scientists continually debate the Steady State theory of the Universe as opposed to the Big Bang theory. Or is the cosmos so complex and marvellously made that surely there is the hand of a Creator behind it?

Do you feel that the horrors of natural and man-made evil and the pointlessness of so much human suffering makes it hard or even impossible to believe in the idea of a perfectly just and eternal God? Then what about a more pragmatic approach – that the divinity – whomsoever she or he may be – takes rather a 'hands-off' approach by creating an autonomous universe and giving us complete freedom to love or not to love, to obey or disobey, to believe in a divinity, divinities or cosmic consciousness, or not to believe in anything above and beyond what we can see and experience empirically?

When I interviewed Karen Armstrong, ex-nun, religious scholar and author of the controversial *A History of God* on my radio show, she told me firmly that God is man-made and that religion changes as man progresses through history. During man's collective 'infancy' the world was filled with people whose sole existence was characterised by hunting, gathering and surviving.

'Religion can be described during this period as playing the "parental" role when gods and goddesses of all shapes and sizes ruled the earth,' said Karen Armstrong. 'Men prayed for rain, for food, for health, for children. There was a whole host of strict do's and don'ts which man followed, and he prayed to oracles for advice and inspiration.

'As man developed further he entered the turbulent phase

4

of religious "adolescence". War and rebellion, aggression, colonisation and Holy Wars characterised this period in our religious history.

'The next "adult" stage of religion occurred when Jesus, Buddha, Mohammed, Krishna and many other prophets or "Sons of God" appeared on earth to experience life as "men". This age is described as "adult" and religion now is characterised by "The Holy Spirit".

'Are we,' Armstrong asks, 'living now perhaps in the most peaceful, positive, wonderful period of all?'

A few weeks later, when British writer Brian Appleyard, author of the highly controversial book *Understanding the Present*, came on the show, he disagreed with Armstrong. We are living in an Age of Science, he maintained, and should understand that the 'bitter message' of science is that the universe offers no consolations. It does not exist for a reason, it just exists like some thick-witted skinhead – mute, gormless and callous. Thus science's worst crime is that it ventures no answer to why there is a universe at all.

A few years ago I made a radical departure from my previous broadcasting career. I had been a talkshow host on radio and television in Britain and in South Africa. Now the head of production at Radio 702, South Africa's first and most successful commercial radio station, told me that the station was thinking about doing a programme on spiritual matters. To be called *Believe It Or Not*, it would be a three-hour call-in show about matters of faith, religion, ethics, morals.

'In other words,' Mike said, 'about the way we live our lives.'

Sounds great, I thought.

'But who on earth will you get to host it?'

'You.'

I burst out laughing. 'Me, host a spiritual show? You must be joking!'

But he wasn't joking. And that's when Blind Dan would say that my karma swung into action.

The programme was a first of its kind. We didn't know what to expect or who would listen. We were going to be up against some prime time TV viewing. Would anyone call in? Although I had been fortunate enough to visit many of the great sacred sites of the world, what did I know about matters spiritual? About the major faiths of the world? Should I start swotting up on the Bible, the Vedic Scriptures, the Torah, the Koran? Wasn't there a copy of *The Prophet* somewhere in my personal library of six thousand books?

I needn't have worried.

Our first programme concerned itself with miracles.

I talked to a woman in Bella Vista, California, who had been polishing a chalice when suddenly it turned to gold and began to weep blood. Cyndi Cain now runs a newspaper devoted to other Eucharistic miracles. I spoke with Sang Lee who witnessed the Miracle of the Sun in Naju, Korea, and to Julia in Medjugorje, whose statue of the Virgin Mary has wept tears of blood and flowed with aromatic oil for many years. I listened to Mary Malone, an Irish mystic who has visited Medjugorje and Fatima but sees her visions of the Virgin Mary at Mount Mallory, Waterford, in Ireland.

And I heard a stunned Catholic Bishop Salvador Lazo of Agoo, who heads the Philippine Diocese where a two-foot-tall statue of the Virgin Mary is located, speak about how the crude wooden carving had first emitted a sweet fragrance, then wept tears of blood. 'It did happen. I saw it. It's a miracle.'

I also heard from Credo Mutwa, an African *sangoma* who, with two colleagues – one a Catholic, the other a Hindu swami – simultaneously experienced a vision of a holy woman whilst they were at a small mission station in the northwest of South Africa's KwaZulu-Natal Province. Although she appeared to them all at the exact same moment, each saw her through the eyes of his own culture – the Virgin Mary, a Hindu goddess, the Great Earth Mother of Africa.

I spoke to a woman who had been cured of cancer at Lourdes and to a man, given up as brain dead, who miraculously regained consciousness just as the life-support machines were about to be switched off. And I listened to all the people who called in to the programme to share their own miracles, great and small.

Over the radio waves I've now spoken with hundreds of people from all over the world – famous and unknown, rich and poor, educated and uneducated, real and spurious, champions and charlatans, mystics, ministers, nuns, priests, saints and sinners. And to thousands of ordinary people like you and me. *Believe It Or Not* has also tackled hundreds of topics all concerned with the way we live our lives.

I have been amazed, incredulous, humbled, outwitted and appalled by some of the things I've heard.

Many of the topics I discussed were the same as those you've talked about, thought about, worried over or read about. After all, humankind has been concerned with matters of faith, ethics, morals and theology ever since it could think and then vocalise those thoughts. We're all still at it today. How many TV and radio programmes, newspaper or magazine articles have you seen, heard or read about the Meaning of Life, Is There Life After Death, ESP, Ghosts, Near-Death Experiences, Miracles, Reincarnation, Karma,

Abortion, Euthanasia – to name but a few? Most thinking people at some or other stage of their lives begin to reflect on their spirituality – and that's when the spiritual development begins.

What I have learned, and continue to learn when I listen, week after week, for three hours every Sunday night, to so many different people and varying viewpoints, is that there has to be, must be, more to life than surface.

When the diminutive Joya Pope, author of *The World According to Michael – An Old Soul's Guide to the Universe*, breezed into my studio she fixed her big, wide eyes on mine and tried to convince me that she channels the wisdom and experience of an angel – Michael – and then passes that on to thousands of people worldwide. I have to confess I wasn't convinced.

Betty J Eadie told me by telephone from the States about her minutely detailed Near-Death experience which she describes fully in her bestseller *Embraced By The Light*.

Lyall Watson, who changed our way of thinking with his groundbreaking book *Supernature*, has often appeared on the show talking about everything from his own supernatural experiences to, more recently, the nature of evil.

One of the world's greatest mystics, Douglas Harding, told me by telephone from his home in England that he believes in a cosmic consciousness – a spiritual realm that we can all access. 'Slip into those spaces between your thoughts and listen,' he advised us in his grave voice. And in many of his books he gives us easy techniques to help us do just that.

Deepak Chopra spoke to me from America before he became really famous. He had always believed in combining what the Western medical world knows about stress with ancient Eastern wisdom on longevity. 'The secret to long life isn't just good genes but the way we live. Get rid of toxic relations, emotions and foods and you can influence your lifespan by thirty years.' His bestseller *Ageless Body – Timeless Mind* has since influenced thousands of people around the world. Sceptics may wonder whether he has found the fountain of youth or a road to riches – it's not important – but what Dr Chopra *has* found is the secret of interpreting the abracadabra of healing into 'a language that fascinates people'. Whether his claims that such 'bio-markers of ageing' as blood pressure, bone density, heartbeat, muscle strength and body temperature can be controlled by our minds, or that with 'meditation, exercise, dieting and nutritional supplements' we can live to be one hundred and thirty, as he claims the ancient yogis of India did, is a matter for you alone to decide.

Another doctor, Dr Elisabeth Kubler-Ross, spoke on *Believe It Or Not* about her widely respected and accepted views on the process of dying. How terminally ill patients go through the five classical stages of Denial, Anger, Bargaining, Depression and finally, Acceptance, in their process of coming to terms with their illnesses. Visit any hospice organisation today anywhere in the world and see those teachings in practice.

Dr M Scott Peck spoke about his *The Road Less Travelled*, and contentious Australian theologian Barbara Thiering about her in-depth, revolutionary study and interpretation of the Dead Sea Scrolls. According to her research, Jesus married Mary Magdalene and had three children.

Jesus has often figured in our programme discussions. One of India's most holy swamis, Sadhu Professor V Rangarajan, told us about Jesus' life in India from a young boy until the age of thirty, and I've spoken to many other theologians of different faiths who claim that Jesus did not die on the cross.

We have also examined how the Internet is shaping our views on Jesus, faith and religion by talking to the authors of various web sites.

Dr Larry Dossey spoke about the healing power of prayer and the practice of medicine, as did Dr Herbert Benson, author of *Timeless Healing* which deals with the correlation between spirituality and healing. Terry Waite, the Archbishop of Canterbury's envoy who was working towards the release of terrorist-held hostages in the Lebanon, shared with us how his Anglican faith had kept him from despair when he himself was captured by those same terrorists and held in solitary confinement for over a thousand days. A giant of a man, six feet seven inches tall, who takes size thirteen shoes, he was chained to a wall in a dark cell where it was impossible for him to stand up or to lie down.

I've learned about the complexities of medical ethics – organ transplants, confidentiality, assisted death and doctors playing God. About genetic engineering – when we spoke to the Roslin Institute in Edinburgh, Scotland, whose scientists cloned the first sheep, Dolly the world-famous ewe. Their soft-spoken assistant director was emphatic. Yes, they had the technology. But no, they would never clone a human.

I can tell you about Rat Worship in India, celibacy in the priesthood, the Turin Shroud, Scientology, cults, the rise of the charismatic churches, Islam, Hinduism, Buddhism, Christianity, Satanism, Paganism and the New Age Movement.

*

It's only now, post-Peru, that I realise that during the years of the programme, sometimes consciously, at other times unconsciously, I had been on a continual spiritual learning curve. And although I was not aware of it at the time, there had been incidents, adventures and people in my life that were all key points in that curve.

I now believe that we are all on this curve; some of us will recognise it, go with it and learn from it; for others, the recognition has not yet begun. But take time, take steps, take a journey, as I did to Peru or wherever, and maybe that recognition is nearer than you can possibly believe. Look, listen and learn. We are all on the same journey.

It took me years to realise that I had been on a spiritual path for most of my life. By reading my story, reliving my experiences, I believe that you may well be alerted to your own journey, to your own personal landmarks along its way.

Unbeknownst to me, my spiritual journey had begun many decades ago, as a schoolgirl in a Catholic convent, in a leper colony in Eastern Nigeria, at an Aboriginal sacred place in Australia's dry and dusty heartlands, in the African bush, during the years of my radio programme. It took a magical journey to Peru for me to begin to comprehend that journey.

So if this book *has* a beginning, it is in the cobbled streets of an enchanting little city half as old as time; in the high, rarefied air of the snow-covered peaks in the Andes; or beside the brown, powerful waters of the Amazon.

TWO

The Land of Green Corn

The language of spirituality is loaded and worn out. So we have to invent a new one.

Plastic shamans. Cultural theft. Supermarket spirituality. Instant soul fixes. Crystals, tea-leaves, psychics, tarot cards, I Ching, past life regression, Kabbalah, Tantra, astrology and alchemy. Snake Oil.

It's quite a list, and that's only the start.

Sweat lodges, meditation, yoga, Zen, flower essences, dream journeys, sensing the aura, angels, spirit guides, Reiki, clairvoyant counselling.

Maybe you've tried some or all of these ways with varying degrees of success. Maybe you haven't even heard of some – or only in a vague sort of way. But the millennium has put us all on the alert. Time now to start searching for a spiritual path, because maybe the soothsayers and the religious know-alls are right – maybe the end of the world is approaching.

Whatever the forecasts, it seems clear that never before have so many people been looking for something more than the reality that surrounds them. Another dimension. Many people share a deep, intuitive knowledge that there's more to life than surface. Call it *fin de siècle*, twentieth-century malaise, a move away from materialistic values – the label we give it is unimportant. What *is* important is that many of us are looking for a spiritual way.

Desmond Morris, the English zoologist who first made world news with his seminal book *The Naked Ape* in which he pointed out the similarities between man and ape, said once on my radio show that ancient man, after acquiring language, was instinctually forced to invent his future. That he could deal with his past and his present, but now, in order to deal with and control his future, he invented God and an afterlife. Otherwise the future would be too uncertain. And fear of the unknown is one of our greatest fears. So, bingo – God, or gods, goddesses, instruments to divine the unknown.

Morris believes that man needed religion as a source of control. First, he invented 'little' gods but they soon became insufficient. What was needed was one single, all-powerful, all-wise, all-seeing god, and from all the ancient candidates it was this type that won through and survived the passage of the centuries. In some smaller and less 'civilised' cultures today, the minor gods still rule, but members of most of the major cultures have turned to the single supergod.

Karen Armstrong, an ex-nun of wide scholarship and strong ecumenical credentials, argues in her book *A History of God* that it is clear that the deity is a product of humankind's creative imagination and that God may well be our most interesting idea.

But whether God made man in his own image or vice versa is irrelevant to many people. Or even if there is a God as such. Zoology and anthropology aside, they *know* that there is something beyond this life, whether as a spiritual future or just an elusive 'something' that perhaps can be accessed. If you're reading this book you know what I mean.

I travel a lot. My work as an academic, an author, a journalist and broadcaster has taken me all over the world from Alaska to Argentina, from Ireland to China, from Thailand to Australia, from Africa to Antarctica. How I came to be in Peru is quite another story.

For years I had been working with the same travel agent – let's call her Sharon. Think of Sharon as the archetypal, hard-nosed, tough businesswoman. She's diminutive, bottle-blonde, super-efficient, looks a bit like Dr Ruth and has the tenacity of a Pit Bull Terrier. But these last few months she'd been losing it. Getting flustered, taking on too much work from too many clients, becoming – and this was quite out of character – inefficient.

I had decided to take my leave of Sharon, but as there was some unfinished travel business to be cleared up between us, I went to her office. I had decided it would be for the last time. As usual, she was either constantly on the phone, running about in all directions like a headless chicken, or trying to deal with other people at the same time as me. I felt frustrated and furious.

However, as she scampered off on one of her forays, I noticed a pamphlet which lay facing me on the top of her untidy desk. *Magical Journeys to Peru*. I skimmed through it. Hmm. Something prompted me to pick it up and slip it into my briefcase.

It stayed there for a few weeks but I couldn't forget it – its contents simply wouldn't go away. Previous participants on these so-called magical journeys had described the experience as the 'Ultimate Transformational Spiritual Journey'. Heigh-ho! New Age Poppycock, I thought cynically. But I continued to find myself thinking about Peru at odd moments. It was as if a seed had been planted.

One cold winter's evening when the grass was scratchy with frost and the jackals were calling to the full moon, I finally contacted Carol Cumes, leader of the expeditions. Making contact with a remote farm in the Sacred Valley of the Incas in Peru is not easy from Johannesburg, South Africa. But after some weeks, much determination, patience, and strange, disembodied voices from a fax line in Cusco, the plans were finalised.

Carol told me she had a very small group of people joining her and Rómulo Lizárraga, her Quechua colleague, in September, when it would be springtime in the Andes.

'Why don't you bring your husband along?' Her soft voice crackled over the Andean airwaves. Why not, I thought.

When my husband Alan returned from a business trip to Botswana, I told him we were leaving for Peru in three weeks' time. I didn't tell him it was to go on a spiritual journey – one step at a time. I had, however, found out from Carol that the others on the journey were 'regular' people – no flakes, loony tune numbers or off-the-wall southern Californians.

The following three weeks were crowded and work-packed. Neither Alan nor I had the opportunity to read or talk about Peru, watch videos about it, or do any research on it. We knew about llamas, people in colourful clothes and funny hats, and Machu Picchu, of course. But that was it. Friends and colleagues asked me if I had read Shirley MacLaine's books. I hadn't, and didn't intend to.

In retrospect, the fact that we knew nothing was for the best. We went with no preconceptions, no notions of what we were to do or see, no ideas about what might happen to us. My Irish husband might have described it as being 'pig-ignorant'. No matter. The important thing was that our minds and hearts were utterly open. The brochure might have claimed that we were going on a spiritual journey. For me, it was yet another opportunity to see new places and learn new things. Spiritual journey? Get real, Kate!

However. Something had just happened to me that had made a very deep impression on me. Looking back, I now realise that it was a milestone on my spiritual journey, but unrecognised as such at the time.

Only a couple of weeks before we set off for Peru I had been privileged to meet the Dalai Lama on his first ever visit to South Africa. On a cold winter's morning, Neil Ferguson, my producer at the radio station, and I went to downtown Johannesburg to hear him speak.

His unlined skin was a warm honey-brown. He sat erectly, a man much bigger than he appears in the world media, a mischievous, almost schoolboy look kept peeping out from behind the calm, strong, kind face. Yes, it was kindness that impacted most on the listener. His voice was deep and clear.

> *We must always acknowledge the interconnectedness of all things. Recognise the profound mutual interdependence of everything – it's part of the natural world.*

Somehow I knew those words were going to impact on my coming journey and on my life. At that stage I had no notion as to how, but they resonated with me over and over again as I prepared for my journey to Peru.

✳

There were seven 'pilgrims' on our journey – an Irishman, two Englishwomen, an American husband and wife, a Jewish widow, and a South African divorcee.

Alan, the Irishman. My husband Alan was born and raised in Northern Ireland in a little town called Newcastle, County Down, where, as the song goes, 'The Mountains of Mourne sweep down to the sea'. Although he came from a large rumbustious family, he was a solitary child, spending hours climbing up the grey face of Slieve Donard, the Mourne's highest peak, and communing with the rocks, running brooks and the storm-lashed Atlantic.

Although born and raised in a strong Protestant community, Alan's God, if there was one, was all around him in nature. Since that time, he's been a lumberjack in the Scottish Highlands, a professional army officer in the British Army, a computer systems analyst, an advertising rep, a writer, and now is managing director of his own small publishing company.

Alan was on the magical journey because of me and, like me, would never turn down an opportunity to do something new, visit a strange place, or try a new experience.

Kate, the Englishwoman. I was born in London, within the sound of Bow Bells, a true cockney, but when World War Two came, my sister and I were evacuated to Norfolk on England's flat east coast.

The London evacuees became famous and much has been written about them since that time. In 1939, only weeks after war broke out, thousands of children were evacuated from London and sent, like so many unsolicited parcels, all over Britain and beyond to whoever would house and feed them.

Our parents were told that the German bombs would soon begin to fall, the Nazi onslaught was imminent and thus it was imperative to get the young children away from the coming danger. Mothers with babes-in-arms and children under three were allowed to go with their offspring. The rest of us were separated.

I was four years old, my sister six. It was a terrible, distressing time for all the families involved. I remember the great glass-domed London railway station where thousands of children were assembled. There was a great deal of shouting and blowing of whistles, heavy train doors clanging shut, clouds of steam. I remember looking up and seeing some pigeons flying high in the glass roof against the sky. I thought they were trying to escape. I remember my mother crying, my father stony-faced, as the government officials tied brown paper parcel labels on us with our names, and then we were bundled into the steam trains that were to take us on an unknown journey to an unknown destination.

My sister had been told that under no circumstances was she to be separated from her little sister, and so when we finally tumbled out on to the railway platform at the end of the long bewildering day in the train, we stood hand-in-hand, little fingers clutched fiercely together, waiting for some kind souls who were prepared to take two children into their home.

'I mustn't leave you,' repeated my sister Rita, over and over like a litany. She bit her lip and fought back tears. Because the single children were chosen first, it was only as the sun was finally setting that a farm labourer and his wife offered to have the two little girls.

To this day, even though I have strong memories of my life before I was evacuated, I have no memory whatsoever of the six months my sister and I spent in those flat, desolate, windy marshlands. A case of what a psychiatrist would call Classic Block Out. Maybe I stopped believing in a 'regular' childhood God during those months.

Why was I on this trip to Peru? Because, as Sir Edmund Hillary said when asked why he had climbed Mount Everest, 'it was there'. I now believe I was 'led' to Peru. My friend, Blind Dan, poet, artist, philosopher and seer, has no doubt of it.

Sue, the other Englishwoman. Sue was born and raised in England, but had emigrated to America as a young woman, and was now a successful landscape gardener in San Francisco. Always interested in things spiritual, she had studied alternative spiritual paths for many years, was widely read in alternative religions and now led meditation groups. Perhaps, of us all, she was the most overtly 'spiritual'. A tall, slim woman with glasses and light brown hair, Sue radiated a deep inner peace and spiritual serenity. A trip to Peru had long been on her 'wish-list' and now her wish was being fulfilled.

The American husband and wife. Gordon and Wilma were from Silicon Valley in California. Gordon was a computer consultant and spent much of his time travelling to and from the Far East; Wilma was a librarian. Committed Christians both, they spent most of their spare time helping others – as grief counsellors, with terminally ill patients and, most recently, as hospital clowns. They proudly showed us their clown pictures. Two bewigged, red-nosed, beaming faces atop white ruffled collars and colourful clown suits. Although committed Christians, they were not happy-clappers, proselytisers, or aggressive 'Born Agains'.

They were wise, happy people – very comfortable to be with – whose belief in the divinity was absolute. Gordon had a cheerful, sunburnt face framed by a short, round, grey beard and always wore a venerable, very battered straw hat that he'd bought from some US mail order catalogue and of which he was inordinately fond. Wilma was a pleasant-looking middle-aged woman with thick white hair and a lovely smile. We found out much later that Wilma was a natural healer and could lay healing hands. They were on the trip because they had always been fascinated by the idea of Peru – its past, its people, its spirituality, its supposed sources of energy.

Joy, the Jewish widow. Alan and I had met Joy and her late husband Ian on a trip to Antarctica nine months previously. Ian, a mining magnate, was a larger-than-life character in build, in personality, in intellect – in just about everything. He had died of emphysema a couple of weeks after we returned from Antarctica and Joy, who in some ways had lived in Ian's huge shadow for the forty years of her married life, began to reassess herself and her life.

No intellectual slouch, she was a writer, a psychologist, a former broadcaster and a teacher. Much of her early married life had been spent in desolate mining areas. Her stories of her life in Namibia's Namib desert were compulsive listening. But Joy was heavily into grief. Ian's death was still obsessing her, and she told us that although Jewish, neither she nor Ian had ever followed the faith or believed in the kind of God that Judaism offered, so there was no comfort for her in that direction.

A small, well-groomed and attractive woman in her late

sixties, Joy was the odd one out in the group, the one who found it very difficult to bond with the others. She had chosen to come along on this trip because Alan and I were going; also, she felt that she might find spiritual comfort and solace in some yet unexplained way.

Carol, the South African divorcee. She came to be known as 'Big Carol' to all of us because of her generosity of spirit, which was reinforced by her big physical size.

Big Carol had had a hard life, a couple of failed marriages, painful and difficult times emotionally and financially, and now ran a small hotel at a little seaside town on South Africa's south coast. She was always full of laughs and her tales of the goings-on in her hotel kept us in stitches.

She was overwhelmingly generous, and although she had saved hard and long for this once-in-a-lifetime trip to Peru, she would give unstintingly of what money she had to the local children. Thoughtfully, she had even carried large packets of candies, coloured crayons and ballpoint pens all the way from Africa to give to the Peruvian children she met. Throughout our journey Carol would bring our van to a halt with a shriek of 'Stop!' to the terrified driver, then she would leap out and distribute her goodies to the delighted children she had spotted.

I have one picture of Big Carol high up in an Andean valley, surrounded by snow-capped jagged peaks, standing in the middle of a herd of goats distributing largesse to two little brown-eyed goatherds.

Immaculately groomed at all times, Big Carol wore strikingly elegant outfits at the most inappropriate times. I can still see, in my mind's eye, Big Carol in an eye-catching peach-coloured top and pants outfit, with a matching wide-brimmed peach-coloured hat, walking nonchalantly along a narrow path high up in the Andes with a precipitous drop falling away beside her to a rushing river hundreds of feet below.

Big Carol, with black hair and dancing bright blue eyes, who was overweight and suffered from severe vertigo, underwent an amazing change. I'll tell you about it later.

So Kate and Alan, Gordon and Wilma, Sue, Joy and Big Carol were the seven pilgrims. All with a different agenda, with differing beliefs, with no beliefs.

The other two members of our little group were Carol and Mark, the leaders of the expedition.

Carol, a small, very together woman just turning fifty, had emigrated with her doctor husband to California from South Africa in the Seventies. For fifteen years she visited Peru, studying its people, customs and cosmology, and had become an expert. Her book on the Quechua people of the Andes and their beliefs, co-authored with Rómulo Lizárraga, *Journey to Machu Picchu: Spiritual Wisdom of the Andes*, published by Llewellyn Press in the USA, is a classic of its kind. She finally decided on the way she wanted her life to be. She divorced her husband, left her four grown-up children, and built a beautiful home, Willka T'ika, in the Sacred Valley of the Incas outside the little town of Urubamba.

Carol's partner now is Mark. Formerly a top executive with IBM involved in the cut-and-thrust of a rapacious marketing environment, Mark had none the less been a long-time practitioner of yoga and had followed a path of learning which had wound its way through Indian and Chinese philosophy and religion, the work of European Alchemists, Shamanism, Mythology and the views of Jung. He'd also been a naval officer, with long experience of the African wilderness, and had conducted groundbreaking work in teaching principles for fulfilment and personal well-being to overworked, stressed business executives. A very tall man, dwarfing the diminutive Carol, he had a wicked sense of humour. Twice-divorced, he still possessed a fair degree of cynicism about spiritual journeys in particular and life in general, and was a perfect foil for the more spiritually committed Carol.

The great advantage Carol and Mark shared as group leaders was that they never tried to push their own personal views, but stood back and let all of us experience things in our own ways and at our own pace.

*

On our first afternoon in Cusco, 'Capital Arqueologica De Sud-America Y Patrimonio Cultural De La Humanidad' and a UNESCO cultural heritage site, after resting and sipping copious amounts of *mate de coca* – coca-leaf tea – to stave off altitude sickness (Cusco is some 3 350 metres above sea level), we visit the huge and ancient ruins of Sacsayhuaman above Cusco.

We follow Carol and Mark and Rómulo Lizárraga, Carol's Quechua colleague, up a steep footpath to the eastern side of the ruins, along the valley of the Tullumayo River. The mountains stretch away into the distance, a lone bird calls, and a Peruvian woman in a short, full black skirt, red embroidered waistcoat and multi-coloured shawl, with a big flat pancake of a hat on top of her long pigtails, argues futilely with a reluctant llama with red ribbons in his ear who is refusing to climb one of the lower paths beneath us. The less-than-cheerful llama seems unaware that this is the photo opportunity his owner has been waiting for. As we walk on battle is still joined; the woman grins at us through gap teeth, shrugs her shoulders, and goes back to tugging the stubborn animal.

Sacsayhuaman is one of the most amazing megalithic structures of the old world. Both an Inca fortress and an important religious site, its walls, built in zig-zag formation, tower above the valley floor and dwarf the surrounding countryside and the little town of Cusco. No civilisation of the Old World matched the Inca stonework or spent so much time and trouble on its stone buildings. Sacsayhuaman's largest stone block, of which there are thousands, stands 8,5 metres high and weighs 361 tons. It's a fine example of the Inca building skills, the massive stones fitting together so tightly and elegantly that you would not be able to slip your credit card into a crack between them. This was the heart of the Inca Empire, spreading north, south, east and west – the Incas called it Tawantinsuyo: the 'Four Quarters of the Earth'.

By 1492 the Spanish had thrown out the Moors, thrown out the Jews, and now they were looking to explore what they called the New World. Gold was their motive. The Spaniards claimed that they wanted to spread the word of Christianity, but they had heard that the New World was filled with gold. That's why their ships, with leaders such as Pizarro, set off from Spain. They arrived first in Central America where they heard stories of gold in the south. They were told that 'down there is the land of Wiru', which meant the Land of Green Corn.

Wiru is a sacred corn which comes from the Andes. It's an incredible indigenous maize that produces bigger, better and more nutritious ears than any other known species. Later, at the colourful market in Pisaq, a quaint little market town in the Sacred Valley of the Incas between Cusco and Machu Picchu, we would gaze in astonishment at sacks of *wiru* whose kernels look like the oversize drawings of an ad agency designer on a cornflakes packet.

The Quechua people from the Land of Green Corn would bring gold ornaments and utensils made of gold up from the south to barter for shells. One of the many accounts for the name 'Peru' is that it comes from the word *wiru*. The Spaniards found it difficult to say the letter 'w' in Spanish, so turned it into a 'p'.

As I sit amongst the mighty stones of Sacsayhuaman, I remember the Inca prophecy which foretold that bearded white men would come from the sea and were to be worshipped as gods. The Incas had never seen a horse, so when Pizarro and his men arrived on horseback, the Incas saw them as divine creatures, half man, half horse. They fell to their knees and worshipped them as gods.

In turn, the Christian Spanish saw the Incas as non-believers, pagans. Legend has it that when Pizarro met Atahuallpa, the all-powerful Inca Emperor, the Emperor asked him 'Who is your God?' Pizarro told him that 'Our God is the Bible', and gave him his copy. Atahuallpa is said to have leafed through the pages (the Incas had no written language themselves) and asked, 'Does he speak? What does he say?' Because Inca gods spoke through the mountain spirits, through oracles, received their spiritual messages through nature, Atahuallpa was incredulous. How could this ridiculous book be a god?

Finally ten thousand Inca warriors were slaughtered here where we sat at Sacsayhuaman, in the very last battle between Spanish and Inca.

It was the end of one of the greatest empires the world has known, an empire far larger than anything that had gone before it, stretching from modern Ecuador to southern Chile, from the Amazon jungles in the east to the Pacific Ocean in the west. If the Incas were the Romans of pre-Columbian America, Cusco was their Rome. Using conquest as their means, like the Roman Empire, the Empire of the Incas thrived and expanded for four hundred years. Also like the Romans, the Incas built superb roads, had a genius for organisation and administration, initiated systems of government and land tenure, and colonised the local people effectively.

As we stand in the mighty fortress of Sacsayhuaman, dwarfed by the huge walls and great blocks of stone, we overlook the little town of Cusco, cradled by the surrounding mountains. Its brown-tiled roofs and terracotta-coloured buildings, most with a strong Spanish look and feel, blend in perfectly with its natural surroundings. There is a fairytale quality to the little town, like one of those line drawings in an old story book where pedlars sell their wares, and children with long hair wander hand-in-hand. It is difficult to imagine the scenes of carnage, terror and bloody battle that it had witnessed when the Spaniards, from their high horses, ruthlessly cut down the Inca foot warriors.

My guide book tells me that the city of Cusco is in the shape of a puma – one of the great power animals in Inca cosmology. The puma's head is where we sit – on top of the hill of Sacsayhuaman; its body is the main city centre. Cusco was not only a capital city to the Incas – 'the navel of the earth' – but a holy city, a place of pilgrimage. Every ranking citizen of the empire aspired to visit Cusco at least once in his lifetime, just as today a Muslim will undertake the Haj pilgrimage to Mecca.

The seven of us – Alan, myself, Sue, Gordon, Wilma, Joy and Big Carol – stand, one at a time, in one of the small circles within the ruins. Guides claim that these stone circles are the remains of grain stores or water tanks, but Carol tells us that this is a holy place, used for ceremony and ritual.

'Stand in the centre and feel the vortex of energy.'

When it is my turn, I close my eyes and feel a surge of natural energy – the first of many I am to feel in Peru.

How to describe this natural energy? Well, it isn't as dramatic as a charge of electricity or a bolt of lightning, but there is a definite physical feeling of power – a quickening of the pulse, a hurrying of the blood, an intensification of feeling throughout the body, a kind of mini-supercharge. I certainly hadn't expected to feel anything like this, but it is undeniable. Not so much a 'Wow!' as a shivery 'Mmm'.

'Call out,' Carol suggests. 'For some reason, there's an amazing natural resonance and voice amplification from this spot. Try it.'

I call out and my voice echoes. I remember the time a few years ago when I stood in the middle of the giant amphitheatre of Epidaurus in Greece and heard my voice resonate from the middle of the performance area to the four-thousand-seat spectator area surrounding it.

A similar feeling of awe now envelops me. It doesn't last long and it moves itself quietly to the back of my mind, to be resurrected on future occasions.

Our first evening in Cusco is bitterly cold and pouring with rain. Still strangers, the nine of us huddle together in the little bus on the way to Tampumachay, where sacred springs flow down from the high Andes. Here the Incas worshipped at a small temple whose empty niches today show where golden statues of their deities once cast fear and awe into the conquered Quechua.

Carol teaches us an initiation ceremony. There are three fountains, the uppermost one representing the condor and the upper world of superior energy, the middle fountain representing the physical world dominated by the symbol of the puma, and the lowest fountain representing the inner, spiritual world, symbolised by the snake.

Carol shows us how to anoint our chakras with the holy waters of the sacred springs.

Alan and I barely know what a chakra is, let alone where they are supposed to be on the body, so Carol gives us a quick explanation.

Many spiritual traditions share a common belief that the human body receives nourishment from the cosmos in the form of energy. It is this energy that gives both life to the body and power to the psyche. The energy is drawn in, converted and transferred through specific centres in the body – the chakras.

Although there are seven chakras in most Eastern philosophies, Carol tells us of the five main centres of Tibetan teaching: brain, throat, heart, solar plexus and sex organs. The brow chakra in the middle of the forehead is sometimes called The Third Eye and is intimately linked with one's spiritual life. The throat chakra, in the middle of the throat, is linked with communication, study and the search for truth. Through the heart chakra, situated over the heart, we radiate love, charity, compassion and self-sacrifice, whilst the solar plexus chakra, just above the navel, is concerned with one's personality – one's ego, self-image, will-power and ambition. The lowest chakra, in physical terms, is the sex organs which also power the personality and can be linked to sexual power. In a spiritually evolved person, however, the energies of the base centre are transferred to the brow and throat respectively.

So we each find these five spots on our bodies. Sue, Gordon, Wilma and Big Carol already know about them; Alan, Joy and I have learned something new.

Feeling a little bit foolish initially, we join in the spirit of the ceremony which is a Ceremony of Purification. One by one we dutifully climb first to the Spring of the Upper World where we anoint our five chakras, and then go on down to the other two fountains and repeat the ceremony.

A bemused party of rain-sodden American tourists watches us closely, but my feeling of foolishness and embarrassment has passed. I feel only a kind of peaceful acceptance.

Joy remembers the moment vividly.

'I was at a crisis point in my life. When I left South Africa to go on this spiritual journey, I was very cynical and sceptical, but I was also an extremely angry person, I had had a terrible year. I had lost my husband, who was my soulmate, I'd been held up at gunpoint, I'd been betrayed by someone I trusted who'd stolen money from our family.

'When we arrived at the sacred springs I was suffering from mountain sickness, feeling very heady and battling to breathe. Also I was feeling so cynical – wondering what on earth I was doing in this place with these strangers. After Carol had showed us how to use the water that bubbled out of the mountain spring, I dipped my hands into this mountain water and felt the most extraordinary sensation – it was peace and it was release. I was very emotional about it but I suddenly realised that I was letting go of the personal aspects of my life that had been tormenting me, and that I was ready to take the next step in my life. And the extraordinary thing was that these spiritual experiences kept on repeating themselves wherever we went.'

On that first night in Cusco, after the Purification Ceremony at the sacred springs, our teeth chattering with cold, our hands encased in the alpaca wool gloves we have eagerly bought from the opportunistic local vendors at the springs, we go high up into a cave with two Quechua healers. They have come down from the mountains to make an offering for our well-being and the success of our journey – simple men for whom making an offering to the *apukuna*, the divine lords of the mountains, was as natural as sleeping or waking. What may have seemed a ceremony or ritual to us was part of their everyday lives, because the Quechua live in constant communion with the spirits. The older of the two men has been a shaman for over forty years. The younger, his 'apprentice', for only twenty.

We stoop to enter the small stone cave which just about accommodates the nine of us and the two shamans. Six candles are burning. As we go through the low entrance we pass, lit by the flickering light of the guttering candles, the carved figure of a snake. The idea is that as you go into the cave you shed your skin, you shed your past, you shed the emotional and spiritual baggage that you want to get rid of, and when you emerge, like the snake, you will have shed your skin and be a different person – ready to move on to another phase in your life.

Remember this was only Day One in Peru, and as I watch these two committed and very humble men making their offerings to their spirits – to the Christian God, the spirits of the mountains, the moon, the sun and stars, all of which are indivisible to the Quechua people – my first feeling is of total disbelief and ironic humour. Although a non-Catholic, I had been educated in a Catholic Loreto Convent in England for thirteen years. I think as I watch and listen, 'Whatever would my Mother Superior say if she could see me now?' I smile to myself.

The shaman makes a very careful offering. On a square of white paper he places a coca leaf for each of us amidst a tidy pile of other offerings – gold and silver representing the minerals, flowers for beauty, grain and llama fat for food. He sings and prays as he works. What he is doing is giving back to Mother Earth, Pachamama, the most important of all deities to the Quechua people, all the riches and goodness she has given to humankind. When he finishes his *haywaskka* – his blessings and prayers – he wraps up this square of white paper and its contents into a very neat parcel and burns it on the fire his assistant has prepared outside the cave. When it has been utterly consumed he tells us in a matter-of-fact way that the gods have accepted our offering.

As we stand around the small fire in the bitter cold, the Southern Cross is trembling in the sky – almost as if in anticipation of the next night's full moon. I feel no spiritual mindshift – that would come later – but as we stand 3 600 metres up in the Andes surrounded by these huge peaks, a feeling of wonder and awe suffuses me. There is something very bonding, very emotional, very strong and powerful about being here, with nature, at such an altitude, with such a small group. We are in another world. The cold, the peaks, the jagged mountains against the sky – there is power here, and presence.

I feel the same power and presence the next day amidst the huge temple ruins of Pisaq, which overlook the enchanting little Andean market town of the same name. As dusk is falling we hike a long way up to the pre-Incan ruins and sit on another huge, shaped and chiselled rock, a similar 'Hitching Post of the Sun' to what we will find in Machu Picchu, which the Incas believed connects man to the heavens. It was from this point that the ancient wise men monitored the stars and measured the solstices, gauging exactly when to sow and when to reap.

Rómulo tells us that the Southern Cross is the 'Rector of the Heavens'. Terraces, thousands of years old, step up almost to the mountain peaks, their irrigation systems still functional. Quechua farmers still cultivate their crops on these ancient Inca terraces, practising crop rotation each year.

Carol tells us we may well see the mighty and majestic condor, the bird that connects humankind to the divine. The ten of us sit quietly watching the sun go down. We hear the rushing of wings and look up. Is this the condor?

A skein of ten dapper ducks flies directly over our heads. Ten ducks, ten people. Ducks in the Andes? Yes, says Rómulo, these are Andean Ducks. We know that birds are sometimes believed to be spiritual messengers, but this is too much. We burst out laughing and wave to the ducks as they fly off into the setting sun.

After darkness falls, Venus sets exactly overhead the huge stone astrological instrument. A falling star cascades to the valley bottom. We climb down the steep and rocky terrain in the darkness. Nobody is afraid as we stumble along the steep paths following the contours of the mountain. The stars pulse.

That night we stay in the delightful little market town of Pisaq which is built round a square whose cobbles were laid by the Spaniards over four hundred years ago. Mountains cradle the moonlit buildings as the shadows of clouds skim over the huge tree outside the small church on the west side of the square.

Our rooms are in an enchanting old Peruvian inn, the Hotel Pisaq, which is run by a young woman from Arizona and her handsome Peruvian artist husband. They met when he was studying in the States. The little hotel is a delightful mix of old and new, with curtains and bedspreads imported from America's Southwest happily complementing the murals depicting Peruvian images and stories painted by the tall, dark, young husband.

Carol has invited a Quechua healer from Patakancha to read the Coca Leaf Oracle for those of us who want to know our future.

In the West, coca leaves are synonymous with cocaine, drug lords, bad negative things. Carol reminds us that during the Bush administration, the United States of America used military helicopters to spray poison on the coca fields in the Peruvian jungle and the Andes.

But to Peruvians, the coca plant is not only a magical plant with great symbolic powers, a natural substance which is an integral part of Andean cosmology, a connection to the divine, but also a plant with miraculous healing qualities. Rómulo is to show us coca plants and talk about these qualities in much more detail during the two days we spend on his farm at the foot of Machu Picchu.

The *Pampa misayoq* – the Quechua healer – is waiting for us when we get back to the hotel. He has made a special journey down from his mountain community at 4 260 metres to read the coca leaves for us. He is a medium-sized man with the golden-brown skin, high cheekbones and slanted eyes so typical of the people of this region. His face is lined and wrinkled from the elements, but his age is impossible to guess – he could be anything from thirty-five to seventy. He wears a woven pointed cap of red, lavishly interwoven with other bright colours and with a multi-coloured tassel hanging from the point. His long woven fringed *serape* or poncho is also red and likewise interwoven with strips of different designs and different colours. He emanates goodwill and benevolence, smiling at us not only with his mouth but also with his dark eyes.

He elects to see our group one by one in our tiny bedrooms. Joy and Big Carol tell us afterwards how he had 'thrown' the coca leaves, in the manner that a South African *sangoma* throws the bones to divine the future. Carefully, delicately, he had selected certain leaves and 'read' their messages. Both women had been astounded at what he had told them.

Alan and I decide not to have our leaves read and hear his counsel. Our reason? We know our past, we tell ourselves, we're experiencing our present, and to know the future will be to spoil its mystery and surprise. Some months later I will be thankful that I did not listen to our future that night in Pisaq. It is to be the healer from the Amazon, the *ayahuascero* Felipe, who will foretell a major coming crisis in our lives.

Later, in a tiny restaurant on the edge of the cobbled square, over a dinner of exceptionally good local trout and exceptionally bad local wine, Carol tells us a remarkable story about a group of seven hikers whom Rómulo had taken on the Inca Trail to Machu Picchu where Carol met up with them.

The Inca Trail is only for the very fit. For four days participants hike and camp on an original Inca road which, on the fifth day, leads right into the sacred city of Machu Picchu. It is a tough, demanding, but amazingly uplifting experience – literally and metaphorically. A few days later when our small group is in the ruins of Machu Picchu, we see for ourselves hikers coming off the Inca Trail. Tired, some of them exhausted, dirty and trail-worn, they dance, whoop, and gambol about the old buildings like so many spring lambs. They say their bodies and minds have undergone some major metamorphosis.

We listen as Carol continues her story. Among Rómulo's group of seven hikers was Virginia, a tall blonde business executive from California with a wonderful laugh. But on the very first day of the trail she became ill, and neither the nurse in the party nor any of the latest drugs and medicines they had brought with them from America had any effect on Virginia's severe stomach cramps. Finally, she was put on the back of a horse and carried to the top of a 4 260 metre pass appropriately called *Warmi wannuskka* – Dead Woman's Pass.

At this stage the horse could go no further so Rómulo told Virginia that from then on she would have to walk or be carried. She moaned, 'Leave me here to die.' Rómulo told her that he could cure her in the ancient Quechua way. He prepared the medicine, rubbed it over Virginia's chest and stomach, wrapped her up warmly, and the two stocky porters took turns carrying her for the rest of the day.

The next day Virginia woke up a new person. She was well again. Although she kept remarking that she smelt like a 'dead person', she and the group hiked and sang their way along the Inca highway as it wound higher and higher amidst the towering peaks.

Carol tells us how she had watched a triumphant Virginia

proudly march into the ruins of Machu Picchu.

'Later,' she says, 'I asked Rómulo what was in the magic medicine. He replied, "Coca leaves boiled in water and sugar cane", adding almost as an afterthought, "Oh yes, and urine." '

The two trail porters and Rómulo himself had 'donated' this crucial ingredient to the medicine.

'Virginia never asked me what the medicine was made of, so I never told her,' says Rómulo. 'Or why she smelled like a dead person . . .'

In the morning, we squeeze on to the hotel's tiny, wrought-iron balcony and watch the villagers setting up the Sunday market in the square below.

The grey cobblestones are adorned with a kaleidoscope of colour as handwoven rugs, intricately worked tapestries, bags, blankets, hand-knitted sweaters, hats, gloves and ponchos of llama wool, alpaca or vicuña are set out on the wooden stalls. Jewellery, hand-painted ceramic bowls and pottery decorated with intricate, traditional symbols unique to the area are also carefully displayed alongside amulets for fertility, good luck and protection.

The square is thronged with people in traditional dress, the women in a mixture of styles from pre-Spanish days and Spanish colonial peasant dress, with tight bodices and short full skirts of many layers. Red is the predominant colour. Their hair is braided into two long plaits fastened at the back with a long ribbon, and everybody wears a hat – it seems that in this part of Peru hats are a non-negotiable option.

The women wear Panama-style hats of woven palm fronds or flat, pancake hats made of wool with coloured fringes hanging from the brim. On market days they decorate their hats with fresh wild flowers of all kinds, tucking them into

36

the brim, or pinning them to the flat top. Most of the men wear the traditional woven pointed caps which look more like a tightly fitting helmet than a cap. There's something very pixie-like about these caps.

Each district has a distinctive colour and pattern for its ponchos – you can tell where a person comes from by the way he is dressed.

Walking round the square, chatting to his constituents, is the young Mayor of Pisaq who carries his ancient silver-embossed staff – a symbol of his authority. A small group of musicians playing flutes, guitars and other indigenous instruments I can't recognise, stroll amongst the crowds playing their haunting, peaceful music.

I buy a tape from them. Sometimes now, when I am stressed or anxious, I play my tape and go back to that memorable market in Pisaq. The quality is poor – I don't think the term 'sound engineer' has reached these parts of the mountains – but the purity, clarity and evocativeness of the music is perfectly captured and soothes my soul.

The section of the market devoted to fresh produce is amazing in its colours and variety. Sacks brimming with cereals and legumes indigenous to South America jostle woven baskets filled with superb fruits from the sub-tropical farms near Machu Picchu. Different varieties of corn – brown, yellow, honey-coloured and golden – lie in heaps on the cobbles, whilst bewildering varieties of Andean potatoes are artistically displayed on colourful woven cloths.

Carol tells us that potatoes were first exported from Peru to Europe when the Spanish arrived some five hundred years ago.

We all try a glass of *chica morada*, a drink made from blue corn, which we find sweet and delicious. We decide against the *akkha*, the alcoholic beverage made from maize, a decision we later regret because we never get another opportunity.

What part, if any, did this unforgettable market play in my spiritual journey? I think the answer lies in the accumulative effect that these new, widely differing experiences was having on me. To be in a place so strange, so foreign, so totally different to anything I had ever seen or experienced, distanced me from my usual self, my routine concerns, my ordinary way of doing things. It was like being transported on a magic carpet to an alien yet somehow familiar environment, where people lived at one with the land and their gods, in an ancient harmony that stirred some recognition within me. Even though the sights, smells and sounds were new, there was a feeling of being 'at home', a vestigial recollection of 'belonging'.

I don't mean by these remarks that I was into any Past Life experience. No, it was a whispering recognition that we all once lived in harmony with our surroundings and gods in this way. But don't get me wrong. The life of these people is no pastoral idyll. They work hard, long hours in difficult, back-breaking conditions at impossibly high altitudes. But what they demonstrate to outsiders is that they have made peace with their conditions and with themselves. They may not have heard the Western cliché 'Go With the Flow', but that's what they do intuitively.

Being on a spiritual journey, as I now know, is experiencing these moments of recognition and becoming part of something much older and wiser than one's present self. Of shedding day-to-day concerns and egocentricity, and seeing something beyond oneself. Maybe the recognition is that there is a wider, perhaps total, community of souls in the universe and beyond, and that we can and should be part of this cosmic family.

A few days later, on a bright sunny morning, we drive past clumps of yucca, fertile valleys, snow-peaked mountains and small snotty-nosed boys herding goats, along a rough dirt road to the great circles of Moray, a little-known place off the tourist map that Rómulo Lizárraga, our Quechua guide, has already told us is the holiest place in South America.

Three huge amphitheatres, each of seven grassed terraces, rake down to a central circle at the bottom. Each terrace wall is built of stones and is higher than a man. It takes us a long time to walk down to that central circle. Fluffy white clouds scud across a bright blue sky. Far above, at the topmost rim of the circles, a man and a small boy are watching us. We sit in the bottom-most circle and meditate.

Alan and I no longer feel any strangeness at being asked to meditate. Meditation, far from being a New Age gimmick or Eastern esoteric practice, now means finding a quiet solitary place to sit and think our own thoughts, or to empty our minds of everything and let peace and nothingness seep gradually in. As we sit resting our backs against the warm stones, Carol suggests 'Commune with the spirit of the place.'

Scientists claim that these mighty circles were once Inca experimental crop stations. No way. Nobody would have taken the time and trouble to build something so awe-inspiring and majestic to try out new strains of turnips. These are surely ceremonial places – places of ritual and sacred rites.

As we sit quietly the feeling of energy is overwhelming. This is my first experience of a vortex of energy – something I have read about but never really believed. The sensation I had felt standing alone in the little stone circle at

Sacsayhuaman on our first afternoon in Peru returns to me, but magnified many times. Now the energy surrounds me like a thick blanket – it's physical, tangible and alerts all the little nerve endings in the body. Imagine a small warm swarm of bees buzzing inside you. I get a sense that over thousands and thousands of years this place has soaked up respect, worship, communication with the divinities. I have felt this atmosphere before, at Stonehenge in England and at the Sea of Galilee where Jesus preached the Sermon on the Mount. I felt it also at Uluru, Australia's most sacred site.

At this moment I have a feeling of great numbers of people, of bright robes, and birdlike, chattering voices.

Sue has brought her divining rods with her – thin straight pieces of metal about forty-five centimetres in length. They are bent at one end to form a 'handle' and the idea is to hold them out straight in front of you to see if any exterior magnetic forces cause them to move. We all have a go. I admit to feeling a tiny movement, but the rods do not really move. If I move my wrists a little, I can get them to move. But that's cheating. My tiny bees are still buzzing inside me, but that seems more of a personal response than a cosmic one.

However, when Sue holds the rods they dance, sway and rotate in front of her. Maybe it's practice, I think. After all, she is the most spiritually 'practised' of us all and has used the rods before. As the rods swing in front of her she tells us how at Sedona in Arizona, the supposed site of many vortices of energy, the rods had behaved in a similar way. Although now the movements are stronger.

Joy takes her turn at holding the rods. Although Rómulo has told us that these little-known amphitheatres are the most holy places in South America and are known for their energy vortices, Joy can't believe it when the rods start to twist and turn. She becomes very angry with me because I tell her that I believe she is deliberately making the rods move. She is adamant that she isn't. She says wonderingly that some force beyond her control is at work and thinks to herself, 'Is this telling me something? Should I actually perhaps not be so sceptical?'

As we sit with our backs against the bottom-most grey stone terrace, Sue describes how she is personally experiencing Moray's spirituality. She tells us how she's been looking forward for a long time to coming to Peru and feeling this energy. How she believes that when you come to a place like Moray, Machu Picchu or Ollantaytambo, your vibrations are raised, which means you put more energy into your body and you become a more conscious person. And this is a very important process.

She has read many explanations for places which have high magnetic energy – ancient underground upwelling water which magnifies the forces of the earth, certain minerals such as iron oxide. She feels sure that the Incas put a lot of their religious places in areas like these because they were more sensitive to earth energies than we are today. They realised that if they were in an earth energy situation which was more powerful, and practised meditation and conducted religious ritual, then they would be able to communicate with other dimensions more easily. It gave them a head start, so to speak.

Sue is feeling Moray's energy very powerfully. She feels it as a healing energy and a ceremonial energy. As we talk and listen we realise that three of our group, Sue, Joy and Wilma, whilst meditating, have shared a similar vision, which amazes them at the same time as reinforcing what they believe they have seen. This was the vision they shared – the details were not exactly the same but the general picture was. They had each seen a large Inca statue in the middle of the circle, about three metres tall. It was placed on a revolving golden disc and had some alignment with the sun.

Sue has sensed that the Incas would set the statue up in the morning so it would align with the sun which would then move round the statue and thus be aligned all day long until sunset. She saw this clearly and describes it to us in detail.

We know the Incas worshipped the sun which was a very powerful symbol for them. All three women have also instinctively understood that the Incas had some technology that we have lost today – levitation, mind power, what you will – and have been put in mind of the Incas' incredible stonework. How did they move the huge stones? Where did they come from? How did they get them to fit so perfectly together? There has to be some explanation which is not in our twentieth-century reality.

Sue, the landscape gardener who is tremendously knowledgeable about plants, also tells us how she feels sure that there were sacred plants here at one time. In fact, seeds and pollens and extracts of jungle plants have been found at some of these sacred places high in the Andes.

But she doesn't believe it was agriculture that was going on. For example, she argues, why are the Moray terraces arranged in sevens and threes – mystical numbers in many cultures? There's no reason to do that if you're simply building experimental crop stations. It's not a very effective use of space. So why waste good space on just sevens and threes?

Good point, I think. And tell her so.

'You understand that intuitively because you are an Old Soul,' she tells me.

I remember that Blind Dan told me the same thing, not long before I left for Peru, and how I didn't know or understand then what being an Old Soul implied.

Surprisingly to me, Gordon and Wilma agree. Yes, I'm an Old Soul.

Neither Alan nor I experience any visions in Moray. We certainly feel the energy and an atmosphere of worship. When we talk together that night we are still sceptical about the moving rods, although we cannot deny that Sue, Joy and Wilma have shared a similar 'vision'. We somewhat cynically agree that they had probably read the same books before coming to Peru.

As we climb out of the stone circle, where Sue, Joy and Wilma have 'seen' the golden statue, Alan wanders off to an adjacent circle which is in total disrepair. As he stands looking down some hundreds of feet to its bottom, the small, sloe-eyed, grubby little boy who has been watching us all with his father, walks up to Alan and shyly offers him two yellow flowers, then solemnly walks on. It is a precious moment of absolute innocence.

Our last trip today is to the nearby salt mines of Maras. We walk to where a strong spring, one of five, rushes out of the mountain. We climb down to taste the water which is ten times saltier than the sea. The river runs along a narrow channel at the base of the mountain and then is funnelled off into a number of small, sloping individual salt pans. The effect is of a steeply descending honeycombed terrace of white pools. The water collects here over a three-week period and then the residual salt is piled into heaps, the brown salt (that which has got mixed with earth) for the cows and other animals, the white for humans. The owner and family of each small pan gathers the salt by hand, standing for hours at a time knee-deep in water. A 99-pound sack sells for six *soles* – a dollar. To me the salt mines of Maras look like a scene out of Dante's *Inferno*.

'How do the people endure this life? What sustains them?' I ask Rómulo.

'Their faith,' he answers. 'They believe that if they are good, honest and sincere in this life, then the next life will be better. And they are grateful to Pachamama, Mother Earth, for giving them the gift of these salt mines.'

Another day we climb into our van and head upwards into the mountains. The road is narrow, corkscrewing, and climbs relentlessly towards the distant peaks. Around us in the valleys the rich brown earth is being hand ploughed with mattocks, or with a team of two oxen. Spring corn is shooting up. We stop to greet a family group cutting eucalyptus wood by the roadside. They offer us food – *wiru* – in their outstretched hands, a Peruvian tradition.

We climb, climb, climb to the mountain village of Willoc.

And draw sharp breaths.

We have stepped straight into the middle of a scene out of a National Geographic video. Sitting in a horseshoe around the village leader are over a hundred villagers from the surrounding countryside. This is a village meeting. They are all dressed in shades of red, in handwoven *serapes* of scarlet, vermilion, orange and gold. Even their flat hats are red, vividly contrasting with the monumental dark brown mountains which, although dwarfing them, somehow create a natural synergy with them. Nowhere in the Andes do I experience a feeling of man against nature, of men and women pitting themselves against the hostile elements. I feel, rather, an overpowering sense of harmony, because everything stems from Pachamama, and she is good.

Seventy or eighty schoolchildren, also clad in traditional costume, greet and surround us. But their brightly coloured red clothes are not worn for the tourists – this is their everyday gear. The children are solemn with a natural dignity – it is very hard to make them smile.

The whole scene begs an impressionistic response. Mountains, valleys, clouds, blue sky, thin air like manna, huddled people in red – life going on as it has done for centuries. We, the visitors, are merely a brief punctuation in their business of living.

We have been in Peru for only a few days, but something is happening to my mind, my psyche, my spiritual being, call it what you like. What is happening is that past experiences, past memories are beginning to re-emerge, to make their way out of the jumbled attic of my subconscious, and are beginning to take on some meaning. Experiences with a strong spiritual resonance, which have lain half forgotten on that dusty floor of memory, are resurfacing, but with a different perspective, a different meaning and a different dimension.

I'm beginning to blow the cobwebs off the obscured map of my spiritual journey. My friend and spiritual mentor, Blind Dan, had always told me that I was on a spiritual journey, but I had never been fully conscious of it.

Now as the darkness lifts, I begin to see the milestones.

THREE

The Veiled Prophet

The time has come for me to tell you about Blind Dan, my friend and spiritual mentor.

Dan and I met through the airwaves. He was one of the very first callers to my radio programme *Believe It or Not*. He often offered the 'African' view of the world, an 'African' philosophy, but as his calls became more regular, it was clear that he was also steeped in Western philosophy, religion and culture. One night he told me and the other listeners that he was blind. I became determined then to find out more about this fascinating man whose intense, passionate way of articulating his unique point of view had become a part of my professional life. Now he was to become part of my personal life too.

Dan lives in a Home for the Blind in Johannesburg, in an area that was unfamiliar to me. I had called to ask if I could come and see him. Yes, he would be delighted.

His directions as to how to find him were atrocious – maybe because he is blind. It was one of those hot, summer highveld afternoons when the thunderheads were building up on the horizon. The Friday afternoon traffic was also building up as I drove round and round getting uncharacteristically more and more flustered, frustrated and finally angry. I very nearly gave up trying to find the place.

'Right, one more try,' I told myself grimly, turning my car round and heading back in the direction I had just come from. I felt like Alice. As if everything was becoming more and more surreal. Johannesburg's skyscrapers loomed in the distance, heat mirages shimmered in front of me and the tar was melting on the roads. All I needed now was the White Rabbit to surface and remind me that 'I'm late, I'm late, I'm late.'

After even more wrong instructions from pedestrians who claimed confidently that they knew where the Home for the Blind was, even more garbled directions from enthusiastic garage attendants who knew nothing, I finally nailed a sympathetic passing police car whose friendly driver restored my faith, hope and equilibrium at one stroke.

'Follow me, lady. I'll take you there.'

I had so nearly given up the quest, but had I done so, I believe my life may not have changed. That my spiritual journey would still be unknown to me. Because it was Dan who first alerted me that I was on a spiritual journey – as everyone else is, unconsciously or consciously – and that I must look out for milestones along the way. Milestones in my past, milestones in my present, and milestones still to be reached. I listened without hearing. I didn't really understand what he meant. It was only as my journey through Peru progressed that his words took on meaning.

Dan had dressed up for this first meeting with me and was sitting quietly and patiently on his bed as I knocked and went into his room. A piece of paper pinned to his door warned passers-by and other residents that he was meditating and was only to be disturbed by appointment.

I apologised for being so late.

He told me that he hadn't been at all worried. 'I knew you would come.'

I looked around me. I was in a small bedroom. There was a bedside table with his precious radio on it – precious because it was his lifeline to the outside world, a rather dilapidated armchair in danger of losing its stuffing, a wardrobe, a window, and a dramatic, brightly coloured, eye-catching print hanging above his bed. My eyes were drawn back over and over again to this print as the hot afternoon drew to a close. A small kitchen led off this bedsitting room with a sink, a fridge, a couple of cupboards and two empty red wine bottles.

Dan rose to greet me, then sat back on the bed, offering me the chair. We sat in silence for a moment, assessing each other, getting a feel of each other.

I saw a man of medium height who looked frail. He had a whitish beard, small, smooth hands, and a gap in his front teeth which, when he smiled, made him look like a mischievous imp. He was dressed almost rakishly in a brightly coloured short-sleeved African embroidered shirt of the sort favoured by Nelson Mandela, blue jeans and a black velvet beret. Round his neck was a strikingly attractive blue and white beaded choker necklace. I commented on it. Dan told me proudly that his grandmother had given it to him long ago.

'I won't go anywhere without this necklace. I'm not complete without it.'

Over the subsequent months I began to feel that I knew

Dan well. We had bonded instantly on that first meeting, and Dan had told me that he had foreseen our relationship and that it was meant to be.

So who is Dan? Who is this man who has played a crucial role in my spiritual development?

Dan Sefudi Rakgoathe is an artist, poet, philosopher and mystic. Born in 1937 in Bongweni, a black township in Johannesburg, South Africa, even as a little boy he intuitively knew that he was 'different' from his siblings, with the gift of foreseeing. He would foretell simple things like the visit of a relative, or more dreadful happenings like the death of a loved one.

He was at Fort Hare University when his father died. At our very first meeting he told me what had happened. One night he had dreamed he was in a mortuary and had suddenly felt a sharp electric shock hit the back of his neck. When he turned round he saw his father's face, young and smiling. His father told him to stop searching because he was no longer in this world. He likened himself to an empty matchbox – 'There is no fire there. I am here.'

The next day Dan learned of his father's death. At the funeral, as Dan was looking sadly at his father lying in state, he felt his father's arm around him and heard his father's voice saying, 'Don't worry, I'm all right.' It was at that moment that he recalled the pact that he and his father had once made. That whoever died first would come back and reassure the other.

We sat quietly for a moment and then I commented on the striking picture above Dan's small, neatly made bed. 'I've been aware that you keep looking at it,' said Dan. 'It's one of my favourites. I did it over twenty years ago.' I was astonished. How could a blind man produce something like that!

He felt my palpable surprise. 'You didn't know I was an artist, did you?' he laughed. 'I can feel your shock and surprise. But I wasn't always blind, you know.'

I found out that Dan was well known and highly regarded for his etchings, woodcuts and linocuts. When I visited an exhibition of his work at Grahamstown's Festival of the Arts in 1996, not long after our first meeting, I saw the full range of that work for the first time. The exhibition, called *Behold the Mystic Sign*, was featured in the Festival programme as one of the highlights.

I found myself responding to his work in the same way as I had done on my first visit to the Home for the Blind. It struck some chord in my consciousness.

Striking, colourful, bold and imaginative, it conveys his personal philosophy as a mystic with a great awareness of the spirituality of human existence. Dan transmits his unique personal vision of man's metaphysical journey through the cycle of birth, death and reincarnation through which he explores cosmic consciousness. His evocative images are powerfully expressive and are imbued with a mystical aura. He uses concepts like 'awakening' and 'the illumination of the soul through divine inspiration' in his art, and symbols such as the sun, moon, male and female. Web-like shapes and interwoven lines reveal his holistic awareness and his strong belief in the interrelatedness of human beings and cosmic forces in the universe.

I was drawn to one linocut, *The Unfolding Man*, again and again. Its central image, a crucified figure surrounded by strong designs and whirling shapes, was surmounted by a beneficent sun spreading its rays. When I went to see Dan, after returning home from Grahamstown, he gave me his poem of the same name that is in the USA's National Library of Poetry. When Dan wrote it, he did not yet know of the tragedy that would befall him – the greatest tragedy of all for an artist.

> *Now, I know I am crucified*
> *To this wasting shell I called Me*
> *Yet – I did not know here to fore*
> *That this mortal MATTER was never true me*

> *Now, I begin to grow with wisdom*
> *In learning from painful passion*
> *That – I am expanding more and more*
> *As every pang arouses rapturous awareness*
> *Of the good that comes out of painful experience*

> *Now, I begin to understand in depth*
> *That I am GOD in GOD and all that is GOD*
> *A GOD – forever unfolding in all CONSCIOUSNESS*
> *That I am ONE with all BIG and SMALL*
> *FOR GOD – the OVERALL dwells in ALL*
> *I know . . . I know . . . I know*

As I finished reading the little room fell quiet. I didn't know what to say, how to express my compassion. I fought back tears. Dan picked up my distress and saved the moment by remarking, 'It's not pure poetry, you know. Not poetry for poetry's sake. I use poetry to make my mystical message clearer – as a kind of supplementary to my visual work.'

Dan grew up in a small, poor home in one of the black ghettos of Johannesburg during the apartheid years, when blacks were looked down upon, discriminated against, abused and often reviled. Considered by many white Afrikaners to be of inferior intelligence, little better than a lower form of animal life, black people were second-class citizens, without a vote, without access to a decent education, and often without hope.

Dan, with the help of his father, whom Dan describes as 'a great philosopher, though unrecognised', and through his own gifts, unique vision and hard work, not only overcame the repressive system by managing to acquire a Bachelor of Fine Arts degree with Honours from a black South African university, but also went on to win a Fulbright Scholarship to the University of California where he took a Master's degree in Fine Art, African Literature and Philosophy. All this at a time when it was almost unheard of for a black person to overcome the restrictions of the ghetto, let alone be admitted to tertiary education.

In the early Eighties he was a successful art lecturer in Soweto, his work unfolding more and more successfully, when suddenly a hideous and ironic tragedy struck. Dan became blind. The cause? Diabetes.

One day we were having lunch at a Portuguese restaurant near the Home for the Blind – a great treat for Dan who doesn't get much opportunity to leave his little room. We were discussing the impact of his blindness on him. He told me that although he had always had fore-knowledge of his blindness, and had even produced a prophetic self-portrait twenty years before his blindness struck, even so, when it happened it was so traumatic that he had seriously contemplated suicide. He had kept thinking about the best way to take his life. He was never afraid of death because he felt that death was one of the blessings that nature bestows upon living creatures. Because death is not an end but a transition.

I asked him, over the chicken peri-peri, what he meant

by transition.

He meant reincarnation. He *knew* reincarnation existed.

'How do you know that?'

'Let me explain to you, Kate. People often get it wrong nowadays and concern themselves overmuch with their past lives. Past lives are not important. Nobody should waste his or her time trying to recall who they were in a past life. Past lives are a closed book. You are now continuing from here, this moment. You are going forward, and if you believe in the law of reincarnation' (Dan used the word *law* emphatically), 'you should be preoccupied with what you will be in the next reincarnation, rather than what you were in the past.

'Time doesn't exist. How can you talk of the future when the future has not been, has not yet occurred? Yet people talk of the future as if it is there. How can you talk of the past, because the past has been and gone. It does not exist as an entity.'

'If there is no time, then what is there?'

'Time exists only in human consciousness.'

We continued to argue about reincarnation, as we had from the moment we met. I simply cannot bring myself to believe in it; Dan is adamant that reincarnation exists.

'It's no good, Dan, you're never going to convince me.'

'Let me try to put it another way. Maybe you'll understand better. There's an error many people make when they think of reincarnation. Do you know what most people believe? They think of the return of the *individuality*, which is not true. You won't return as Kate. You won't return in the same individuality as you are now. You will not be the person who was Kate in the past incarnation. But if you look closely, if you did take the trouble to find out who you were in the past – although as I've told you I don't believe in delving into past lives – then you will find a trend that will clearly show itself. In your next incarnation you won't be Kate. You won't be doing what Kate is doing now. Rather, you'll be doing at an advanced stage what Kate is doing now.'

'Will I still be Kate?'

'No. Reincarnation is the return of the soul personality, so it won't be "Kate" who reincarnates, but her soul. Let me tell you, and this is what The Masters have told me during my visions and meditation. It will be your soul.'

As our relationship grew and developed I began to 'listen' to Dan more closely. At first, I had not really heeded or listened closely to many of the things that he told me, simply because they seemed so strange to me, and irrelevant to the hectic life I was leading. I've always been a goal-oriented person, accomplishing one thing, achieving another, too busy to think about things spiritual.

But as I learned more and more from the people I met on my radio programme, gaining a greater understanding of many of the spiritual topics we discussed, so I began to question my own beliefs. Where did I stand spiritually? At this stage, pretty well uncommitted. But there was a growing awareness that there was more to life than surface.

Dan finally confided to me that he belongs to one of the great Mystical Orders of the world – the Rosicrucian Order, an ancient order wrapped in mystery, mysticism and theosophy, of which he is one of the Healing Illuminati. They have given him the name the 'Veiled Prophet'. That same day he said to me, out of the blue, 'You're an Old Soul, Kate.'

The way he said it made me feel that this was a good thing to be, but I didn't know quite what to make of it, what being an 'Old Soul' meant.

'What's an "Old Soul"?'

'Let me tell you first what it's not. Some people believe that being an Old Soul means having reincarnated many times. That's rubbish, nonsense. Reincarnating, that is repeating reincarnations, doesn't necessarily make you an Old Soul, because you might be so lazy and idle in each of those incarnations, that you never make any progress forward. So if you are born three times within a period where you have been very lazy, not trying to expand and improve yourself, then you are not making any headway. So in spite of having three incarnations, you are still at the same stage of evolution as you were.'

His gaze became still and he took my hand in his frail one.

'Kate, it's time for me to tell you something. In your next incarnation you are poised to become a prophet or a prophetess.'

As I started to laugh and protest a charge of electricity passed from him to me and I shuddered involuntarily. He did not know that I came from a long line of Yorkshire witches whose family name was Ashburn. One woman of each generation since the 1600s has had the gift of second sight. Only twice in my lifetime has it come to me, and several times to my youngest daughter. The last occasion was when she was studying in the United States and, not knowing that her father was critically ill with cerebral malaria, she had called *knowing* intuitively that something was desperately wrong with him.

Dan continued, his small, smooth hand pressing hard into mine.

'Do you know what makes me know this? Because of what you are engaged in presently, that shows what you are

heading for. The radio programme you are involved with –
that programme could not have accommodated anybody
except an Old Soul, somebody who could lead it through
with such empathy and experience as you do. What you're
doing is drawing from your subconscious old wisdom that
you have garnered through your past. That is what attracted
you to your radio programme – that is why you decided to
do it even though nothing before in your broadcasting career
had been even remotely similar. Your radio station took an
absolute flyer – they couldn't have known, even if they'd
hoped for it, that a programme that dealt with spiritual
matters would catch the public's imagination. And that's over
four years ago now.'

I phoned Dan excitedly when I learned that I was going to
Peru.

'What do you think?'

'I don't think, I *know*,' he said mysteriously.

'Know what?'

'That now is the perfect time for you to go to Peru. Ten
years ago would have been too soon. Even five years ago, a
year ago. You are now ready.'

'What do you mean – "ready"?'

'I've told you so often, Kate, that you're on a spiritual
journey. Now you're going to find out the truth of that for
yourself.'

'That sounds a bit heavy!'

'Shhh, Kate. Hear me out. Listen to that voice inside you.
It's been getting louder and louder. I've heard it myself when
I talk to you. It is unmistakable. It will always guide you if
only you will give it a chance to guide you. You take your
hunches and intuitive impulses for granted – we all do. We

often don't even want to listen to them, we don't want to reflect upon them, or meditate upon them. But listen to that voice. It's like the connecting cord of a phone – with somebody speaking at the other end. The connecting cord between the lower self and the greater self, which is cosmic. That connecting cord is intuition and it is only through intuition that we can become enlightened. Trust me. *Bon voyage*.'

The phone went dead at the other end.

I put down the receiver slowly. I sat and thought for a few moments, then I dialled his number.

'Yes, Kate?'

'How did you know it was me?'

'I knew.'

'You talked about this cosmic cord which connects us all. But what does it connect us *to*? Divinity? Cosmic power? A great pool of spiritual knowledge?'

Dan was emphatic.

'Please get this clear. Cosmic consciousness is not something objective and isolated from us. We are part of it. That which people are hunting for frantically – call it God, whatever – is just this whole cosmic wisdom and consciousness of which we are all a part.

'In Sotho we have a term which applies so well. *Morati – From Me To You Beloved.*

'Goodbye, Kate. Have a wonderful journey.'

FOUR

Willka T'ika

Let's return now to Peru.

After the high ruins and crowded market place of Pisaq, the salt mines of Maras, the story book village of Willoc, we arrive at Carol's home and spiritual sanctuary Willka T'ika.

Willka T'ika – Sacred Flower – is a special place of beauty and harmony in the heart of Peru's Sacred Valley of the Incas. It's the culmination of a dream for the slight, determined woman who made her own path by walking it.

For many years Carol was married to a doctor. Together they raised four children and lived a comfortable life in Southern California. Carol first started leading groups to Peru nearly fifteen years ago. What was at first an attraction to the land and its peoples, slowly grew into a compulsion which culminated in her divorcing her husband and moving permanently to Peru, where she built Willka T'ika, her farm.

But the word 'farm' fails to paint an adequate picture of what the place is really like. It's much more than a farm. Situated between the quaint, historic little town of Cusco, perched some 3 350 metres up in the Andes, and the towering peaks of one of the most sacred and spiritual places on earth – Machu Picchu – the two acres of Willka T'ika nestle in the valley of the Urubamba River.

Built by local craftsmen, it combines the traditional sixteenth-century Spanish colonial style with the indigenous handwork used by Peruvians for thousands of years to construct their temples and cities.

Huge, solid wooden gates lead into the farm. In front of the wooden, ranch-style buildings are masses of brightly coloured flowers tumbling in glowing profusion about the green lawns – delphiniums, snap dragons, carnations, cosmos, verbena, alyssum, gypsophila, lupins, geraniums, salvia, marigolds. Nasturtiums climb the walls and jostle clumps of fuchsia.

Handmade ceramic pots spill out yet more flowers, watched over by the head of a puma – a potent Peruvian power animal – carved between the cobbles of a handmade stone path. Curved terracotta tiles protect honey-coloured adobe walls, handmade wooden balconies jut out beneath eaves, and curved windows and doors add to the feeling of peace and harmony. Ceramic tiles, wall hangings and plaques, made by the village potter, decorate the walls. Grey boulders, placed haphazardly around the main house and guest buildings, complement the uneven walls surrounding the farm – each wall raised by hand, stone by stone, in the time-honoured method of centuries.

We feel our minds and bodies relax as we unpack our few belongings in the cool whitewashed rooms where handwoven curtains, bedspreads and rugs echo the ancient designs of a centuries-old civilisation.

The mountains tower high above Willka T'ika, offering a

sense of beneficence and protection, but also a reminder of the power of nature and the *apukuna*, the divine lords of the mountain.

One by one we wander out into the peace of the gardens and admire the huge stalks of *wiru*, the sacred corn of the Andes, thrusting up from the rich, brown earth. Joy and Big Carol sit under the shade of the five-hundred-year-old Lucma tree and absorb the pure energies of the mountains, river and valleys. They raise their faces to the sun and close their eyes.

Sue is the first to follow the stone-edged paths, planted with sacred and healing plants, medicinal herbs and yet more flowers, of the walk-around spiral that Carol told us is intended to lead you on an external and internal journey to examine your innermost thoughts and feelings.

Gordon and Wilma, holding hands, rest on the raised wooden Andean meditation platform and gaze out at the high snow-peaked mountains. Alan and I take a look at one of the special sites used for traditional ceremonies such as offerings to Pachamama – Mother Earth.

As I write, a dried sprig of tiny yellow flowers falls out of my notebook on to my computer keyboard. It is from Willka T'ika. Its delicate, evocative fragrance envelops me.

'Something brought me to this particular spot in the Sacred Valley,' remembers Carol. 'And when I found the ancient Lucma tree, I knew it was my place. I was determined that everything should be done in the old way – even though it took years and a lot of patience to achieve it. Everything inside and outside the house comes from our natural surroundings – the wood, the stones, the bricks, the glass cut to the shape of the arched windows, the floorboards cut from local wood. Willka T'ika is a revival of ancient technology – bricks, mud, wood and straw.'

Only one thing is 'unnatural'. The Quechua housekeeper, Antonia, 'planted' into the garden the plastic rose that Rómulo Lizárraga's daughter Indira had given Carol on Mother's Day.

'Never give flowers,' she had scolded the well-meaning little girl, adding darkly, 'Flowers are for the dead and the saints', as she pushed the waxy red rose into the earth. Defiantly, it 'blooms' on over a year later, as if to say that kindness and thoughtfulness can be as fertile as the dark soil surrounding it.

We spend a night in this lovely, peaceful place and I awake the next morning knowing that I will return one day.

In the morning our group of seven pilgrims makes its way to the picture book village of Ollantaytambo high in the mountains where the people still live the same way they have for centuries. We climb to the top of this once-mighty fortress and sit on one of its stone-walled terraces. Here, one of the Spaniards' most feared enemies, Manco Inca, made his last stand. We look down on to the open square hundreds of metres below and imagine the scene as the proud Spanish horsemen and their troops were routed.

A contemporary account describes the battle. 'We tried to creep in at dawn and surprise the Incas, but it was a horrifying sight! As soon as we came within bow shot thousands of eyes were upon us and dark figures rose up above all the ramparts.'

Manco Inca had manned the terraces with bowmen from the Amazon forests and with Inca troops armed with slingshots and javelins. When the terrified conquistadores tried to retreat, Manco Inca diverted the river Patacancha to flood the low ground, so that their horses foundered and became bogged down.

Here at Ollantaytambo the Incas built a great temple to the Sun and another to the Moon. High on the surrounding mountains, about two-thirds of the way down from the tallest peaks, the remains of huge stone storage rooms still cling strongly. Here grain and crops were stored in a system of natural refrigeration as the high winds blew around the stores and kept them cool.

We are 3 650 metres up when we reach the Temple of the Sun. Huge red granite blocks, once fitted together with seals of gold, interlock as tightly as a completed jigsaw puzzle. I remember standing at another place in another time a few years ago, in Egypt's Valley of the Kings. It seems to me today that this ancient Inca temple would not have been out of place there. The similarities in architecture, design, decoration and atmosphere are strikingly similar. But the carvings adorning this temple's façade are uniquely Peruvian, a reiteration of the Andean cosmology: the condor, for the world of the spirits; the puma, for this world; and the snake for Pachamama and our inner life.

Something strange has happened within our group. Big Carol, as we call her affectionately, as opposed to the slight figure of Willka T'ika's Carol, has always suffered from vertigo. A large, comfortable woman, always short of breath, she had worried about the heights and the climbs involved before finally deciding on her Peruvian Magical Journey. Friends and relations told her not to go. 'You won't make it.' 'You'll be a drag on the other people.' 'Lose some weight first.' There are over three hundred steep steps up to the top of Ollantaytambo. We all climb them with difficulty. Carol experiences no more difficulty than the fittest member of our small group. She is suffused with a natural energy and keeps shouting with joy at her physical achievements. Her vertigo has vanished. She attributes this to the fact that she feels that she has been in this place before – in a previous existence. Her feet seem to know the twists and turns of the paths as she walks lightly and confidently above precipitous drops to the valley below.

Big Carol shared her experiences with thousands of listeners to my radio station some months after our return home from Peru.

'Nobody would believe this, but I was home. I mean, I felt at home, that's the only way I can describe it. It sounds really corny, but I felt at home in so many of those high places. It was the same feeling at Machu Picchu. I *knew* I had been there before. I felt my greatest strength there – I was in command of everything there. I can't explain it any better than that – I was home.'

We are soon swiftly returned to the world of the here and now when we take the local train from Urubamba on a two and a half hour journey to Rómulo's farm at the foot of Machu Picchu. In the local Quechua language *machu* means 'ancient' and *picchu* means 'summit' or 'mountain top'. The train track runs along the bottom of the Sacred Valley of the Incas, and the train journey through this valley with its white water torrents, raging river and spectacular scenery must compete for one of the most beautiful in the world.

Never is there a sense of menace, danger or destruction. The whole spirit of this part of the Andes can only be called benign. The traveller feels safe, secure, at peace and at home. A young flute player, dark-eyed, soulful, with an *unkhuna* – a small cloth of vivid, glowing colours – around his shoulders, wanders from carriage to carriage playing lilting tunes on his Andean flute that bespeak joy, peace and harmony.

The train makes a special stop for us (although 'pause' would be a better word because we have to tumble off in great haste before the train picks up speed again) at the beginning of the steep, downward rocky path that leads to Rómulo's farm. We inch down it in the dark, cautiously navigating the uneven terrain by the light of two inadequate flashlights. We hear a rushing and a tearing sound.

Suddenly, we are on the banks of the Urubamba River, a tributary of the Amazon which tosses and rages a hundred feet below us. One by one, too amazed and incredulous to be nervous, we sit astride a small wooden platform, an *oroya*, legs dangling either side, heads to one side to avoid being decapitated by the thick metal cable winching us across the turbulent river below to the opposite bank. No one feels alarmed, no one feels afraid or threatened. It is pitch dark, which is as well. Had we seen the drop or the antediluvian method which ferried us across high in the warm night air, even Big Carol's newfound courage might have deserted her.

Big Carol, Joy and Sue sleep in a low adobe hut accessed by a flight of rickety wooden stairs. Gordon and Wilma, Alan and I share a large wooden cabin divided into two by a wooden partition. We are warned to be careful when we go outside our cabin – just the other side of the bushes there's a sheer drop to the river below.

After a soup made of local squash we fall into bed. The rushing of the river is the last sound we hear.

Rómulo and his family are Quechua *campesinos* (farmers) who have farmed here for generations. The next morning we see that this farm is not made up of fields and terraces as so many of the hillside farms, but is rather a camp surrounded by wooden and adobe buildings. It clings to the mountainside amidst sub-tropical vegetation that somehow seems unlikely in this place of high, snow-clad peaks. Hens pick their way about, guinea-pigs constantly 'vacuum' the hard dirt floors, two kittens play in the sun and a couple of well-fed dogs doze peacefully.

We drink lemon grass tea and the best coffee in the world. Pancakes are made over a wood-burning stove and we eat them with fried plantains and bananas. The guinea-pigs run about busily under our feet mopping up any stray crumbs. Guinea-pigs – *kkowi* – are found in all Quechua homes and perform a triple bill. They double as vacuum cleaners, they are used for healing, and when extra protein is needed in the diet, an older male *kkowi* is selected, its neck is swiftly snapped and it goes into the cooking pot or is roasted over an open fire. We are not invited to eat *kkowi*, but Rómulo tells us that the meat tastes like poultry.

There's a special vortex of energy at this farm – it is palpable. We feel remarkably energised – as if our old batteries have been replaced by brand new, super-charged ones. We wash in spring water from the mountains and I hang out some washing on a line strung between two buildings. Far, far above me, the mysterious cloud-wreathed peak of Machu Picchu is unfurling itself from the early morning mist. By noon, it will appear in all its glorious awe-inspiring clarity – no wonder the Incas built a sacred city here. The outlines of faint paths clinging to the contours of the mountain can be seen. This is an aspect of Machu Picchu that is rarely seen by the tourists who ascend the other side of the mountain in cheerful, loud buses which wheeze their way up and round the precipitous mountain paths. We feel privileged to share

Rómulo's simple home with him.

The conquistadores never found the ancient city of Machu Picchu – that is why we are able to see it in all its glory today. The Incas never finished the city and, in fact, had abandoned it before the Spanish arrived some four hundred and sixty years ago. It is said that the history of the Incas is sixty per cent speculation, thirty per cent probability and only ten per cent established fact. Most of what we know about the Incas comes from the biased reports of the Spanish conquerors and latter-day archaeological research. Historians put Manco Inca's founding of Cusco and the Inca civilisation as such at around AD 1100. But we also know now from the work of modern archaeologists that Cusco had been inhabited by unrecorded pre-Inca cultures for thousands of years before.

What we do know for sure is that it was The Inca, believed to be the Son of the Sun, who ruled absolute. As Son of the Sun he ruled by Divine Right because the Inca people believed their race to be the children of the sun and the moon. To challenge The Inca, therefore, was to challenge God.

Rómulo tells us the Inca creation myth.

Once upon a time, when the world and its peoples were in darkness, the Great Lord, the Sun, sent his only son Manco Capac to earth to spread culture and enlightenment. At that time too, the Moon sent her daughter, Mama Occlo, to be Manco's bride. They appeared on earth, emerging from the waters of Lake Titicaca at the islands now known as the Islands of the Sun and Moon.

Manco Capac had been told by his father, the Lord of the Sun, to travel day and night, near and far, until he found a rich, fertile place into which he could easily plunge his golden staff. After long wanderings the couple finally found such a valley, and when Manco plunged his golden staff into the ground it sank and disappeared into the rich earth. Manco Capac named the spot Cusco, 'the navel of the earth', and here founded the Inca capital and empire.

But although the Incas subsequently controlled and ruled over an empire of six million people with a hundred different ethnic groups speaking twenty languages in a territory as big as the Roman Empire, they were missing one crucial cultural component – they had no written language.

One of the most moving moments of my pilgrimage was when I stood in Lima's Gold Museum before a mounted wall-hanging of the twisted knots known as *khipu* that the Incas used for their 'language'. Unlike Egyptian hieroglyphics, which could be interpreted and read after the finding of the Rosetta Stone, nobody yet has been able to decipher the meaning of these intricately knotted strings, although Dr Alberto Villodo, a medical anthropologist, psychologist and author, and expert on the Incas, told me that during his research he had met with descendants of the ancient Incas who had fled the conquistadores and were now living in villages 5 800 metres up in the Andes. He said that these people could still interpret the *khipu*.

That the knots form patterns and have meaning we know from the accounts of the conquistadores, and as I stood before this dusty museum exhibit I thought what stories these tongueless pieces of cord could tell, if only they could 'speak' to us. An invisible barrier of time, culture and meaning lay between me and this poignant reminder of a once great past. I felt strangely moved.

Dr Villodo also told me, when I interviewed him in Johannesburg, that these descendants of the first Incas had recently been driven by moral imperative to come down from their mountain eyries to tell the world of their ancient prophecies. As with many other millennium predictions, these prophecies tell of cataclysmic events, natural disasters and a swing by humankind back to the traditional ways where reverence for nature and empathy with Pachamama will be restored.

Professor Hiram Bingham from Yale University was first credited with having found the ancient 'lost' city of Machu Picchu, and his highly readable account, *Lost City of the Incas*, is a classic of its kind.

Although Bingham's theories are now outdated, his fascinating tales of treasure, buildings buried under jungle creepers, explorations and wondrous discoveries still excite the imagination and did much to create the mystical and magical fame that surrounds Machu Picchu – a fame that today draws millions of visitors from all over the world to this remote spot in the Andes.

But the local Quechua had always known about the sacred city at the top of the mountain and many had seen small objects of gold and silver that had been pilfered from the ruins. Gold was known as the 'sweat of the sun', silver as the 'tears of the moon'.

Rómulo tells us how his mother, Senora Lizárraga, still remembers the coming of the Americans in 1911 and the six years of excavation that followed. She heard stories of treasure at Machu Picchu as well as tales of mysterious deaths. She and her family saw heavy crates being carted out of the ruins, and shortly afterwards the first tourists began to arrive.

Hiram Bingham liked to think that he had 'discovered' Machu Picchu, but Rómulo's forefathers had always known it was there. After all, their ancestors – the ancestors of today's Quechua society – lived in these Andean areas long before the *Inkakuna*, The Children of the Sun. The *campesinos* have lived here for how long nobody knows, continuing their pastoral way of life and quietly maintaining their ancient rituals. For thousands of years the traditions and spirituality of the Andean people have been passed down orally from generation to generation.

During our two days at Rómulo's farm at the foot of Machu Picchu mountain, before we visit the legendary city for ourselves, we learn about the 'true' discoverer of the ancient lost city of the Incas.

We sit in the afternoon sun with our backs against the adobe walls of the small buildings. The two kittens are playing with some coffee beans which have fallen from their drying stand, chickens scratch busily around us in the way of all chickens worldwide.

We ask Rómulo about the vestigial paths that we can see leading up the sides of the great Machu Picchu peak.

He tells us the story of his grandfather, Angel Moriana Lizárraga who, in 1875, was leasing land at San Miguel along the edge of the Ahobamba River. San Miguel is the area at the foot of Waynapicchu (Young Mountain), which rears up over the ruins of Machu Picchu. If you're feeling energetic and have strong legs, you can climb Waynapicchu when we go to the ancient city, Rómulo tells us. Angel's brother Agustín, who helped him farm, was always on the lookout for more fertile farming land to cultivate the family squash, yucca and cereal crops.

One day when he was burning and clearing a valley at the foot of the Young Mountain, he stumbled across an ancient stone stairway. Curious, he climbed it to its very top and found himself on a level stretch of ground – the area today known as the Sacred Plaza of Machu Picchu. Agustín was thrilled to find level areas filled with rich soil, apparently waiting to be cultivated, but then he realised that these areas were terraces which formed the outer ledge of a vast, mysterious city hidden in the jungle.

So, says Rómulo triumphantly, it was my great uncle Agustín who really discovered the Machu Picchu ruins. And I can prove it. When we go up there I'll show you the great Sacred Rock where Uncle Agustín carved his name: *A.Lizárraga 1901*. And, as promised, when we go to Machu Picchu, he shows us the stone with Agustín's 'signature' carved upon it.

Where there was an ancient Inca city there had to be treasure, and Agustín found corn cobs and other objects made of gold and silver which had been placed by the Incas in niches in the walls of many of the buildings.

Soon the rest of the family got to know about the treasure and talked about the corn cobs made out of gold and the other fine items. But unlike Agustín, they had no desire to remove them from the ruins. They knew it was a sacred place and did not want to touch or remove any of the objects for fear of being punished by the ancient beings of the city.

But Agustín was young and rebellious and was more tempted by the treasure than respectful of Quechua traditions. It is said that he removed some beautiful objects within easy reach and sold them to a family of commercial merchants and traders, the Lomellini family from Italy. Years later, this family was known to be the most wealthy and admired in Cusco, thanks to their secret business with Agustín Lizárraga.

A scruffy ginger kitten jumps on to my lap and begins to purr loudly. Then it stretches and goes to sleep. We gaze at the faint outlines of the old stone stairways leading up the back of the mountain and think about Agustín and his treasure.

But Agustín couldn't keep the good news of his finds secret and shared them with his friends – Agustín's parties were legendary for their largesse. And so, of course, word of this man and his treasures reached the ears of Hiram Bingham – the 'true' discoverer of Machu Picchu.

I think of David Livingstone's 'discovery' of the great Victoria Falls in the country that is now Zimbabwe – 'scenes so lovely must have been gazed on by angels in their flight', he wrote in an uncharacteristically emotional manner in his 1855 diary entry. But of course the indigenous people had always known about *Mosi-Oa-Tunya*, 'The Smoke That Thunders', just as Agustín and his family had long known about Machu Picchu.

The sun is setting behind the great peak as Rómulo finishes his story. We look up again at the green side of the mountain and the narrow curving path that led not only his great uncle Agustín to Machu Picchu, but also led the way for Hiram Bingham and for our own footsteps.

Big Carol and Joy lean against the warmth of the adobe wall. Sue sits quietly on a wooden bench with one of the dogs lying over her feet. Wilma and Gordon hold hands. Alan's eyes are closed but I know he is very much awake, reliving Rómulo's story in his mind. I gaze up at the distant mountain and wonder what brought me to this place. Is there a reason? I'm beginning to believe there is.

Rómulo takes us for a walk through his farm. A few months before a landslide washed away half of it. But he was lucky. His sister Clothilda's farm, five kilometres further on up the mountain, was totally obliterated as a thick stratum of mud, layers of slime, and huge boulders, some the size of a large house, destroyed everything in their path. She and her husband lost everything – the farm building, furniture, crops, livestock, and the money for the children's school fees that was under the mattress of their double bed. Waking up in the middle of the night, they had heard the landslide thundering down the river valley towards them and had run for their lives. Their neighbours, a family of eight, were all killed – buried under tons of mud and debris.

Rómulo shows us banana, grapefruit, avocado and coffee trees on our way down to the banks of the Urubamba River.

He stops before a coca plant. 'The greatest problem in South America,' he tells us.

He describes how this 'wonder' plant, rich in so many healing properties, has been abused and debased by twentieth-century man. 'The coca plant has fourteen alkaloids – all with healing properties. But modern man has taken, processed, and marketed only one of those fourteen alkaloids – cocaine. My people chew the leaves for comfort and relief as we have done for centuries. When we mix them with a paste made from the banana flower, the resulting substance allows us to walk comfortably and easily for a hundred miles or more.'

Certainly when our group chews coca leaves to stave off altitude sickness or to hike the uphill path to Clothilda's farm, we feel the effects immediately. The taste is bitter, the texture scratchy and fibrous, but the leaves do their work well. We feel buoyant and full of energy.

But the coca leaf has a far greater power than warding off fatigue, hunger or altitude sickness. The leaves have a great symbolic power because they connect man to the sacred and divine energies of Andean cosmology. They act as a channel of communication between humans and the gods. Excavated burial sites show that coca leaves were used ceremonially thousands of years ago. Today the Quechua people use the leaves in their daily lives as well as in ceremony and ritual.

Rómulo describes one of the most frequently used offerings: the *kuka k'intu*.

He explains that a *kuka k'intu* is a brief ritual offering of coca leaves to the Andean deities, Pachamama or the *apukuna* – the lords of the mountain. The *campesinos* or peasants (words that are used with dignity and no negative connotations) offer a *kuka k'intu* before beginning the work of the day. It also is offered at all Quechua ceremonies, at the commencement of a special journey, before visiting a sacred site, and on many other occasions.

'We obtain leaves of the best quality and arrange them in threes, with the upper, dark green side facing the top,' explains Rómulo. 'We lift the *k'intu* in front of the mouth, and without letting them go, blow on them once. The blowing is called *phukay*. Then we respectfully call upon the local *apukuna* and the Pachamama, and may offer a silent prayer or make a request before beginning to chew the coca leaves. The leaves are a form of payment or offering to the Pachamama, *apukuna*, and the other divine energies of the mountains.'

We are now sitting on the gravelly river shore below Rómulo's farm gazing at the surrounding peaks. In places, lush, sub-tropical vegetation fringes its banks. High, high up on a mountain side, a lonely *campesino* burns some new ground. Immediately below him, his crops flourish.

This has always been the way of life and the same three ancient 'commandments' still govern the daily lives of the Quechua people as they have always done: *Ama sua, ama llula, ama quella* – 'Don't lie, don't steal, don't be lazy'. As we watch the farmers about their work, again there is an almost irresistible temptation to idealise them and to see their ancient way of life as a pastoral idyll. But although it's a life romantic to look at, it's a life that is back-breaking to live.

Rómulo tells us that there are hundreds of varieties of Andean potatoes existing today and we remember the different varieties spread out on the colourful cloths at Pisaq market. *Sara* – corn – is the sacred crop of the Andes and its origins have intrigued scientists from all over the world. It appeared in the Andes more than four thousand years ago and is a hybrid between theosinti and a perennial grass in the *cia* family. To the ancient Andean people, *sara* was a gift from God – the most sacred crop of the Inkakuna. Rómulo's great uncle Agustín and his friends found golden replicas of corn cobs in the ruins of Machu Picchu and others have been discovered in temples and holy places in Cusco and elsewhere in the Andes.

We learn about cereals such as *kiwicha*, *kinuwa* and *kkaniwa,* which are indigenous to the Andes and known as 'Food of the Gods'. They contain 10-25 per cent protein, much more than wheat and barley. They also contain significant quantities of calcium, phosphorus and magnesium. One of the proteins in *kiwicha* is called *lisina* and it enhances virility, strength and sexual prowess. The Inca men were known far and wide as fearless fighters and tireless lovers, but when the Spaniards found out about the properties of *kiwicha*, they banned its cultivation in Peru and replaced it with wheat and barley imported from Europe.

For nearly five centuries the magic grain was lost to us, but recently archaeologists have retrieved seed from old sites and it is once again being grown in the Andes. We saw sacks of *kiwicha* on sale in the market place at Pisaq. This potent plant has even orbited into space. NASA's laboratories discovered that *kiwicha* is not only full of protein and energy, but also low in calories and cholesterol. It's now not only the 'Food of the Gods' but food for astronauts as well.

'We have thousands of varieties of medicinal plants with unique healing properties,' Rómulo tells us as we sit by the rushing river. 'Quechuans use these plants to heal anything from a torn ligament or fractured bone, to kill internal parasites or cure burns.'

We discuss the controversial plant *Maca* – the plant containing substances that fortify the human immune system. Known to stimulate fertility in animals, studies by Peruvian and European scientists have shown that the plant tuber contains certain alkaloids that benefit the human immunological system. In Mexico *Maca* has been used to treat AIDS sufferers.

Later that day we hike up past a spectacular waterfall to Rómulo's sister's farm – or where her farm used to be. Clothilda and her husband Ramon have just finished building a small wooden shack to replace their former dwelling and are trying to put their lives back together. A lone turkey cock which survived the disaster struts importantly about the small clearing high on the banks above the river, still brown and muddy from the recent landslide.

Clothilda has made us soup. It is the gracious local custom to offer visitors food, however poor or needy the host may be. Clothilda shows us her new puppy – a small indiscriminately coloured female creature of high energy and sharp needle-like teeth. She suddenly singles me out and falls asleep on my lap. Clothilda shyly asks me to give it a name. I suggest 'Thandi', a South African name for a loved one. I often think of that dog high up in the Andes – surely the only dog in Peru with a Zulu name. I hope it brings joy and good luck to Clothilda and Ramon.

There are many caves in this area at the foot of Machu Picchu. The local people believe them to be the resting place of an ancient people called *Machukuna*. Rómulo had seen these caves as a boy and a few years ago Carol persuaded him and his brother Julio to take her there. It was an eight-hour hike from the family farm on the Urubamba River and Rómulo was not even sure if he would be able to find his way back to those ancestral caves. But after hours of hiking through almost impenetrable vegetation, with the brothers hacking at the tall grasses, bushes, trees and vines in their path, they arrived at a large, flat rock that overlooked the entire valley. This rock was a remembered landmark.

Carol, Rómulo and Julio held hands for a moment and asked for permission from the ancient spirits of the valley to enter the next valley where the caves were. Then they each took turns offering a *k'intu* of coca leaves to the Pachamama and local *apukuna*. The *k'intus* were then placed into the ground and covered with earth. They rested a while and the men chewed the coca leaves.

An hour later, Rómulo and Julio found the caves.

Carol stepped up to one of the caves and crouched down to peer inside. She saw some very large skulls, huge femurs and other bone fragments. At this moment the men took out a small bundle filled with wheat, corn and other grain that their mother had prepared as an offering, set it out on the ground for the spirit ancestors of the caves, and said silent prayers.

Carol tells us of the intense energy she experienced around those caves where the air had been undisturbed for many,

many years. She shows us a photograph of the ancient human relics. The huge skulls stare silently at the offerings, dwarfing the outsize corn cob placed reverently in front of them on the cave's loamy floor.

The old people say that behind Machu Picchu, in the Ahobamba valley, are more of these caves filled with the remains of the *Machukuna*. As neither Hiram Bingham nor subsequent archaeologists have found sites such as these in Machu Picchu itself, Rómulo and his family believe that the Incas buried their dead away from the sacred cities in valleys such as these.

As the three of them left the cave that day, making their downhill journey back to the farm, Carol looked up into the distance. She saw an old Inca pathway leading down from Machu Picchu into the valley they were leaving. Rómulo and Julio confirmed her sighting. It was one of the paths that Uncle Agustín had used to go in and out of Machu Picchu nearly a hundred years ago.

On the steep climb down from Clothilda's farm, I walk ahead of the group. Sue is picking flowers and marvelling at the gorgeous orchids lining the narrow path. Big Carol and Joy are deep in conversation about a past life. Gordon and Wilma are looking down on the river at the havoc caused by the landslide that destroyed Clothilda and Ramon's farm. The banks are piled high with mud, fallen trees and huge boulders, many as big as buildings.

I am walking in front of Alan with my mind in neutral, content to soak up the atmosphere surrounding me. Suddenly a long green snake slithers across the path in front of me. It is a bright, iridescent green. I am excited but don't know why. Alan catches a glimpse of its tail as it vanishes into the thick undergrowth.

I tell Rómulo about the snake.

'You are lucky,' he says gravely. 'Very few of us see such a snake. It comes from the *Ukhupacha* – the inner world, and brings wisdom.'

Looking back to that moment, I wonder if this rare sighting was another milestone on my spiritual journey. I believe it may have been. Before Peru, it would just have been any old snake – we get plenty in Africa. The serpent in Peruvian cosmology symbolises the inner life. As in the tradition of many Eastern beliefs, it awakens in the secret place at the base of the spine and rises up through the chakras, towards the head, activating the spiritual life and becoming *shakti* – divine energy.

I still wonder today if this green snake heralded the beginning of my spiritual wisdom, or if it was just another serendipitous coincidence.

❋

I've been doing a lot of thinking as the trip progresses. About things I've never really thought about before, or not in any meaningful way. I've become aware for the first time that, as Dan has always told me, I am on some sort of spiritual journey. I'm also becoming aware of some of the past milestones in that journey. Times, places and people come back into my mind – things I haven't thought consciously about or dealt with before . . .

FIVE

In His Name

When I was five years old, and my sister Rita was six, my mother and father 'rescued' us from being evacuees and brought us back to live with them. Once again we were a family. This was only now possible because my father had given up his job in London and had got a new job in Hertfordshire at De Havilland's aircraft factory. My parents had rented a new house between St Albans and Hatfield, where the factory was situated.

It was a modest three-bedroomed house, but its greatest delight was the back garden which sloped down into a wild wood. In springtime this wood was a riot of colour with huge red rhododendrons, white wild cherry blossom and carpets of bluebells. There were rabbits and foxes, blackbirds and robins, and enough thicket and undergrowth to delight the heart of any imaginative child.

I remember vividly the day we moved in. I was wearing a blue silk knitted dress which had been made for me by one of the patients at my Auntie Phyllis's lunatic asylum. (She was the assistant matron there.) There was a flagstone path leading down the back garden which stopped short of the wood. My sturdy little figure, with long pigtails and a stubborn expression, walked down this flagstone path very slowly. Then went back to its beginning and skipped down it. Then back to the beginning again to hop from one big stone to the next. I knew exactly what I was doing.

I had seen this path in a dream I'd had shortly before my mother came to fetch us from Norfolk. I knew exactly what it looked like and exactly what I was going to do – first of all to walk slowly down it, then to skip, then to hop. I was much too young to understand that I'd had a premonitory dream. I happily told my mother: 'I like this house. I'm glad we came here.'

Years later I told her of my dream. It didn't surprise her. At the time she had observed that I moved about the house on that first day as if I knew exactly where I was going. I had even told her before we got to the house that I wanted the little bedroom at the front.

Both my parents were remarkable people. Denied education because of their social class and lack of money, they had educated themselves. My father left school at twelve to go down the coal mines in the north-east of England. He came from South Shields and was a 'Geordie'. My mother had worked hard on him to eliminate his broad Geordie accent.

She said when she first met him at a dance in London, although she couldn't understand a word he said, she was determined to marry him. By the time I was old enough to remember my father, he spoke with hardly any accent at all. He was what used to be called in the old days, 'one of Nature's gentlemen'. He could charm the birds off the trees. Tall, dark and handsome, he was one of the gentlest souls I've ever known, had a great sense of humour and could sing and yodel like an angel.

At fourteen my mother was apprenticed in the Rag Trade. She reported to a fearsome French 'Madame' who instilled fear into the heart of all the apprentices (except my cheeky mother) at the same time as teaching them superlative seamstress skills. Doris, my mother, made dresses for the Queen of Spain, handstitched underwear of the finest silk for the princesses, and years later sewed pearl beads and tiny crystal flutes on to a ball gown for Queen Elizabeth, Queen of England.

My mother came from a colourful, noisy, ambitious and clever family. Her father, Johan Frederick Ahlquist, was a blond Swedish Viking, born in 1863 on the island of Gotland, which floats in the Baltic Sea between Sweden and Latvia. He ran away from home at the age of twelve and stowed away on a sailing ship which had put into Slite, the tiny fishing port where his father was a carpenter. Years later, in our early teens, Rita and I visited his family home. The big wooden house, its timbers darkened and weathered over the years by the howling Baltic winds and salty spray, stood as firm and reassuringly as when his father had first built it. Even in the early Fifties, my grandfather was still a local legend, although he never once returned to the little town of his birth.

He made the sea his career, sailed with Joseph Conrad, was becalmed in the Sargasso Sea, jumped ship and trekked across Canada in the coldest winter in living memory, was flogged by a brutal Yankee skipper on an American whaler, had two of his toes bitten off by a shark, and finally came to rest in the port of Hull in Yorkshire, after falling from the mast and breaking his leg. By this time he had worked himself up to Ship's Master.

Whilst in hospital in Hull he met my grandmother, Edith Ashburn, who came from a long line of Yorkshire witches and who could dance and sing like the Music Hall star she aspired to be. I have a photograph of her at this time in gypsy costume, holding a beribboned tambourine and laughing at the camera.

Edith and Johan fell in love, even though Johan spoke very little English. They instinctively knew that the north of England was not the place for a couple with plenty of ambition, intelligence and drive, but with no money.

They moved to London, to the Isle of Dogs in the heart of London's docklands (where Canary Wharf is today) and my grandfather went to work as a stevedore at the City of London docks. He rose to become the manager of the East India Dock – no mean feat for a foreigner in the xenophobic England of the time.

My mother was brought up to the sights and sounds of another era – of the Pearly Kings and Queens, of the great Shire horses pulling kegs of beer on long carts behind them, of the annual visit of the chimney sweep when all the furniture would be covered up with sheets, of the cries of street vendors, and the rattling wheels of the hackney carriage over the cobblestones bringing the top-hatted doctor always just too late to deliver the baby. (Apparently the doctor always made sure that the midwife got there first but that he collected the fee of one guinea.)

Doris used to talk about the tea clippers proudly sailing up the Thames and of how once she saw one of the folding bridges cut off the legs of a friend who was sitting on the bridge and didn't get off in time. Parrots, parakeets, monkeys and a chameleon shared the tall old London house with Edith,

Johan and their young family of five children. My mother remembered that the house was always full of mysterious visitors – men with dark complexions and foreign accents, skippers and sailors, carpenters and sailmakers, who brought the children exotic gifts and interesting things to eat.

She grew up determined one day to travel herself, and after she was widowed at the age of forty-seven, in my first year at university, she made her wishes come true. She worked her way round the world, as lady's maid, as dressmaker, as barmaid, as a lady's companion, as a housekeeper, a nurse and a school matron. She lived and worked in Africa, in Australia, New Zealand, Europe and America. She lived for two years with my sister in the remote Western Highlands of New Guinea where she taught my sister's cook, who wore Bird of Paradise feathers in his hair and a bone through his nose, to read and write in English. She was horrified to find out that the locals still ate human flesh – 'Long Pig' – but was somewhat mollified when she discovered that they only ate the tax inspectors.

At the age of seventy-four, Doris went to Saudi Arabia to be nanny to the children of an oil sheik.

'Why are you going to Saudi Arabia?' Rita and I asked her, knowing that she'd never been a nanny and that she wasn't too keen on small children.

'Because I've never been there,' came back the swift reply.

She stayed for a year in Riyadh, taught her small charges Christian hymns and the names of all the teams in the First Division of the English Soccer League, tried (unsuccessfully) to get the slave girls to revolt, and nearly got one of King's soldiers castrated when she complained to the King that the hapless fellow had put his hand on her knee at a picnic in the desert.

At the age of eighty-nine she lived alone in a spotless little apartment in Hove, Sussex, had boyfriends, went dancing, read ten books a week (by special dispensation from the local library), and still wore black satin underwear because, she maintained with a twinkle in her eye, 'You never know . . .'

Altogether, Doris was a remarkable woman.

Along with her thirst for travel was a thirst for education, and a ruthless determination that her two daughters would have the education she had never had. She and my father saved every penny possible and sent Rita and me, aged seven and five respectively, to Loreto College in St Albans. We were non-Catholics – my mother had been brought up as a Methodist, my father as nothing at all as he was an orphan. Later, after my father's death, my mother converted to Catholicism, but it was only ever a half-hearted sort of conversion and she always harkened back to the days of her youth and the 'Chapel' where she had enjoyed a great social life, if not a religious one. The reason she chose the convent for Rita and me was that it had a fine academic reputation, and would certainly make us 'ladies'.

(We both later acquired pretty good academic reputations ourselves, but I've never been sure about the 'ladies' bit.)

Thanks to my mother and grandfather, I was brought up in a house which boasted the Complete Works of Shakespeare, the Complete (signed) Works of Joseph Conrad, and the Complete Works of Charles Dickens. I had read all of Dickens (my favourite author to this day) by the time I was ten, and the rest soon followed.

My father was an ardent socialist – he had been on the infamous Jarrow Hunger March in the Twenties, when thousands of miners marched down to London from the north of England to complain about their conditions of work and pay. He told us how men had fallen by the wayside from hunger and exhaustion during the week-long march. He himself had fainted a couple of times and had been supported on the shoulders of other, older and stronger miners. His contribution to the household's reading matter was the Complete Works of Sidney and Beatrice Webb. English pioneering social reformers, the Webbs were early members of the Socialist Fabian Society and founded the London School of Economics in 1895. They were among the first to argue for social insurance and had written many influential books, including *The History of Trade Unionism* and *Soviet Communism*.

I can still see the shelf of clothbound red books which my father unsuccessfully tried to get me to read. One winter, when I was forced to stay home from school for weeks because of bronchitis, and because I had read everything else in the house, I forced my way through some of those books. I'm sure that my aversion to and lack of interest in politics stems from those chilly days when my young mind wrestled with the ideas of political systems.

Ironically, had it not been for the sweeping social and educational reforms of Clement Attlee's socialist government which came into power in Britain in 1945 after World War Two, neither Rita nor I would have gone to university. The government's groundbreaking Education Act recognised and rewarded academic merit with university scholarships. Previously, entry to a university had been a matter of money or class.

My sister Rita, who always knew she would be a teacher, honed her early teaching skills on me by force-feeding me a world of information (often garbled) and the entire contents of Arthur Mee's ten volumes of *The Children's Encyclopaedia*.

But I was an avid pupil and we would give each other 'tests' on the pantheon of Greek gods and goddesses, on the inventors of the telephone, on Albert Schweitzer's and Wolfgang Mozart's early lives, and on the history of English literature.

Highly precocious readers and dedicated students, night after night, when the air raid alarms were going off, and the wood pigeons were cooing in the wild wood, we would sit in bed and read our encyclopaedias. It was the best early education that a child could have wished for.

But Rita had other plans for me. I was to go on the stage and make the family fortune by becoming a famous actress. She inspired me with stories of the great English actresses Sarah Siddons and Sarah Bernhardt. I had Sir Joshua Reynolds' portrait of Sarah Siddons in a big blue hat stuck to my bedroom wall.

By the age of eight, Rita had made me memorise everything from Keats' *Ode To A Grecian Urn* and Blake's *Tyger, Tyger Burning Bright* (which I loved), to parts of Abraham Lincoln's Gettysburg Address and the famous sleepwalking speech of Lady Macbeth. I can still remember appearing dramatically from behind the sitting-room curtains, clad in an old green silk dressing-gown of my mother's, with a yellow knitted tea cosy on my head, exclaiming heroically, 'Out damned spot!' to the assembled cheers and jeers of my friends at my eighth birthday party.

Looking back, after the horrors of evacuation were behind us, my sister and I had an idyllic childhood.

But we worried and argued a lot about God.

✳

There can be both positive and negative milestones on a spiritual journey, but sometimes the negative ones produce positive results. The milestones that I now recognise – and there may be many more as yet unrecognised – were of both kinds. My evacuation – such a negative experience that to this day I have no memory of it – convinced me that there is no One, Kind, Good God of the Old Testament School, and perhaps that was the first milestone in getting 'regular' institutionalised religion out of my system, thus leaving me more open to other spiritual possibilities.

I have vague memories of occasional visits to church on Easter Sundays and Christmas mornings with my mother and father before the war, when I had a woolly mental image of this old white-bearded man in a long white gown sitting on a cloud (which puzzled me even then – why didn't he fall through it?), smiling down benevolently on earth. Angels sat around him and played harps, which even then I suspected was a very boring thing to do. There was also someone called Jesus who suffered little children to come unto him and seemed a nice man, in spite of his strange long hair. I had been taught in my childish evening prayers that God and Jesus would look after me. But of course when the crunch came, they didn't. They allowed me to be taken away from my mother and father and sent off to a desperate and desolate place, for all I knew, for ever. To this day I have a horror of separation – psychologists who follow the works of R D Laing would have a field day with me.

At school, however, I was prepared to give God and His Only Begotten Son another try. The non-Catholics worshipped alongside the Catholics – although in different pews – in the school chapel, a beautiful little place with parquet floors smelling of scented beeswax and incense.

Along with this daily worship we learned the Catholic catechism, how to say the rosary, to put ash on our foreheads on Ash Wednesday, and because Rita and I had good singing voices, to sing in the choir and at Midnight Mass.

I loved the Midnight Mass every Christmas. I sometimes felt that I could almost become a believer as our sweet voices drifted up into the air, curling up to the chapel roof with the incense and breathy prayers of the congregation. I sang like Dylan Thomas' Christmas aunt – like a full-throated thrush. The Midnight Mass meant taking the late Christmas Eve bus in to school and then being allowed to stay in the boarders' dormitory after the Mass was over. It was an exciting and thrilling time. The nuns spoiled us and fussed over us, making us drink hot water swirled around in newly empty jam jars because the resultant thin liquid was supposed to be good for our voices.

I loved the Plain Chant, the Gregorian Chant, the sung responses and the flickering candles. I did observe that the hymns weren't as jolly and cheerful as the Anglican ones, because now my mother sometimes took us on a Sunday to St Albans Anglican Cathedral, a beautiful old building with flying buttresses, grey stones and a wonderful two-arched façade. On these occasions I abandoned the Catholic music and lustily sang 'All Things Bright And Beautiful' or 'Abide With Me'.

But, Protestant or Catholic, Rita and I were firmly in the milieu of a Christian God, who became more and more complicated as time went on. But we were never really in His grip.

'How do we know there is a God?' declared Rita heretically when she was about nine.

'There must be,' I answered quickly. Too quickly.

'How do you know?'

'Well . . . (my seven-year-old mind faltered) . . . because everybody says so,' adding triumphantly, 'and there are lots of pictures in books.'

'You mustn't believe everything you see and read.' This from a sister who had been 'educating' me mercilessly from books since I could first remember.

As the years went by, I longed to be a Catholic like Mary Darney, the boarder with the long black hair and pale complexion, who wore a Children of Mary medal and a white veil. She was very holy because there had been some family 'trouble' and she had prayed and fasted and overcome her woes. We found out later when we were cynical teenagers that there had been a terrible, not-spoken-of scandal in the Darney family when Mary's mother had run off with the local Protestant schoolmaster, ruining her chances of future social acceptance and salvation in one fell swoop. Needless to say, Mary became much more interesting in our eyes as a result of her glamorous, if murky, past than all her holiness and pale loitering had ever achieved.

And so I tried to make myself more holy and to become more convinced about what so many of the other girls, and certainly the nuns, fervently believed in. I tried to access the Christian God and all that went with Him. I would sneak into the chapel during my free periods and kneel at the feet of the statue of the Sacred Heart, an anguished-looking character with a pained expression and a huge, protruding red three-dimensional heart. He also wore a crown of thorns. Altogether not a very attractive image. I prayed fiercely for some sign. No-o-thing.

I then turned my spiritual attention to the Virgin Mary, Mother of God. She stood across the aisle from the Sacred

Heart and looked much more amenable. I would fix my glittering eyes intently on her pink and white plaster face, like some mini latter-day Ancient Mariner, and *will* her to move. I was very into the Children of Fatima and St Bernadette of Lourdes (having just wept through Jennifer Jones' heart-rending performance in the movie *The Song of Bernadette*). If the Virgin Mary could appear to *them*, maybe she might give *me* some sign. But she never did. Not so much as a twitch of her blue robe nor a wave of her stiff fingers. Her basilisk stare met mine in a true case of the Irresistible Will against the Immovable Object. Greek met Greek.

In desperation, I asked for an audience with our Mother Superior, a slim ethereal creature of surpassing beauty and chill demeanour who struck terror into all our hearts. She taught maths, and would ridicule and dismiss sarcastically the pupils who could not attain her high standards. To this day, I am convinced that I could have been much better at maths if I had not been so afraid of asking her questions. Almost to spite her, and to prove that I was not a mathematical slouch, I passed matric maths by learning all the geometry theorems off by heart and because I could do quadratic equations. (But I have never understood the problems where two trains were rushing towards each other at death-defying speeds and we were expected to make complicated deductions about this foolhardy, if not fatal event. When we were asked to calculate how many men it took to dig a ditch in how many days, I always got half a man. Mother Immaculata thought I did it on purpose, but I didn't. I longed with all my heart to get *whole* men like everybody else.)

To ask for, and be granted, an audience with Mother Immaculata was no mean feat.

She greeted me icily.

I explained that I wanted to become a Catholic (a course of action I had discussed with no one, not even my sister).

To her eternal credit, she turned me down, but suggested that I might like to attend the Catholic Doctrine classes. Which I did. I believe, by the age of fourteen, I knew more about Catholic dogma and doctrine than any other non-Catholic in the country. I learned about the Immaculate Conception, Heaven and Hell (the demons never made sense to me or acted as any kind of moral deterrent), the Holy Trinity and the Holy Ghost.

I've always had problems with the Holy Ghost, never quite sure who or what he or it is. Today, when Born Again Christians call in to my radio programme and tell me passionately about the Holy Spirit, I am equally confused. Is the Holy Ghost tongues of fire, a sweeping wind, an infusion of joy, or a signal to start rolling around and frothing at the mouth? Beats me.

By the time I left school at the age of seventeen, eager and excited to go up to university, I was one of the most knowledgeable non-Catholics about Catholic Doctrine in the country and I had given up religion. I was cynical, self-assured, well-read, confident and full of myself in the way only a successful seventeen-year-old schoolgirl can be.

But the Catholic Doctrine came back to haunt me. My son Simon was born at a Catholic mission hospital called Anua, in the wilds of Eastern Nigeria, run by the Medical Missionaries of Mary. It was the only hospital for hundreds of miles and a two-hour drive over very rough roads from the tiny village on the banks of the Cross River where my husband was stationed. My baby was the only white baby amongst hundreds of black ones – the nuns didn't even have to put an identification band round his wrist. I was twenty-three years old. However, the night he was born, as I lay in labour in the hot, humid little room I had been given at the hospital, with the myriad sounds of the tropical night drumming, thrumming, rustling and creeping around me, a terrible thought suddenly occurred to me. The Catholic Doctrine rushed back into my fevered brain with a terrifying jolt.

'Catholics kill the mother and save the baby!'

I shouted for the Sister-Matron who, highly alarmed, came running. Up until this moment I had been a model patient. So much so, that the nuns were using me as a guinea-pig for the Dr Dick Grantley-Read Method of Natural Childbirth which had just hit the obstetrics and gynaecology world.

'What's the matter? Are you all right? What's the matter with her?'

This last comment was addressed to the sixteen-year-old African probationer nurse who had been sitting with me, encouraging me to 'Breathe!'

'Catholics kill the mother and save the baby,' I sobbed, convinced now that I was in the hands of so many be-robed and be-rosaried Angels of Death.

I poured out my fears to the Sister-Matron, insisted that she summon Sister-Doctor Mary Nolan, the doctor who was to deliver the baby, and that my fears be put at rest.

Sister-Doctor Nolan calmed me by telling me that I was in no danger. But to this day, I'm not quite comfortable in my mind as to what would have happened if it had been a life-and-death toss-up between my baby and me.

I met Malcolm, my first husband, when I was eighteen and he was twenty. He was a student at Oxford University, I was at London University.

It was the long summer vacation and Rita and I were working as barmaids in an old London pub called The George. With its small-paned windows, long wooden counters and polished pump handles for pulling the beer, it was a pub straight out of a Dickens novel. Even the regular customers had a Dickensian look about them – old, thin men with pinched red noses, blowsy intimidating old women in the style of Mrs Gamp, and a tortoiseshell cat obviously escaped from The Olde Curiosity Shop. But it was also a student pub, and regulars and students rubbed shoulders with aplomb, although the old resident piano player with grey, greasy hair and a limp who fell in love with my sister and would play *Blue Moon* soulfully on the piano every time he caught her eye, used to complain bitterly about 'bloody students!'

One night Malcolm came in with a bunch of friends, asked for half a pint of draught bitter and confidently told me, 'I'm going to marry you.'

'Don't be daft!' I ignored him and went back to pulling more pints.

Two years later we were married. Malcolm got a job with the United Africa Company and went out to Nigeria nine months ahead of me whilst I finished my degree. It took nearly a week for me to get from London to the tiny trading post of Itu, on the banks of the Cross River, deep in Nigeria's Eastern Region where Malcolm had been posted. We were a hundred miles from the nearest town – itself only a dot on the map – and apart from two missionaries and a German doctor at the Itu Leper Colony, I was the only other European woman for hundreds of miles.

We lived in a tall wooden house on stilts, with an eccentric diesel generator that provided electricity on a sporadic basis. If the generator was still running when we went to bed at night, we used to call out in pidgin English to the Night Watchman, 'Quench Fire!', which was his command to turn it off. There was no running water. The gardener used to carry up buckets of brown river water for our baths, whilst rainwater for drinking was collected in huge barrels positioned under the roof. We slept under a double mosquito net, but were eaten alive by mosquitoes. I still have faint scars on my legs from those days.

The kitchen, where the cooking was done over a coal fire, was a short walk from the house. Bassey, our cook, who had six toes on one foot and sharply filed teeth which gave him the appearance of an amiable vampire when he smiled, could rustle up amazing meals in this antiquated coal oven – from freshly made bread to suet pudding and guinea-fowl stew.

Itu was a strange and exceptional village deep in the heart of Iboland. It was a haven for the *oṣu* – the outcasts. An *oṣu* was a person dedicated to a god, a thing set apart – a taboo for ever, and his children after him. An *oṣu* could not marry a free-born person, and had to live apart from the community. An *oṣu* could not attend a ceremony of the free-born, nor go into their houses. The mark of an *oṣu*'s forbidden caste was long, tangled, dirty hair, because they were forbidden to cut it or use a razor. When an *oṣu* died, he or she was buried apart from the clan in an area known as the Evil Forest. For some reason, Itu had become a haven for the *oṣu*. On moonlit nights the drums would beat even louder and more power-fully than on other nights, and the *oṣu* would gather on the river banks below our house. Strange screams and noises would go on well into the night.

The young District Officer, Charles, told us not to worry. 'They're only sacrificing a goat.'

We didn't worry and lived cheek-by-jowl with the *oşu* and other villagers. My best friend was the sixth wife of a trader. She spoke a little pidgin English and would bring her fat baby to see me. She enjoyed her status as sixth wife. She was the spoilt favourite wife – spoilt not only by her husband but also by the senior wives who looked upon her as a little sister. We used to sit together on the rickety wooden veranda overlooking the slow swirling river, and watch the tiny bejewelled kingfishers darting over the water.

Once we saw the dead bodies of a young man and woman float by. They had been bound together. I understood from Regina that they had committed some crime against their community – an illicit forbidden love – and had been condemned to death by drowning. I suspected that the missionaries had not always been as successful in their conversions to Christianity as they believed.

I was knitting baby clothes – very difficult in a hundred degrees of humidity because the wool and needles stick to your fingers. Regina was embroidering a flowered table-cloth for her baby's bottom drawer. I've often wondered what happened to that table-cloth and where it is today.

All my life I have loved and studied birds, and I am an enthusiastic amateur ornithologist. At Itu I decided that I would like a bird feeding table. The ancient gardener, who would raise his battered hat respectfully to me as I sat on the open-sided toilet, was set to work. Finally the bird table was finished. I put out all sorts of leftover food and fruit and waited expectantly for the birds to come. The next morning I went out to the veranda and looked down at the garden below to see if my offerings had been accepted. They had.

Three large vultures perched precariously on the bird table. They eyed me malevolently but hopefully. That was the end of the bird table.

One evening, not long after we arrived in Itu, there was a great commotion on the river banks below the house. The chief and villagers were crowded on the bank, waving rusty old Dane guns and antiquated muskets at the river. Wild shots were being fired. What was going on? We found out that a solitary hippo, who had drifted downstream from the Cameroons where the great hippo herds were, had capsized a villager's canoe, and bitten him in half. The village were now out to shoot the hippo, which they finally did after many unsuccessful and noisy attempts. Charles, as District Officer, was called formally to the scene. He discovered that the late hippo had an enormous abscess on one of his huge front teeth – surely the reason he had become bad-tempered and been thrown out of the herd. One of my most prized possessions to this day is a large yellow tooth – a non-abscessed one – from that hippo.

Once, when I was four months pregnant, Malcolm and I went by engine-canoe to visit two young Catholic priests who lived way up-river in a lonely outpost. I was the first white woman ever to have visited the outpost. They had cooked a meal of chicken, rice and okra, a slimy vegetable which is regarded as a delicacy by many Ibos. The meal was practically inedible – but was memorable for the love and care that had been lavished on it. After lunch, Father Pettit, a country boy from County Cork, politely and euphemistically asked me if I needed to use the 'Ladies'. I did. I was shown along a little path leading into the bush. At the end of the path was a freshly dug hole in the ground, surrounded by woven palm leaf walls. A stick had been thoughtfully planted by the hole so that I could hang on to it as I squatted. The 'Ladies' had been built especially for me.

The two young priests, so far from their Irish homes, told us tales of witchcraft and juju, of mysterious beans which when eaten could kill you and leave no trace, of the fear felt by their tiny congregation when a chief died. A chief was required to be buried with as many followers as possible. Potential 'followers' hid in their houses or ran into the bush for fear of being buried alive with their chief.

My rejection of organised religion which took place over many years when I was a child and schoolgirl was, I suppose, the first major milestone on my spiritual path. The second, which was not an accumulative process, was a dramatic, unforgettable event which happened during the year I spent at Itu.

Founded 1928 – In His Name is inscribed on the Gateway of the Itu Leper Colony. This remarkable sanctuary for lepers was run by Dr and Mrs A B Macdonald of the Church of Scotland, who had come out to Nigeria in 1921 and had spent the best part of their lives helping sufferers of this ancient, dreadful disease, called by the local Efik community *Akpamfia* – literally 'The White Death'. Here in Itu a battle was joined where dedicated men and women came to grips with the ancient horror and defeated not only the disease, but the helpless, hopeless attitude to it which had persisted through the ages.

Dr Macdonald used to say, in his broad Scots accent, 'It seemed that as all the forces of light gathered to pursue the enemy, ignorance of it faded away. We can say to the new patient who may still come with the fear that he has been given a death sentence, "It is not so. There is every possibility that like the majority of your fellow patients you will go out free of this thing in a little over two years." '

In 1958, the Itu Leper Colony celebrated its thirtieth anniversary. I was halfway through my first pregnancy and running the Colony Brownie Pack. This is a distinction I have always savoured. There can be few women in the world who can lay claim to being the Brown Owl of a Brownie pack in a leper colony. And a pregnant Brown Owl to boot.

In 1957, the year before we arrived in Itu, Queen Elizabeth had visited the old slaving port of Calabar, two hours down the river from Itu. The mission launch had come to the Colony beach and taken all the leper Scouts, Girl Guides, Cubs and Brownies to line the route and see the Queen and the Duke of Edinburgh. My Brownies used to relive that day over and over again, telling me about it with shining eyes.

One afternoon, after our Brownie meeting was over, I popped in to the Macdonalds' humble house where Mrs Macdonald was making tea. Come rain, shine, flood, or famine, Mrs Macdonald served tea every afternoon at four o'clock sharp, with Dundee cake which was sent to her in round tins by the parcel load from Scotland.

Dr Macdonald was reading a letter that had just been delivered to him. It was from the Moderator of the Presbyterian Church of Eastern Nigeria, the Reverend A O Anicho.

After he had finished reading it, he gave it to Mrs Macdonald.

When she finished reading, she said to her husband, 'May I give this to Kate to read?'

He nodded and she handed the letter to me with tears running down her thin face. 'We would like you to read this.'

It was a moving, emotional letter.

*We of the Presbyterian Church of Eastern Nigeria are proud
and happy to have been associated with the Itu Leper Colony
from its beginning, thirty years ago. All of us, ministers,
evangelists and members, had come to think that leprosy was
incurable. We could only mourn with the families of those
upon whom this ancient curse had fallen. We could not say
'Go to the Mission Hospital', and we knew how they wasted
their money and slowly lost all hope as the magician and local
doctors failed to work the miracle they had promised. We
thanked God when our beloved Dr and Mrs Macdonald left
the Itu Mission Hospital and went into the Colony to live
with the lepers. But at first we believed that a place where the
wretched sufferers could die in peace was all that the Colony
could ever be.*

*And through the years what have we seen? We have
seen this great miracle of God's love. We have seen those we
counted as dead, given new life. We have seen the great Church
of the Colony crowded with men and women and children
whose faces shone with hope and thankfulness. And we have
seen these people – our people – coming home with their
certificates of cleansing, to take a foremost place in their
congregations . . .*

*We rejoice with you. We rejoice that our Lord and
Master chose one of us to renew His work of cleansing, and
that it was because this work was begun in Itu that sufferers in
all Nigeria and indeed in all Africa, can now have hope. We
thank God for all in other lands who have joined with us in
prayer for the Itu Colony, and for all those who have given
their skill and their gifts for the comfort and the healing of
those who had once had no hope.*

There was a knock on the door. Dr Macdonald was needed at the Colony hospital. After he had left I asked Mrs Macdonald if I could make a copy of the letter.

'I'm sure Dr Macdonald would have no objection,' she said in her quiet Scots burr.

She gave me a sheet of paper and an indelible pencil. To this day, I can't say why I asked her if I could make a copy. But it lies beside me now, as I sit at my computer keyboard, the yellowed paper dog-eared and torn, with the Reverend A O Anicho's words copied out in my girlish handwriting.

I now recognise, of course, the Dalai Lama's 'The Interconnectedness of All Things' and that something inspired me to copy out those words, so that in another part of Africa, more than forty years later, I would look back at that moment and it would prompt me to recognise another milestone on my spiritual path.

Itu Leper Colony was recognised as a 'second-class' township. The epithet 'second-class' was not a value judgement but a designation of size.

By 1958, when I became a small part of its life, it had some one thousand patients, covered some four to five square miles of land, land which was originally dense tropical forest but which had now been cleared. Formerly the haunt of pythons, crocodiles, leopards and monkeys, the Colony grounds now held six villages for the patients, the school, houses for the African and European staff, a workshop of two acres in extent containing thousands of pounds worth of machinery, a palm oil mill, a school with eight hundred children, a Church seating two and a half thousand people, a hospital and all the subsidiary buildings, fifteen miles of roads, a canal three miles long, water and electricity laid on, and hundreds of acres under agricultural and oil palm plantations.

The palm oil produce was the main source of the Colony's income. An island in the swamp made an ideal pasture for the Colony herd of about a hundred and fifty Maturu cattle.

One year there had been over four thousand resident patients on the roll. The Macdonalds used to tell Malcolm and me that one of their greatest joys was that they had lived to see the introduction of the sulphone drugs and the wonderful effect they produced. They would talk of one day in particular, when nine hundred and sixty-one people were discharged symptom-free. These included many people who had been with them for ten to eighteen years.

When Malcolm and I first visited the Colony, a couple of weeks after we arrived in Itu, we were beset by fears of what we would see and what might happen to us. We'd seen movies and read sensational books about leper colonies, about limbs and fingers falling off, running sores and the terrible risk of contagion.

Dr Macdonald briskly put our fears at rest.

'Put a wee drop of Dettol' (a popular disinfectant) 'in your bath at night and the Lord will take care of the rest.'

As is often the way when confronted with the sheer, blinding kind of faith the Macdonalds had, the Lord did indeed do the rest. From the age of two weeks until we left Itu when my son was three months old, I used to weigh him on the Leper Colony hospital scales using pennies as weights. To the best of my knowledge, by the age of forty, which he is now, nothing has fallen off him.

The people who lived and worked in the Colony, other than the handful of European staff, were all lepers – the teachers, the judge and judiciary, the police force, the ordinary men, women and children who made their homes there. The worst cases, those people who had open lesions or were desperately ill, were kept in the hospital. I only went into the hospital a few times as Dr Macdonald felt that during my pregnancy it might be too risky an undertaking.

If the weather permitted, when it was the dry season, the mothers of newborn and young babies would breastfeed their babies in a small, outdoor area under the shade of a huge cottonwood tree. The mothers would be draped in clean white sheets, with two holes cut out for their nipples to poke through, and they would sit and cradle their babies in the age-old fashion of all nursing mothers. After each feed, the babies would be taken back to the Baby House and the mothers would return to Women's Town. Girl nurses from outside the Colony had been trained to look after the babies, and as soon as a mother was pronounced free from leprosy, her healthy baby was given back to her on a full-time basis.

Once a week there was a film show, and we would all sit together on long wooden benches under a star-studded sky, whilst the leper projectionist worked his film projector from the mud and wattle hut with the palm-mat roof behind us. I vividly remember watching Laurence Olivier's film of *Hamlet*, in the company of hundreds of lepers all quoting from memory in perfect syncronicity with the great English actor, 'To be or not to be, that is the question.'

When Malcolm and I arrived in Itu in 1957, Mr Isaac E Obianwu had been Chief of the Colony for six years.

He was a gentle, smiling man, usually dressed in a shabby faded green embroidered cotton shirt of the sort favoured today by African politicians. His features had the charac-teristic appearance of someone who has suffered from leprosy for a long time in that they were 'leonine' – a term used by the doctor and nurses who treated the lepers. His nose and cheeks had broadened and his forehead was lumpy. He had also lost some fingers and toes.

Isaac was a remarkable man. He had lived in the Colony for twenty-six of the thirty years since its founding, and he told me that he owed his life and everything that makes life good to the Itu Leper Colony: 'I never stop marvelling at what has been done for me and my countrymen "In His Name".'

As a child he had been taken from one indigenous healer to another, but they could not cure him. Finally he was taken to Port Harcourt to see Dr Braithwaite, 'the big European doctor', who told his mother about Itu and said that he should be taken there at once.

'It was a very wonderful thing to come to Itu Colony,' he told me. 'The most wonderful thing was that people no longer looked at me with fear and with pity. In the Colony we are all one.'

Isaac became a member of the choir, and when Dr Macdonald brought out the brass band which some kind person in Scotland had donated to the Colony, Isaac became one of the first band boys, and eventually the bandmaster. One day, when we were sitting outside Dr Macdonald's office, Isaac told me how late one Christmas Eve long ago, when the band was good enough to play carols, Dr Macdonald had piled them all into a big canoe and taken them up the river to Itu town beach to play to the villagers. The villagers were astounded. Isaac was very nervous about going in the canoe as he was unaccustomed to travelling in one, and felt happy and relieved when he was back in the Colony.

He often used to tell me about the early days when the

Colony was being built and beginning to grow. The men and women were divided into companies for work. There would be about twelve or fifteen men or women in each company, and there were 'strong' companies and 'weak' ones. Some people were so weak that they could not do any heavy work, and they were put into town garden companies, or cleaning companies. Every Thursday, all the head men and head women gathered at one place, early in the morning, and each was told what his or her company should do for the following week. This distribution of work was still going on when I lived in Itu.

The Colony school had much shorter hours than the outside schools. All the teachers were patients, and many of them had not had much schooling themselves, but they were keen to teach, and the children were very keen to learn. There was also an adult education school which met in the evening after the day's work was over. I remember watching the group of men and women of all ages sitting in the open air, their books and papers lit by hissing gas lamps, as the fireflies danced around their heads. When the adult students were deemed able to read well enough, they were given a Bible in their own language.

Most of the patients had been subsistence farmers before they entered the Colony, but they often left it as carpenters, bricklayers, engineers and electricians. Many became teachers and one became a minister of religion.

I asked Isaac what being the Colony Chief entailed. He said that one of his most important functions was to meet every new patient who came in for treatment. Many of them were downcast and unhappy, and he tried to cheer them up and give them a positive attitude. Then he would read them the rules of the Colony which they had to agree to keep.

These rules were administered by the Colony court, of which Isaac was president. The Colony's uniformed police, men and women, helped to keep order and administer the rules. The men patrolled the men's towns and the women the women's towns.

There were three special occasions in the Colony that I will always remember.

Part of Isaac's work was to see that every patient had a house in the Colony. Usually there were two people to one house. Every Wednesday morning at seven o'clock, with other members of staff, Isaac would inspect the towns. Everybody was expected to keep the houses and streets neat and clean.

Not long before Christmas, I noticed that there had been much more bustling, sweeping, cleaning and tidying-up than usual. Everybody was very busy indeed. I asked Isaac what was going on. He told me that every year there was a Special Inspection and prizes were given for the best-kept street. A few days later, at the annual concert, a very jolly, festive occasion, the prize was awarded. That year Opobo Street was the winner, and assembled cheers and groans went up as the winners rejoiced and the losers complained.

I suppose Isaac is dead now. But he lived long enough to be given a clean bill of health. For years his condition had worsened slowly but steadily, apparently hopeless, but he was given the precious gift of life again by the sulphone drugs. This had been some years before we got to Itu.

The second memorable occasion we witnessed at the Colony was the Feast or Distribution of Presents which took place after the Christmas Day Service. In the old days, said Isaac, cows were bought and there was much feasting. At the ceremony Malcolm and I attended, Dr and Mrs Macdonald handed out clothes, rice and blankets to much noisy joy.

The third occasion, which became a major landmark on my spiritual journey, I only recognised for what it really was during my trip to Peru when, for the first time, I was trying to piece together that long, often obscure journey.

Dr and Mrs Macdonald invited us to a New Year's party. I didn't know much about how the Scots celebrated New Year's Eve, other than that everybody got rip-roaring drunk, very sentimental and sang *Auld Lang Syne*. I wondered if there would be a piper – you never knew, the Colony Band might boast a set of bagpipes – and if there would be dancing.

We knew who the other guests were, certainly: Charles, Malcolm and me; Sisters Moss and Clanahan from BELRA (the British Leprosy Relief Association) who worked in the Colony; Mr Drake, Mr Owen and Mr Boyd, also from BELRA; Dr Philip, the medical superintendent and his wife, and the Macdonalds. I squeezed my burgeoning body into a pretty party dress and off we went to the Macdonalds.

We all sat around rather uncomfortably in the Macdonalds' hot little parlour and made small talk. It was an excessively humid night and soon we were all wet with perspiration. I could feel my starched petticoats drooping as we sat.

Never mind, a drink would set things right. We were offered fruit juice. And then more fruit juice. I met Malcolm's eyes across the room and he shook his head imperceptibly. There wasn't to be so much as a dram of whisky; it was a 'dry' evening. My heart sank. It sank even further a few moments later when, about forty minutes before midnight, Dr Macdonald announced that we would now make our way to the Colony Church for the Watch Night Service.

'This sounds like a barrel of fun,' I whispered to Malcolm, as we shuffled along the mud streets towards the church.

Neither of us had been in a church since we were married, and before that, not since I had left school.

I had seen the church many times from the outside where it stood beyond the old, spreading, scarlet-flowered Flame-of-the-Forest tree near the entrance to the Colony. We'd often heard the robust, melodious harmonies swelling out from the band, choir and congregation on Sundays and could hear the music from our wooden house nearly a mile away. The great, rambling, red church with its roof of palm fronds was never the geographical centre of the Colony, but it was the centre of the life of the place and from it stemmed the spirit that was Itu. Its Sunday services, Sunday school and Bible classes gave life to the Colony.

I'll try to describe it, but really, all the words in the world could not do justice to it.

It was a huge, sprawling, one-storeyed building hand made of red clay, and was a natural development of the first palm grove where the patients and staff had come together to worship in the early days. Then, like Topsy, it just 'growed'. Every time new space was needed, more red clay was added, more walls were built, the roof was extended and, inside, more red mud pews were added. Now this logistically impossible structure could hold two and a half thousand people.

'Impossible' is the accurate description, because it was an architectural miracle. According to visiting architects, who came from all over Nigeria and beyond to wonder and examine this theoretically unachievable natural cathedral, it shouldn't, couldn't stand. It should have collapsed years ago. But it hadn't, and, to my knowledge, is still standing to this day – a paean of praise to the God the Colony all worshipped so fervently and believed in so implicitly.

New Year's Eve, 1957 – the inside of the church was packed. There must have been over a thousand people crammed into the pews, sitting on the freshly swept red earth, leaning against the polished red mud walls, standing shoulder to shoulder in the remaining spaces. Like me, the lepers had put on their party clothes, with multi-coloured *lapas* or cloths tied round their waists or thrown over their shoulders Roman-style. The women wore huge, intricately tied turbans, and many had pinned bright tropical flowers on to their clothes. The atmosphere was more like a teeming market day than a church service. There was jostling, shoving, resettling, constant movement from the cheerful and expectant crowd.

At this stage, I had no idea what I was about to see. Certainly, it seemed an occasion like no other I had yet witnessed in the Colony. Perhaps this was the way the Colony always celebrated New Year?

Dr Macdonald led the Watch Night Service, which was mercifully short. His interpreter hurried through his duty of translating the English into the vernacular at lightning speed. It seemed as if everybody was waiting for something to happen. If the heat and humidity had been bad before, now in this jam-packed gathering it was almost unbearable. My dress was sodden; my hair, glamorously twirled up on top of my head for the occasion, was wet and strands were coming loose all over the place. Malcolm, who had been wiping his face non-stop with a handkerchief like the other men in our party, had now given up the futile exercise.

A couple of hymns were sung, the final prayer was said, and we all sat down.

'What now?' I whispered to Malcolm. 'I can't wait to get home and have a drink!'

The Colony clock chimed twelve times. It was midnight. I started to move in order to kiss 'Happy New Year' to the rest of our group sitting on the red, raised platform. But nobody else moved, so I sat still. A sense of expectancy hung in the air like a tangible, heavy blanket. The heat grew more intense. It was as if the world was holding its breath. Never before or since have I so clearly understood the expression 'You could hear a pin drop'.

Finally, after what seemed an age, Dr Macdonald broke the stillness and rose to his feet. Dr Philip, the medical superintendent, handed him some sheets of paper with writing on them. Dr Macdonald looked down at the lists, because that is what the pages were, cleared his throat, and began to read out names. We now understood that these were the names of the lepers who had been 'cleansed', who were leprosy-free, and could now go home. Some of the people on the list had been in the Colony for as long as fifteen years; all had been there for at least two.

I believe that it is rarely given to anyone to witness joy of such purity as I saw that night.

As each name was called out, the man or woman would cry out with happiness, dance, sing or drop down to their knees to thank the God who had healed them in this way. I did not, do not, believe in miracles, but these sights were and are among the most wonderful things I have ever seen. There was no doubt that God was alive and well and living in the great, red mud church of Itu that night. Tears coursed down my face. We were all crying.

As Dr Macdonald called out each name, there was a hush, an intake of breath and then a roar of delight, wonder and excitement. There was spontaneous singing, dancing, whistling, crowing, shouting and hooting, as the chosen person advanced up the aisle and came up to Dr Macdonald to receive his or her Certificate of Discharge. Every available space in the church was thronged with processions of cured lepers, singing in ecstasy.

Why do I say that this moving ceremony was a major milestone on my spiritual journey? Because that night I implicitly understood for the first time that there is a Divinity that can be accessed by human beings. Maybe Divinity is too prescriptive a word. Perhaps it's better to say that there is something beyond our present reality that is good, loving and caring. For those lepers in Itu Leper Colony that night, God was everywhere, in their hearts, minds and souls; in their neighbours, in Dr Philip, in Dr and Mrs Macdonald, even in Malcolm and me. Their unshakeable faith in a Christian God had been miraculously rewarded; they had been restored to life again with the precious promise of health and strength by His grace.

When the band, led by Isaac the bandmaster, struck up 'Here, O my Lord, I see Thee face to face' we left the church and went out into the velvety silent night.

*

Never again could I be cynical about the Christian God who had so failed me as a child. I still do not believe in Him, but at Itu that night I saw how He lived in others.

*Nearly forty years later, the words inscribed on the archway leading into the Colony – **In His Name** – came back to me as I sat in the ancient 'pagan' ruins of Machu Picchu. We had come to the Sacred City of the Incas after leaving Rómulo's farm.*

On the way Carol's partner Mark had been telling us a lot about

Zen Buddhism. I knew very little about it, nor did any of the others. One thing he said made a great and lasting impression on me. Zen Buddhism, he told us, points to enlightenment being found in the **present moment.**

As I sat with my back to the Hitching Post of the Sun, at the very top of the Machu Picchu ruins, that hot African night in the church of polished red mud became part of the present moment. I realised how important that experience had been for me. I consciously articulated in my own mind for the very first time that religious ritual and intellectual analysis are not necessary for the attainment of spiritual liberation. Experience, and being open to experience are. Awareness is all.

Later, back in South Africa, I did some reading into Buddhism and came across these words in a Mahayana text. To me they sum up the essence of what I felt and saw in the Itu Leper Colony church.

> *Words are not the highest reality, nor what is expressed in words the highest reality. Why? Because the highest reality is an experience which cannot be entered into by means of statements regarding it . . .*

I had been given the opportunity to revisit past spiritual experiences because of the nature and strangeness of the journey I had made in Peru. I could see a pattern emerging – first my childhood and schooldays experiences, then Itu . . . now Peru.

SIX

Inkakuna – The Children of the Sun

After two unforgettable days and nights on Rómulo's farm behind the great mountain of Machu Picchu, we say goodbye to the dogs, kittens and guinea-pigs and continue our journey towards the ancient city.

From the sun-dried earth of Rómulo's farmyard we have seen the mountain itself in many of its moods, but as yet have had no glimpse of the ruins themselves. We have sat at the foot of the mountain and watched the sun come up behind it and then set, and we have seen the mountain wreathed in early morning mist and shrouded by the falling darkness. Now it is time to go up to its peak.

Once again, this time in daylight, we are winched one by one on the rickety wooden *oroya* over the rushing Urubamba River. We climb up the steep slope on the other side to wait at the sleepy railway halt where we are to pick up the train from Cusco to Machu Picchu. This is not the smart tourist train recommended by the travel agents, but the daily local train.

We are to spend the night at Agua Calientes, the little town at the foot of the Inca ruins where American movie star Shirley MacLaine had an Out-of-Body experience in its famous, hot, medicinal mineral baths. We sit on the edge of the platform and wait for the train to come.

It turns out to be the worst train journey I've ever taken, definitely a not-to-be-repeated experience. My notebook entry has one word – 'Hell!'

The carriages are packed with local folk on the way to market, families off to visit friends and relatives, hundreds of people with overflowing baskets, bulging string bags, lumpy suitcases, fresh vegetables, loudly squawking fowls and crying babies. This is no pretty, picturesque picture book scene. Rather, a pretty squalid one.

Young backpackers from all over the world with heavy, awkward-looking bedrolls add to the congestion. Sitting is out of the question – either on a seat or on the floor – there's simply no room. Thank goodness we have been allowed only one small overnight bag each – even toting this is a Herculean task.

I become separated from the others in the throng and find myself squeezed upright between two dirty, surly German backpackers. After what seems a never-ending journey, I hear the cry 'Kate! Kate!' being passed down the train. 'Message for Kate! Get off the train at the next stop!'

The train lurches to a halt. Literally walking over the people sitting on the carriage floor, flailing my elbows left and right, using brute force to push my way through the crowds, I manage to jump off the train just as it begins to move again. My companions, who have been anxiously looking out for me, breathe a sigh of relief as I tumble down the high iron step.

We're staying overnight at Agua Calientes to ensure that we can be on the first bus up to Machu Picchu the next morning.

Our hotel, if indeed the collection of small dark rooms, communal toilets and showers can be called a hotel, is on the train platform where a full-scale market operates. Stalls, itinerant pedlars, flute-players, men selling hand-carved chairs, little boys clutching big round yellow cakes – ten cents a slice – and any number of the oddest-looking dogs and crowds of people give the little station a festive air.

The lively, gala atmosphere soon disperses the nightmare memories of the train, as we sit round a long table on the edge of the platform drinking the local beer and bargaining with the friendly people for their colourful wares. Occasionally a train goes by and we all wave. This is fun.

'Get your swimsuits, it's time to go up to the baths,' announces Carol. We cross the railway tracks and make the very steep climb to the mineral baths, passing through a small cobbled square decked with bright bunting on our way. I'm not sure what to expect. No, I hadn't read Shirley's book – although I've visited such hot springs before in Europe and Africa. They were clean, well-laid out places with excellent facilities.

Well, the hot springs of Agua Calientes may have been sacred and OK in ancient times, but today they are pretty unsightly. A recent landslide has washed mud and dirt down the mountain into the area of the springs, and mounds of earth are piled up all around in wet, spongy profusion. The surroundings of the springs are bare, muddy and bleak.

The baths themselves are small rectangular cement pits, in which waist-high, dubiously coloured water bubbles and steams. The smell is like that of a run-down public swimming pool. To make matters worse, these cement pits, the largest of which is only about three metres square, are crowded with people of every shape and description. Obviously this is where the locals take their daily bath. Whole families, including small naked babies with snotty noses, joke and laugh as they soak off the day's dirt. Travel-stained backpackers, some of whom have just come off the arduous five-day Inca walking trail where there are no ablutions en route, dreamily watch their layers of grime and sweat float away. A few of the young bloods of Agua Calientes lean nonchalantly against the pitted cement sides of the main bath and size up the foreign talent. One big, blue-eyed Swedish blonde attracts a lot of attention.

I think grimly that Mother Teresa herself would have been hard put to have had a spiritual experience here. However, we undress in the unsavoury changing rooms, bite the proverbial bullet and gingerly squeeze ourselves down a couple of rough, uneven steps to join the other bathers. The water is pleasantly warm – I feel as if I'm standing in a kind of primordial soup.

'Well, I've been here, done that, and will definitely *not* get a T-shirt,' I think to myself as I walk back down the hill to the train station.

Do I feel good? Purified? Uplifted? No way. I can't wait to get back to our tiny hotel and take a shower, even if it means standing in line.

The hot, medicinal, mineral springs of Agua Calientes can at best be described as a character-building experience, rather than an Out-of-Body one.

At seven o'clock the next morning we pile into the first bus of the day – destination Machu Picchu. Our driver navigates the hairpin bends, steep drops and stony roadside edges on the steep ascent with all the bravado and enthusiasm of a Formula One racing driver. At the top we check into Machu Picchu's Tourist Hotel, which stands just outside the ruins and whose limited number of crowded but comfortable rooms is booked out a year in advance, and make our way to the ticket kiosk, a few yards from the hotel.

We can't wait to see one of the wonders of the ancient world. We hurry through the gates, but Rómulo, Mark and Carol will not allow us to see the ruins from here. They want us to have the best and most spectacular view possible. Our first sight must be our best sight.

So we follow a narrow pathway up the side of the mountain and climb to a grassy plateau where a large funeral stone, about the size of a rowboat, rests at the highest point of the ruins, close to the city's original entrance. Three steps, symbolising the three Andean cosmological worlds, are carved into the side of the stone. Scholars and anthropologists believe that this canoe-shaped stone, carved with rings and pointing to the west, was central to an ancient initiation ceremony where initiates underwent a symbolic death and 'resurrection'.

Carol tells us how once, on an early visit to Machu Picchu, she had accompanied Don Eduardo Calderon, a healer from Trujillo, to the 'Sunboat' as it is popularly known. He had recited the following prayer:

> *May the winds of the south take the canoe to the regions of silence and death and then back to life . . .*

Carol tells us that the spirits of the dead were believed to pull the Sunboat, with the initiate lying on top of it, west towards the sunset. When the sun rose, the initiate would return from the east with new life as one of the *Inkakuna*, the children of the sun.

The ten of us – Kate and Alan, Gordon and Wilma, Carol and Mark, Sue and Rómulo, Joy and Big Carol – join hands and stand silently around the mystical stone. The air is thin beneath the blue, clear sky. As it is still early, there are few other people about. We let go hands and walk to the edge of the small grass plateau where the stone rests, and look out at what lies below.

No words can fully describe the impact that the first sight of this ancient city makes. No pictures can prepare you for this moment. One's breath is simply taken away. I hear the others gasp at the same moment as I do.

Machu Picchu beggars description – one of the few man-made wonders of the world that not only fulfils one's expectations, but exceeds them.

Because the 'ancient city of light' was never discovered by the Spanish invaders, its ruins are not the remnants of a conquered citadel like Sacsayhuaman outside Cusco, but are ruins made beautiful by the passage of time, enhanced by the weathering of the elements. The decay is natural, organic, unaffected by human hands. Temples, granaries, roads, squares and houses – one design for the priests, a lesser one for the soldiers, a still lesser one for the craftsmen – cluster together in raked terraces at the foot of the pointed peak so familiar to all armchair travellers.

As I stand above the mighty ruins, I can almost believe that the Inca Empire still exists and that the ordered life of the fourteenth and fifteenth centuries is still going on in the valley below.

It takes the rest of the day to explore the ruins. We take

our time, unlike the parties of rushed, mostly elderly, American tourists who are being raced round the ancient complex, presented with some very dubious facts and potted history, force-fed an indifferent lunch in the noisy cafeteria of the hotel and then, after this whirlwind tour, are herded back on to the tourist train for the two-hour return journey to Cusco.

Viewing Machu Picchu, soaking up its ambience and absorbing its history and religion takes time. When you go there, make sure that you allow yourself that time – even if it means making those hotel reservations a year in advance.

There's so much to see. Machu Picchu rises from the banks of the Urubamba River and when we look down the mountainside from the Sunboat site, we can see the roofs of Rómulo's farm far below us in the distance.

We enter the city through its mighty stone gates and spend leisurely hours marvelling at its wonders – sacred altars, where the *apukuna* were worshipped; the striking stone carving of a condor representing the *Hanakpacha*, the upper world of the Andean spiritual universe; the three high windows of the sacred temple, behind which Rómulo's great uncle Agustin entered the city in 1901; the *Intiwatana*, the sacred sundial known as the 'Hitching Post of the Sun', a colourful if inappropriate analogy because the Incas had no horses. This carefully carved rock, with its flat table top and narrow pillar made of stone which juts up from the top at a ninety degree angle, is positioned at one of the highest places in the city. To the original inhabitants of Machu Picchu, *Intiwatana* symbolised the point of communication between the sun, the Sun God, and his earthly followers, a physical place where divine forces connected with man.

Carol tells us about Andean Beings of Light, highly

evolved spiritual beings who supposedly lived millions of years ago. These Superbeings brought electromagnetic energy from the universe to Earth, which was a space station, and infused the inhabitants of earth with spiritual energy. Huge monuments and stone temples, built on special vortices of energy were home to highly evolved souls who had been incarnated in these holy places and guarded the wisdom of the ages.

I listen to her quiet voice. An attractive if way-out proposition I think, but one which finds no resonance with me. However, Sue and Big Carol are totally sold on the idea. A few months before coming to Peru, I had heard Graham Hancock, author of the bestselling *Fingerprints of the Gods*, speaking at a dinner in Johannesburg. On that occasion I had felt the same mixture of cynicism and fascination as I was feeling now. Spiritual energies, yes. Inexplicable building methods, yes. Forgotten technologies, yes. Space stuff, a definite no.

Carol, Sue and Big Carol join in an animated discussion of how energy paths connected temples of the sun to the sacred sites of other civilisations, such as the Mayan and Aztec. Today we have forgotten our connections to other planets, forgotten ancient secrets and mysteries and are now mere three-dimensional beings, unable to travel in time and space.

I sit dozing in the late afternoon sunlight.

But then I am jolted back to the presence of the Dalai Lama and the message of the 'Interconnectedness of All Things' that he had given us on that cold winter's morning in Johannesburg just before I left for Peru.

Carol is telling the others how the Andean Masters believe that we are all part of the universe and connected to all things.

How over the millennia we have forgotten who we are, where we have come from and where we are going. And how we are really multi-dimensional beings, functioning simultaneously in many dimensions and levels of consciousness.

I gaze at the ruins before me and the mountains around me and try to make some sense of what Carol and the others are talking about.

Is it possible to function simultaneously on more than one level of consciousness, I wonder?

Their words and arguments will come back to me with a sharp clarity when I experience my 'Everlasting Moment' in a simple wooden hut beside the Amazon River.

Late that night, we re-enter the ancient city. Flashlights are forbidden so we follow one another closely, holding on to the walls, picking our way carefully along steep pathways, ducking under low arches, moving on and up, higher and higher until we reach the *Intiwatana*.

The air is pure, the silence profound. Our little group, so different in so many ways, but now bonded together by our shared experiences, is totally alone in Machu Picchu – one of the great holy places of the world, one of its most sacred sites. It is a precious, privileged time, one to hold on to for always. We each find a solitary spot under the stars. I feel divorced from the here and now, my mind floating somewhere above the dimly seen but intensely felt mountains. There is much spiritual energy here, and great peace.

✳

If, Dear Reader, as Jane Eyre might have called you, you have travelled with me thus far, I hope that you have been sharing with me some of the thoughts, ideas and sensations that I was experiencing. Maybe some of the ideas and notions are already familiar to you. Maybe you have already discovered your own spiritual path and have recognised the milestones along it. Maybe not. All I can say to you is to keep your minds, spirits and hearts open.

Credo Mutwa, the well-known African *sangoma* and *sanusi*, the human repository of so much of Africa's traditional spiritual past, advised listeners on my radio programme not long before I travelled to Peru that each of us must learn to build our own individual spirituality. We can listen to and learn from other people's wisdom and mistakes but, finally, it's up to each and every one of us to find our own brand of spirituality, the one that suits and satisfies us best.

'You cannot build a temple on the shifting sands of confusion,' he said. 'So you must first sort yourself out. Take time to think about your life and of what part, if any, spirituality plays in it. Because before you can build your spirituality, you must look at your past, examine that past, throw out the rubbish and gather from it the things of value – only you will know what those are – and use those things, those experiences to build your spirituality.'

Most of you, like me, will have been on a spiritual journey all your lives. Some of you, again like me, unknowingly. Some of you will have already clearly recognised your path, some only dimly, others not at all.

It took a strange and magical journey to show me my way. Blind Dan had always asserted that I was on a spiritual journey, and now I was beginning to believe that what he had always insisted on was true. In my case, it had taken a literal journey to an unknown, unfamiliar place to unravel, and then put back together again, the threads in my own life that made up the fabric of this journey. For me, Peru was the catalyst.

However, a more down-to-earth event – the death of a loved one, an illness, the birth of a baby, a new book, a magazine article, a television programme, the words of a friend – might be your inspiration, your route map, your catalyst.

I have no doubt though, if you're a thinking person and know that there has to be more to life than surface, you will also know that it's essential to keep your options open, to stay aware, to be open-minded. You will be surprised at what may occur. Look for things to happen, connections to be made, and I believe they will.

Seven years before I went to Peru, I visited Australia and experienced many strange and wonderful things there that were memorable to me at the time, but which over the subsequent years I had filed away in my spiritual memory bank.

Their significance had not yet been revealed to me.

Mark, a keen, lifelong student of Zen Buddhism, had told us that enlightenment is found in the *present moment*.

On the night that we had sat among the ancient ruins of Machu Picchu, my experiences in Australia re-entered my consciousness and took on a spiritual shape and meaning. I became aware that they also had been landmarks on my spiritual journey.

For the Aboriginals of Australia, one of the world's oldest people, time is unspecific. In a physical and spiritual landscape with no boundaries, the concept of immortality is fundamental to a vision where there is no past, present or future.

As I sat in the dark with my back to the great stone

Intiwatana at one of the highest points of the Sacred City of Machu Picchu, my past and present also merged into one and became part of my future too . . .

SEVEN

Landscape With No Boundaries

A few years before my visit to Peru, I had visited Central Australia – the Red Heart of the Continent – one of the driest and most barren places on earth. As the memories begin to resurface, come back in time with me as I remember . . .

It was winter Down Under. Although the shadows were lengthening, the raw heat of the day was still oppressive. William and I had been walking since morning in the West MacDonnell ranges. Those red mountains surround the little town of Alice Springs in the heart of Australia's Red Centre where William, who was a senior ranger with the Conservation Commission of the Northern Territory, was stationed. My nephew is an expert on the bush, its flora and fauna, and had just been posted to Alice from Australia's 'Top End'.

In a land of contrasts, there can be few more dramatic than that between the Top End, the north, and the Red Centre, to the south. The north has endless eucalypt woodlands, sandstone plateaus, lush tropical forest, wild rivers and vast wetlands. In the south, where long droughts are the rule rather than the exception, rainfall is unpredictable. It is a stark landscape of sand and rock, but when the dawn lights up the age-old hills or the rocks glow red with the setting sun, it is one of the most beautiful places on earth.

There is little surface water in the dauntingly dry landscape of the south, although earlier in the day Will had shown me a deep narrow cleft filled with icy water. Dozens of Bony Bream, the Red Centre's largest fish, named for their many finely branched rib bones, were lying dead on the banks.

'They can't stand the frosty nights,' Will explained. 'We call it the "winter die-off". Apparently the cold, low oxygen conditions stimulate the growth of parasites in their gills and the fish can't get enough oxygen from the water. So they suffocate.'

We'd been carrying our own water all day and as evening approached had just enough to get us back to where Will's old 4x4, a Russian Lada, was parked near the Visitors' Centre. We hadn't seen a soul all day. We sat down on a smooth, red rock and drank the now brackish water from our water bottles.

I heard a faint rustling in the scratchy spinifex grass beside me.

'Don't move. Freeze.' Will's voice was soft, urgent. I sat motionless as a huge mottled brown snake, at least two metres long, slithered past my feet. Thank goodness for sturdy boots, I thought. Each scale on its thick body had a dark or light tip, giving it a kind of criss-cross colour pattern. We watched it as it moved on purposefully past where we were sitting and disappeared behind another big rock.

Will whistled softly through his teeth, expelling the breath he had been holding in for the last few moments.

'Well done, Auntie Kate,' he said in his soft Australian drawl. 'You've just seen a King Brown – the largest and most dangerous snake hereabouts. You're lucky, that's quite an honour.'

As I sat in Machu Picchu thinking about this episode in Australia's dry desert seven years earlier, I was very aware of the bright green snake I had seen just a couple of days before on the way back from Clothilda's farm. Rómulo had told me how lucky I was to see such a potent symbol of wisdom.

'An honour?' I asked Will.

'Yeah, a big powerful snake like the King Brown is very important in the Aboriginal Dreaming.'

Later on, in Arnhem Land in Australia's 'Top End', my sister's great friend and mentor, an Aboriginal elder, who by Aboriginal law may not be named because he has since died, would tell me about the Dreaming.

The King Brown, or Mulga, was to be the last memorable sight in a day that had been full of memorable sights.

We had set off early from Alice Springs, affectionately known by Aussies everywhere simply as 'Alice'. Alice is surrounded by desert on all sides, and its Outback population is scattered on sheep and cattle stations, some as large as Belgium. Neville Shute first made the little town famous in his novel *A Town Like Alice* which became a hugely successful television mini-series starring one of Australia's best-known actors, Brian Brown, as the Australian soldier who survives crucifixion in a Japanese prison camp in World War Two to go home to Alice. The cult Australian movie *Priscilla, Queen of the Desert*, which delighted audiences all over the world, also features the little town whose tar roads blister in the heat of summer and crack open with ice in the below-freezing winters.

But although these weather extremes are part and parcel of life in the Red Centre, they can also affect the country as a whole. Less than twenty years ago, a prolonged drought christened the Big Dry withered the entire country. Strong winds whipped up the parched soil from the Outback and carried it to the cities of the south and east, blinding motorists and clogging machinery. Australians still talk about Ash Wednesday in 1983, a bitterly ironic date, when gale-force winds drove bush fires along 750 kilometres of coast from Adelaide to Melbourne. In some places the fires caused a vacuum into which fireballs were sucked at speeds of more than 160 kilometres an hour. Seven townships were wiped out, two thousand homes were destroyed, and more than seventy people lost their lives.

The Big Dry lasted for two years. Many farmers were ruined financially, selling off prime ewes that would normally have fetched 30 dollars a head for as little as 10 cents each, because of the lack of fodder and pastureland. Worse was to come. Six months later, major floods caused the worst flooding in ten years.

Droughts, floods and cyclones are all familiar weather hazards in the Outback. No Australian will forget Christmas Day 1973, when the little town of Darwin on Australia's northern tip was struck by Cyclone Tracy, which, with tremendous force and mighty winds (although the exact force of the wind is not known because the Darwin Airport anemometer broke when registering a speed of 275 kilometres an hour), blasted the roofs off buildings and cars and demolished everything in its path. By the time Cyclone Tracy had whirled past, sixty-seven people had died and 90 per cent of the buildings in the city had been devastated.

Darwin was rebuilt, but its inhabitants know that a cyclone can be expected to pass within 100 kilometres of the city once every six years. The easy-going inhabitants shrug their shoulders. 'No worries,' they say in typical laid-back Aussie fashion. 'It's happened before – it'll happen again.' Darwin has now been flattened three times. Once by a cyclone in 1897, then by Japanese bombs in World War Two in 1942, and then by Cyclone Tracy in 1973.

Natural disasters like droughts and cyclones typify the harsh nature of this continent but also, paradoxically, form its unique beauty.

Will and I had spent the day walking through Simpsons Gap National Park, one of the largest parks in Central Australia. The Park, as its name suggests – the Aussies typically don't go in for fancy, romantic names – incorporates a number of scenic gaps including Simpsons Gap, one of the most prominent and dramatic of the breaks in the towering red peaks of the MacDonnell ranges.

We had first climbed Cassia Hill to get a superb, elevated view of the MacDonnells and the whole Simpsons Gap area. On our way to the summit we had passed through groves of witchetty bush and mulga.

(A few nights later, I was to eat a witchetty grub, the larval stage of a moth that feeds on the witchetty leaves. One of Will's Aboriginal friends, Sam, had offered it to me as a great delicacy. I tried hard not to think too much about what I was eating as I slowly chewed the fat, white worm which, thankfully, had been fried. I had eaten fried grasshoppers in Nigeria many years before when, as an English teacher in a village school, I attended the birthday feast of one of my

Nigerian pupils. The taste was pretty much the same – dry, scratchy, vaguely prawn-like, unmemorable.)

We walked most of the day through steep-sided ridges and timbered creek flats and past huge ghost gums. The mighty white trunks of the ghost gum trees gave off an aura of other-worldliness as the sun reflected off their papery, silver-white, dead-looking bark. But I only appreciated their ghostliness fully when I camped out in the Outback with Will and Sam.

One very cold night, under the brilliant stars, snug in my swag (a camping bedroll), I watched the ghost gums quiver and glisten in the moonlight as the dingos howled. Scary stuff, even for a bush baby from Africa. Sam was sitting propped against one of these white giants a few feet away, his blue-black face lost in the shadows. Only his eyes glittered in the firelight. I heard a chortle and then saw his teeth shining whitely as he laughed at me. An owl had been calling since dusk and its soft 'boobook' calls punctuated the night until dawn.

After our encounter with the King Brown at Simpsons Gap, as Will and I walked back to the Lada, we caught sight of the elusive rock wallabies who had ventured out of the shady hiding places in the rocks where they sheltered in the heat of the day. Like so many of the other strange creatures that dwell in this land at the bottom of the world, their uniqueness seemed both familiar and startling. Sitting up on their long hind legs, strong tails acting as a balance behind them, short front paws clasped in front of their chests, they watched us with bright, beady eyes. It was getting cooler, but even in July, the coldest time of year, we wore hats and carried water bottles.

'You don't take chances with this heat,' said Will. 'One of

our guys got lost a few months ago and ignored the golden rule of not moving away from his vehicle. We found him forty-eight hours later, but he was a goner.'

The only people who truly know how to live in harmony with this relentlessly demanding, unforgiving landscape are its first inhabitants, the Aboriginals, whose history goes back some 50 000 years. And only now, in the latter years of the twentieth century, is their culture, status, importance and spirituality being recognised.

In the space of less than two hundred years, one of the world's most ancient peoples were dispossessed, wrenched from their culture and forced into a marginal existence on the fringes of white society. When the first settlers disembarked at Botany Bay in 1788, it's estimated that there were about 300 000 Aboriginals in Australia and Tasmania, including the deserts of the Outback. Between them, they spoke more than five hundred different languages grouped into about thirty related language families.

But they were not a unified, homogeneous group. The Aboriginals themselves never used one collective term to describe themselves. And no individual Aboriginal, at that time, would have known or guessed at the existence of many of the other Aboriginal peoples and regions in a continent which covers nearly three million square miles – almost the size of the United States.

Their culture, rich, complex and subtle, was incomprehensible and therefore inaccessible to the first settlers who initially considered the Aboriginals a nuisance, to be driven off into the vast emptiness which surrounded the pioneer settlements. But the nuisance quickly became a threat when the Aboriginals retaliated as the invaders pushed into the interior from the coast, taking more and more land as they did so. Now Aboriginals were hunted down and killed, and when they tried to fight back with their own form of guerrilla warfare, they were swiftly dispatched by the white man's superior technology.

But this is history – a history that has many parallels in most of the other continents of the world. What is important today in Australia is that ancient wrongs are being redressed, and the land that formerly belonged to one of the oldest peoples in the world is being returned to them. Spiritual sites are once again recognised and we, in the rest of the world, are privileged to have the opportunity to learn about a culture which resonates strongly with modern man in his quest for a spiritual path and an understanding of a confused world.

Aboriginal people know that Uluru (Ayers Rock) and Kata Tjuta (Mt Olga) were created and shaped into their unique forms during the Tjukurpa or Creation. The Tjukurpa ('chook-oor-pa') is fundamental to the life of the Aboriginal people. The Tjukurpa is the law which gives meaning and order to all aspects of life. It provides explanations for the origins of life and all living things, as well as for features of the landscape. Each individual feature of Uluru and Kata Tjuta represents the visual imprints and physical proof of the activities of the ancestral beings of the Tjukurpa. Although archaeological evidence suggests that they have lived in the Uluru area for at least ten thousand years, the Aboriginal people know that the landscape of Central Australia has been a part of their culture since the beginning of time.

Will, his friend John from Darwin, and I made the trip to Ayers Rock from Alice. Our small plane took off shortly after dawn and flew northwest, past the Australian/American Joint Space Research Facility at Pine Gap which gleamed whitely in the early morning sun.

'Nobody really knows what goes on there,' said Will, hinting darkly at nuclear goings-on and sinister technology.

At Simpsons Gap the plane turned and flew west along the West MacDonnell Ranges past Standley Chasm and Ellery Gorge before turning south to Hermannsburg Aboriginal Community, an old Lutheran Mission established over a hundred years ago. The first superintendent of the settlement, Pastor Kemp, produced an Aranda language dictionary, and his successor, Pastor Strethlow, translated the New Testament into Aranda. My imagination pictures these two good men from the north, accustomed to the icy snows of northern Europe, bent over their God-inspired work by the light of a guttering candle in temperatures that can fry an egg on a rock. Today, the motivation of missionaries like these has been severely questioned. Was their work in the name of God or in the interests of colonial aggrandisement? Presumably only their God knows.

Ironically, Hermannsburg Mission is perhaps best known today not only for the pioneering linguistic efforts of its early supervisors, but also as the alma mater of one of Australia's most famous Aboriginal artists, Albert Namatjira. Little mention is made of its religious impact on a people who had followed their own spiritual way thousands and thousands of years before the birth of Christ.

The cluster of old buildings receded into the distance as we flew over the Finke River, reputedly the oldest river in the world, to Palm Valley, where we looked down upon the ancient cabbage palms, rare plants and ferns that are found nowhere else in the world. These species of plants are the descendants of those that once lined the foreshore of the great inland sea that existed here many millions of years ago. Not far from Palm Valley the plane lost height again to give us a closer look at the Amphitheatre – a large, semi-circular valley used extensively in the ancient sacred rites of the Aranda Aboriginal tribe. Our pilot, Bob, told us that this enclosed valley has the same acoustic qualities as the classic Greek amphitheatres of Delphi and Epidaurus. Our amplified engine noise startled a herd of brumbies, wild desert horses, which galloped off in alarm.

Next, we flew over the spectacular rugged scenery of the Krichhauff Ranges, past Areyonga Aboriginal Community, the James and Middle Ranges, towards Kings Canyon. Will had spent the previous year as Ranger at Kings Canyon. It is spectacular from the air, but even more so on foot, he told me. The Lost City, an extensive series of rock domes and terraces which overlooks the head of the canyon and its sheer cliff face, resembles the ruins of an ancient civilisation.

On we flew to Lake Amadeus, named by its first white discoverer after Amadeo, King of Spain, part of the chain of salt lakes which is all that remains of the great inland sea. And then to Uluru – one of the greatest natural wonders of the world.

Nothing prepares you for The Rock. I'd seen photographs, watched videos. I'd read that it is geologically unique, the largest formation of its kind in the world, 600 million years old. But like everybody else who first catches sight of this great, mile-high, smooth red monolith, I was astounded. It rises sheer from an unending featureless plain dotted with spinifex grass. Because of its rounded surface and exposure to the elements, no soil can cling to its bare stone surface which changes colour dramatically with the changing light of day. It looks as if it is sculpted out of red marble.

A small bus met the plane and took us to the foot of the Rock.

'See you back here in six hours,' said Bob cheerfully. 'Don't break your necks.'

Yes, of course we were going to climb the Rock. For me to have come all this way from the bottom end of another fabled continent and not to climb the Rock would have been unthinkable.

I was in full-on tourist mode. Had I not stood on a high glacier in Alaska, ridden to the Great Pyramid of Cheops on a camel, marvelled at the ruins of Masada in Israel, picked poppies in Thailand's Golden Triangle? Had I not had my picture taken on the top of the Leaning Tower of Pisa, climbed down into the Grand Canyon and up to the top of the Empire State Building, waltzed with a Chinese dancing instructor in a square in Beijing, and even kissed the Blarney Stone? Now I was going to climb Ayers Rock, and might even buy a T-shirt to wear afterwards, *I Climbed Ayers Rock*.

No thought of this being an ancient Aboriginal sacred site crossed my mind. My radio programme *Believe It Or Not* was still two years away, was still undreamed of. Instinctively I had always known that I was a 'spiritual' person, but in the media world I worked in, being spiritual was hardly a recommendation – that sort of thing was reserved for flakes and Born Again Christians. Spirituality was decidely uncool.

What do I mean when I say that I instinctively knew that I was a spiritual person? It's hard to articulate, but when I watched the stars at night, saw a rose unfurl, stood among the great pillars of Stonehenge or trod on the stone steps of Canterbury Cathedral, steps worn smooth by the feet of pilgrims over the ages, I had felt something deep and atavistic stir within me. But being consciously spiritual and seeking a spiritual path was for other people. I was much too busy with the here and now to bother about what might lie behind present reality.

At Ayers Rock that day, Will, who is now a reformed alcoholic, was suffering from the worst case of DTs he had ever experienced. White and shaking, he told me that he didn't think he could make the climb.

'Rubbish,' I said briskly, with no notion of how traumatic his condition was.

John was suffering from a bad case of bronchitis, croaking and spluttering like a frog in extremis.

Stepping out with all the vigorous enthusiasm of a Brown Owl leading her troop of Brownies (shades of the Itu Leper Colony!), and cheerfully ignoring the printed signs at the foot of the climb which gloomily warned us of how many lives had been lost in climbing the Rock, we set off. We were not, however, a merry band. As we inched up the slippery red stone, hanging on to the chain which stretches up into the unseen distance, my confidence began to take a dip. Will was brushing off unknown creatures which were 'attacking' him from all quarters whilst John's wheezes and sneezes were growing worse.

But we persevered, and a couple of hours later found ourselves standing on the top of Ayers Rock. We signed the Visitors' Book, and as I did so I remarked to Will and John that somebody, somewhere, some day, would recognise my name in this book and tell me about it. (It hasn't happened yet, but it will.)

We each found a private space on the wide, flat summit

and sat down. I gazed at the limitless horizon. Like the empty sky, this landscape has no boundaries.

A surge of inexplicable feeling engulfed me. I lay down on the smooth rock, pressed my cheek to its warm surface and cried my heart out.

I was not crying because of the severity of the climb. I was not crying with relief at having got my two sick boys to the top. I was not crying for Will, nor for his pregnant wife who had left him because of his remorseless and terrifying drinking. I was not crying for my widowed sister, who was watching her brilliant and talented only son drinking himself to death.

I was crying for joy.

Seven years later, on top of another mountain, Machu Picchu, another of the earth's most sacred places, I realised why I had been crying that day. It was because for the first time I had been in touch with my own spirituality. The feelings I had experienced – and they returned to me with great intensity at Machu Picchu – were of being enveloped in a cosmic love, in tune with a cosmic consciousness, and enfolded in peace. I was only now able to recognise these things, because I had begun to experience them here in Peru.

When you have a spiritual experience of this kind for the first time, (a) you may not recognise it (I didn't), and (b) you don't know how to handle it (I didn't). I sat alone, a little stunned, very confused.

Then I felt a pair of strong arms around me. It was Will. He looked well again and in control.

'Are you all right, Auntie Kate?' he asked anxiously, adding, 'If it helps, I know what you're feeling. I've just felt it too.'

The three of us – a middle-aged woman, an alcoholic

and an invalid – literally skipped down the Rock, holding hands like a bunch of kids. We whooped and sang, shouted and carolled our joy to the empty spaces that echoed back our voices. Climbers on their way up smiled a little nervously at our antics as we reassured them, 'No worries! Keep going. Don't give up. It's worth it!'

As I sat under the bright Andean stars, I relived that spiritual experience, accepting it for what I now knew it was. I could now appreciate its significance fully as it reinforced my growing conviction, first experienced long, long ago, on New Year's Eve in a remote corner of Nigeria, that there is more to life than the physical world, much more to life than surface.

*

There aren't many people who are lucky enough to venture into the interior of Australia's Red Centre with their own personal ranger. Will took me to remote places well off the tourist map. We camped in the Outback. He showed me where he was building a new trail through the MacDonnells, walked with me in Rainbow Valley where the setting sun shines directly on to a stark range of richly coloured sandstone, swam with me in the deep waterhole of Ormiston Gorge, and took me to meet many of his Aboriginal friends.

Will was born in the Western Highlands of New Guinea where his young father had been an Assistant District Officer before he died tragically of cancer when Will was only five years old. The family had always been a pioneering lot – Will's paternal grandfather had single-handedly explored much of New Guinea's uncharted territory at the turn of the century.

Because my sister's time was largely taken up with running a school for the indigenous people of Minj – people aged from five to seventy – writing textbooks for them, setting up a system of more formal education, teaching them everything from how to read and write to Shakespeare, Will's upbringing had largely been left to Joe, the Papuan man who served as cook, housekeeper and nanny. A photograph of Will as a baby shows him proudly clasped in the arms of a very fierce-looking man with Bird of Paradise feathers in his hair, a bone through his nose, and his strong near-naked torso wrapped in a very small loincloth.

Will could speak the local dialect before he could speak English and on many occasions had been taken to visit his protector's remote village. Thus when Will came to Australia he found it easy to mix with the Aboriginal people and formed strong and lasting bonds with them. He was neither a 'bleeding heart' (an Aussie term of opprobrium for people who take up trendy liberal causes) nor a politician. There was no hidden agenda. Will soon found he was spending more time with the Aboriginal people than anybody else.

Ultimately, two of them in particular saved his life.

In Alice Springs today, with his reconciled wife and two small sons, Will lives his life on a spiritual basis. He has found that this deeper perception has diluted his fear not only of his own daily predicaments but also his ability to accept the world's. He believes that he has been prepared for this awareness through meeting particular people.

Will had lived and worked in the bush for most of his life and had embraced isolation and wilderness unequivocally as his soul's balm.

He had gone to live with his mother, my sister Rita, in

Arnhem Land after a particularly destructive episode in his life. Arnhem Land in the Northern Territory of Australia is maelstrom country, affected only by the flow and flood of rivers, the wet season and 'The Dry', fire and regrowth and the sweeping tidal reach of the Arafura Sea. His mother was running a school on Elcho Island, part of North East Arnhem Land. They were both adopted into the Aboriginal community and given 'skin' names, a true honour in those days. These names are more than titular: they represent a kinship network within which you are able to conduct your daily affairs with the comfort of belonging.

Will had met Barney (he was not allowed to reveal Barney's real name because of tribal taboo) as a result of his own addictive, destructive lifestyle.

Barney was tall, obsidian, elegant and graceful in manner and movement. He was a hereditary landowner, a man of power or 'Mala' leader. It was Barney, Will told me, when we met in London for his sister's wedding a few weeks after I came back from Peru and was telling him of my own spiritual awakening, who first took Will on his own spiritual journey – a journey that was to bring Will to where he is today.

Will first met Barney through his mother, a very strong woman in her own right. Their friendship continued and grew through Will's interest in and deep love of the bush. Barney was a master in his own country and taught his young disciple about bush 'tucker' (food) and native medicine. He intuitively knew that Will was soulsick, and as time went by he showed him things that would help.

Will told me how he remembered being angry, resentful, cynical, disillusioned, feelings that are all encapsulated in the word 'fearful'. He and Barney sat on top of the ochre cliffs above the bay. Snake Island was a speck on the queasy monsoon horizon. The Aboriginal Elder told Will to look at the sun directly and briefly and then to close his eyes and look away, to *will* away the hideous red and black speckles on his lids. Will did this, and as his lids cleared and became opaque the poisonous backlog ceased. Barney told him that he was only ever to repeat these actions if in extreme distress.

Barney's totem or animal spirit was the whale; his was a relationship with the ocean. Over the years he would often anoint himself with copious quantities of 'Reef Oil', an aromatic suntan oil. Will thought it whimsical, almost amusing, but always dutifully purchased it for his Aboriginal mentor while on leave to the mainland.

'But my cynicism was dispelled on a day in my journey I will never forget,' Will recounted. 'That was the day Barney chose to reveal himself and the power of his totem.'

They had returned from a fishing trip to one of the Island's tidal estuaries. Will felt high on life and stuffed with coal-cooked fish and bush onion. The home beach was nondescript, it was a grey day, neither here nor there.

As they sat on the beach, exhausted, Barney smothered himself in copious quantities of Reef Oil and then spoke. It was a conversation of fellowship with the rolling massive tides, the acres of sea grass, dugong plains, turtle, shark, stingray. Still speaking, the grey, long-limbed old black man strode into the riffle of low tide, sank to his knees and anointed himself with ocean, his voice weaving into the surround. His murmur rose and fell as he spoke his centuries of verse, and refreshed his spirit. After a while he arose and walked back from the ocean towards Will. He was younger, his hair black, his body tauter, straighter, powerful.

Will watched, silent and amazed.

Life returned with the bite of sandflies. Some time later, Will could not say how long, Barney became his old self again. His eyes twinkled as he shook his grey head and smiled wryly as they rose stiffly, brushing off the sand, to head home.

Will left the Islands of North East Arnhem Land not long afterwards, still too selfish, he told me that cold December night in London, to realise the gifts within. He landed up on the Western border of Kakadu National Park in the Alligator Rivers region, *Crocodile Dundee* country. It was there that he met Alfred (also not his real name), the traditional Custodian of the area. He was a mischievous old man whose snowy beard grew or didn't, depending on the number of anthropologists in the area.

Alfred and Will travelled widely together and Will instinctively felt that he would be taught another spiritual lesson. Alfred showed him how to read *his* land and the essence of his belief, not something taken on board, but coming from within by birth and honed by being.

After Will left the territory, Alfred appeared again at crucial moments in the lives of Will's family. At a kitchen window in troubled times in Alice Springs to Margo, Will's wife. At a screen door late one night in Darwin to his mother. In an intensive care unit in Adelaide.

Will believes that this is because Alfred showed him his *Tehuringa* stones, the documents of his clan and totem. With this act, Will's family was incorporated into the life story of the clan, and Alfred's task as Custodian was to succour *all* his clan. Will also believes that his part of this gift is to grow in faith and to be open to all things.

As a recovering alcoholic and drug addict, Will feels that he is inextricably linked to and dependent on faith in powers greater than himself, and that they are there in myriad forms. These stories relay only some of Will's own story; men and women and places of power abound, but he could only access some of them through the virtual destruction of self as he was.

As we sat in my niece's apartment in London the night before her wedding, two months after I had sat with my back to the Hitching Post of the Sun and relived my experiences in Australia, Will said to me, 'Unfortunately I can't tell anyone else "How To", I can only tell my story and live my life. I met Barney nineteen years ago, and Alfred fourteen. It's taken me a long time to receive their messages.'

EIGHT

Lightning Dreaming

John and I flew up to Darwin without Will. By now he was becoming very ill and had been hospitalised.

'Give up drinking or you'll kill yourself,' the doctor at Alice had told him.

Remember that bizarre bar somewhere on the frontiers of space in *Star Wars*? The locals – oldtimers, young 'uns, creatures two-footed, four-footed, human and otherwise, permanent or just passin' through? The atmosphere – way-out, hyperactive, frenetic and more than a little off the wall? The noise – a super-decibelled babble of alien tongues?

OK, that pretty well sums up Darwin at the Top End of Australia's Northern Territory. It's a clean, modern little city which has grown from a tiny pioneering outpost a hundred years ago, to an unofficial 60 000 plus today. Darwin boasts the highest rate of alcohol consumption in Australia – 40 per cent above national average – and one of the highest in the world. Only in Darwin do the inhabitants hold an annual regatta for rafts made out of empty beer cans, always in plentiful supply in this thirsty little town.

Its reputation for transience and impermanence derives not only from the devastating cyclones of its past, but also because it has a floating population of newcomers from other parts of Australia, as well as English, Greek, Chinese, Timorese, Lebanese, Vietnamese, Yugoslav and Italian immigrants who make it look like a temporary cantonment for exiles in spite of its modern hotels and thriving casino.

There's a great spirit in Darwin – always has been. Its inhabitants still live constantly at the frontiers of change, excitement, safety and the unknown. Perhaps it's this spirit that makes Darwin a place of exceptional, hard-living, hard-working, warm and generous people who are bound – citizens, residents and non-residents alike – in a spirit of sharing and friendship that is less common elsewhere in Australia.

Darwin is the gateway to one of the world's great natural wonders – Kakadu National Park, which lures visitors from all over the world, from well-heeled oldies to young backpackers. Listed as a World Heritage Site because of its outstanding wetlands that are of international importance, and the significance of its present and past cultural history, Kakadu is unusual in that it qualified for World Heritage listing on the basis of both its natural and its cultural values.

The name of Kakadu is derived from *Gagudju*, one of the several languages of the Aboriginal people whose traditional lands and culture provide the foundations for one of the world's finest national parks. Over 200 kilometres from north to south and 100 kilometres east to west, Kakadu includes approximately 17 500 square kilometres of the Alligator Rivers region in the tropical north of Australia. The park covers six major topographical regions including the spectacular Arnhem Land escarpment (which some estimates put at 400 million years old), and has undulating wood-lands, precipitous waterfalls, docile-looking water buffalo, forests full of animals and birds, extensive floodplains and mangrove-covered tidal flats.

In Kakadu I learned more about the ancient ways of looking at life. It's hard today for us to remember that it is only really in the last two decades that the rich and ancient culture of the Aboriginal people has come to be appreciated and understood. Perhaps distinguished travel writer Bruce Chatwin started it all with his memorable, evocative book *Songlines* which became a global bestseller. He was one of the first to write with integrity and credibility about the strong environmental ties of the Aboriginals – a part of their culture which attracts many urbanised city dwellers and nature lovers from all over the world – ties which are based on complex spiritual beliefs.

These beliefs centre on the arrival of the 'First People' in a creation era now referred to as the Dreamtime. Before the Dreamtime the landscape was empty. Then the First People arrived and created the landscape by 'singing' it and everything in it, even the people themselves. They also founded the religious ceremonies, marriage rules, food taboos and other laws of human society. This was the beginning of everything significant for all Aboriginal people, not only those who have lived in Kakadu for at least 25 000 years – possibly 40 000 to 50 000 years. Aboriginals know that they have been part of the land from the beginning, since their legendary ancestors in human and animal form fashioned the landscape and all living things.

There is a whole pantheon of these Ancestral Beings. But the Dreamtime also has a parallel reality in the present because all men are the descendants of these mythical ancestors, irrevocably linked to them and to the land they created. In the old days, before the coming of the white man, every Aboriginal knew each feature of his tribal territory, and that every rock, tree or waterhole contained the spirit of his ancestors. He not only knew his way around his land, but also could as easily navigate its history, myths, legends and spirits. He knew that he was identical, one with his ancestors, and therefore the land he moved through was his own creation too.

Past and present are inexplicably intertwined. 'Dreamings' are Ancestral Beings who are part of this past and present. Their spirits are passed on to their descendants. Witchetty Grub Dreaming, Water Dreaming, Wild Yam Dreaming, Bushfire Dreaming and the hundreds of other Dreamings known across Australia are part of the spiritual identities of those Aboriginals who claim them as their Ancestral Beings or totems. Groups, clans and tribes may share the same Dreamings which provide much of the spiritual reinforcement of traditional communal title to land. To falsely claim the Dreaming of another group is a serious infringement of Aboriginal law. In the myths, Dreamings are born, live and sometimes die, but they are always eternally present in the Dreamtime.

The attainment of religious knowledge began with initiation during adolescence and became a lifelong quest. There were specific male and female religious ceremonies, and individuals held specific aspects or segments of mythic information. There were many religious ceremonies, some secret, some public, usually accompanied by dancing, singing and mime, which were integral parts of everyday life. Children were first taught children's dances, but after initiation the more complicated and ritual steps are revealed to them. Audience participation is crucial; not everyone plays an individual role but everybody joins in the dancing and clapping. Sticks are clapped together and the deep, doleful sounds of the didjeridu accompany and punctuate the action. This huge woodwind, now familiar to people all over the world, was originally made from the branch of a tree hollowed out by termites. It originated in North East Arnhem Land.

The western edge of Arnhem Land, a steep escarpment whose spectacular cliff is over 200 kilometres long and 300 metres high, overshadows the adjacent wetlands.

John and I took a short plane trip to get a bird's-eye view of Lightning Dreaming, the escarpment home of Namarrgon, Lightning Man.

As we prepared to touch down at the tiny airstrip after a thrilling and very bumpy ride, our wheels got stuck. The young pilot seemed unfazed, and zoomed off again to have another try.

'No worries,' he assured us.

After three more abortive attempts at landing, we finally crunched to a halt. I was not afraid for one second. The spirit that entered my soul at the top of Ayers Rock had made me feel strong and protected. The spectators on the ground, however, were shaken and pale.

My sister Rita said, 'I thought that was it. That your bones were coming to rest in one of the oldest places in the world.'

But it was only my spirit that had come to rest.

Kakadu is one of the few places left in Australia where the original inhabitants maintain personal and spiritual links with traditional lands.

These links can best be seen in the unique Aboriginal art sites – one of the greatest collections of ancient art in the world. Rock painting is a tradition that has continued in Kakadu for thousands of years. Some paintings are believed to be more than 20 000 years old, which would make them some of the oldest human works. Some are as recent as 1985.

Aboriginal rock art, as with other forms of Aboriginal art, isn't always easy to understand – even among the Aboriginals themselves it's not fully understood by the uninitiated. Western views on its meaning, significance and artistic 'value' have differed greatly since the time the work was first 'discovered' and attempts were made to analyse it critically.

What *is* known is that the single most common subject matter of Aboriginal art is landscape-based myth, but the Aboriginal artist is not painting a landscape as a pretty picture. His images of landscape are representations of instances of Dreamings, because in his terms all landscape is someone's home. Some critics have held that it is naturalistic art, depicting the physical, social and cultural environment; others believe that the art is not at all naturalistic, that images are not painted in three-dimensional space but reduced to symbol. These images split the sequence of time – time without tense – when daily events are contextualised in the ideas of original creation, where man and spirit are one, interchangeable, eternal.

No concept of the Western notion of the artist existed in Aboriginal society. Each individual was expected to learn about specific sets of designs and, if called upon to do so, to reproduce them. That's not to say that one person wasn't more talented or skilled than another, but the concept of an artist as commentator, interpreter and muse of his society was unknown.

Although it is now fairly widely known that the world's oldest continuous surviving artistic tradition is that of the Australian Aboriginals, the fact that spontaneity was not part of that tradition is less well known. The elders exercised a firm control over the designs themselves and who could execute them. Why? Because the designs come from the Ancestral Beings and cannot, must not, be changed.

As I stood in the Anbangbang Gallery at Nourlangie Rock, in the rock shelter that has been in use for some 20 000 years, I was reminded of the archetypal images you see in child art, of the San rock paintings and engravings of Southern Africa, of the Palaeolithic cave art of Europe and, more recently, of paintings by Dubuffet, Miro and Paul Klee.

In front of me was Namarrgon, Lightning Man. He had a large head with seemingly empty eye sockets and a long body. The lightning was depicted in lines which joined his head and feet. Painted stone axes were attached to his head, elbows and knees, which was how he made lightning and thunder – by striking these axes against the ground or against the clouds.

But surely these paintings looked fresh and new? How could they be 20 000 years old? Our Aboriginal guide explained.

'In the old days many of us at one time or another painted on the rock faces of our shelters. We didn't feel that we were disfiguring or defacing the pictures that were already there. We were simply expressing our thoughts, our feelings, our thanks – whatever. So in some places you get layer upon layer of paint. But here at Anbangbang, the work of our clan, the Badmardi, has survived. Yes, these paintings are new, but they're painted over much older paintings – how old we don't know. What you see now is the work of Nayombolmi, called by the Europeans Barramundi Charlie. For most of his life he worked for European people, and as he grew older, he became more and more sad and disillusioned when he saw the ancient rituals and traditional ways of our people getting lost and forgotten. He didn't like the kind of art that was being produced for tourists and collectors, he said it was useless and fake. He said it was art with no meaning, no resonance. So in 1964, the year before he died, he came back to this gallery, to Nourlangie Rock, and he painted this large painting on the rock face in traditional X-ray style.'

The X-ray style, as its name suggests, looks through the outer physical form of its subject to the bones, tissue, spirit and very being of the subject beneath. The finished painting looks like a stylised and somewhat surreal X-ray picture of the man, fish or lizard that the artist is trying to portray.

'Barramundi Charlie painted Namarrgon, Lightning Man, the essence of good, and Namondjok, a dangerous spirit representing evil. Beneath them you can see two family groups of men and their wives on the way to a ceremony.'

'Why are the women's breasts so big?' asked one of our group.

'They are full of milk. Barramundi Charlie, or Nayombolmi, is using this symbol of fertility to try and bring life back into this shelter – to breathe new life into it.'

I thought how delighted Barramundi Charlie would be today to see the genuine renaissance of Aboriginal life and thought. Maybe the symbol of the women's milk had worked.

Next, we walked round the art sites at Ubirr. Here, once again, the cool rock overhangs provided shelter and living areas, and the smooth rock faces were ideal surfaces on which to paint important events, animals and spiritual figures.

Ubirr has different styles of rock art. The simple red ochre paintings, unadorned by other colours, are probably the oldest. We gazed at the elongated, stick-like 'mimi' figures of spirit beings, and a painting of a Tasmanian tiger, frozen in time, looking for all the world like a sedate Tigger from *Winnie the Pooh*. Archaeologists say that the thylacine, a wolf-like marsupial, has not prowled Arnhem Land for thousands of years, but although the animal became extinct on the mainland, it seems that there were plenty of the handsome creatures in Tasmania until the turn of the century when bounty hunters shot them out.

One of the special wonders of Ubirr is the mural – two metres deep by 15 metres long – of X-ray fish, turtles and small food animals. Though more simple forms of this style are found elsewhere in the world, the complexity and artistry of these images at Ubirr are unique to this part of Arnhem Land. We also saw examples of 'contact art', so-called because it marks the arrival of non-Aboriginal people – people portrayed with their hands in their pockets and with axes and firearms. Our guide told us that the rock art tradition has almost died out since the arrival of the Europeans, but that the artistic tradition lives on in present-day bark and board paintings.

My sister Rita had a number of exceptional pieces of traditional Aboriginal art which had been given to her when she worked on Elcho Island in the Gulf of Carpentaria. Not 'airport' or tourist art, but original pieces, some very old and treasured, which had been given to her during her four-year stay there by the clan which 'adopted' her. Museums had begged her for these pieces, but they were beyond price because of the context in which they had been given. She always refused to part with them.

After her death, Will, on the last blind bender of his life, took them to a Darwin pawn shop, and with the proceeds bought two bottles of whisky.

But lost things have a way of returning themselves to their owners. I feel instinctively that those bark paintings, masks and ceremonial objects have somehow found their way back where they belong.

We walked to Ubirr lookout and gazed at the sweeping views of the escarpment. A sense of history, mystery, solemnity and peace pervades this sacred place. It's tempting, as it is with the sacred places and rock art galleries of the San, to romanticise and idealise a way of life which was so in tune with everything in the universe. To weigh up what modern man has lost rather than to remember what he has gained – modern medicine, education, access to food and housing.

Not everybody, of course. I am thinking of the people who live in cardboard shacks, *favela*, shanties, with no electricity, no running water, no latrines, and very little hope – people in Rio, in Hong Kong, in Lagos, in Cape Town; the street people of New York, London, Calcutta, Sarajevo, Amsterdam and Alice Springs.

As I watched the great thunderheads building up over the purple crags beyond the green plains, here where people have lived for thousands and thousands of years, for the first time I fully articulated in my mind what it is that modern man has lost.

The Aboriginal culture may not always have been a comfortable nor easy one, but at its heart was a strong sense of continuity, of community, of security within the family or clan. The primary structures of Aboriginal society were based on kinship. Every known person was considered to be kin, either by blood ties or through the imagination. Kinship provided a baseline from which to operate in society. A powerful ethic lay at its heart – that the whole is greater than the one. That no one individual is greater than his tribe. Concomitant with this oneness with each other was a oneness with the entire world, seen and unseen, a close personal relationship with the land and with the spiritual heritage.

That's what we have lost today – the unquestioning acceptance, the unchallengeable certainty that mind and body, spirit and physical form are one. That's why so many people today are searching for a spiritual way. An idea persists that somehow you can acquire spirituality.

But we can learn from this Aboriginal culture that spirituality is not something that you put on like a pair of new shoes, it must imbue every part of your life, otherwise it will be invalid. The spirituality of these ancient people, of the Africans, the Native Americans, the farmers high in the Andes, is inextricably interwoven with every part of their lives. It is not something that is taken out on high days and holy days, dusted off and then celebrated. Spirituality is a quintessential part of life. Only if we recognise this will we be whole.

Some years later, in a mountain cave high up above Cusco in Peru, I was reminded of this moment in Kakadu. The two Andean shamans who conducted the ceremony to bless our Peruvian journey and pay homage to the spirits of the places we would visit, did so with no conscious thought of such a ceremony being 'spiritual', separate in some sense from the rest of life. If you open your heart and mind you will discover your own spirituality – it's there, I promise you.

*

The Yellow Water Boat Tour chugged through some of the most important wetlands in the world, a refuge for migratory birds and other birds – such as the strikingly coloured magpie geese.

I felt as if I could be home in southern Africa as a huge flock of whitefaced whistling ducks, some thousands strong, flew in a great cloud above our heads before settling on the river banks. Small yellow lilies, trees of all shapes and sizes, and thousands of grasses lined the banks.

Our cheerful boatdriver pointed out a big black and white bird as tall as my shoulder, delicately picking its way on its long red legs through the water lilies.

'See that big bird over there? That's the Jabiru – Australia's only stork, also known as the Policeman Bird.'

The Jabiru uttered a low booming sound, made a clattering noise by shaking its long thick bill, and flew gracefully off.

Our boat moved out of the bright waters into a narrow, shaded creek. Sinister-looking, long-legged mangroves appeared to 'walk' in the waters, and we heard a loud splash as a crocodile plunged off his basking spot into the muddy stream.

Our boatdriver pointed to a pair of red eyes that stared malevolently at us from the thick undergrowth.

'A saltie,' he proclaimed proudly. 'A saltwater crocodile. You don't want to go swimming here! If you alarm one of these buggers when he's basking on the bank, you're a goner. They attack with no provocation, and they can out-sprint any of you. These fellas can capsize a boat – no lady, not ours – and can even climb into one. They also love dogs.'

A woman passenger with a small, fluffy poodle on her lap looked anxiously at the red staring eyes and clutched her little dog tightly.

'Yeah, nobody knows why, but they're attracted to the barking of a dog. Keep that mutt on a leash and well away from the water's edge. We also get the freshwater crocs here, but they're small compared to the salties.'

The most famous crocodile in Australia is 'Sweetheart' who, stuffed and mounted, now resides in Darwin Museum. He's really there by accident. Dave Lindner, one of the Northern Territory's great 'characters', whose personal vendetta against uranium mining and buffalo is legend, was attempting to move Sweetheart, then thought to be a female, from one creek to another, deeper one. Sweetheart drowned as Dave winched him from the river head first with his great jaws firmly tied. He should have been hauled by the tail so that he didn't inhale water into the lungs. When the taxidermist cut him open, Sweetheart had obviously just had a snack. Inside his stomach was one whole wallaby, a buffalo leg, and lots of barramundi.

'Let's go and see Sweetheart,' my sister said, when John and I arrived in Darwin from Alice Springs.

I was less than enthusiastic. I came from Africa where big crocs were two a penny. But I wanted to see the Museum's splendid collection of Aboriginal art and Sweetheart was on the way, in the entrance room. This is one big croc – six metres from the tip of his snout to the tip of his tail. African crocs aren't in the same league as Sweetheart. Because crocodiles are notoriously difficult to preserve, for the first few months of Sweetheart's museum life, maggots crawled in and out of his gums. Legend has it that lady visitors of fine sensibilities swooned when they saw the grisly sight.

Crocodiles, which have been on earth for over 100 million years, are very powerful totems in Aboriginal cosmology. As with the San people of southern Africa, the ability to change from human to animal and back to human is central to Aboriginal spiritual belief. In Arnhem Land many tribes believe that Baru, the crocodile ancestor, is the bringer of fire – in modern Aboriginal parlance, 'Boss for Fire'.

Others believe that Ginga, a spirit ancestor of the Gagudju people, came from the sea at the beginning of the Dreamtime with the other creator beings and was responsible for making the rocky outcrops. One day, however, when Ginga was in the shape of a man, he caught fire and rushed into the water, turning himself into a crocodile.

Tribes in other parts of Australia attribute the creation of fire to birds or other animals.

Rita and John took me to see a unique, unforgettable, and unbelievably kitsch feature of the Kakadu National Park: the Crocodile Hotel, built in the shape of a crocodile, 250 metres long and 30 metres across the belly. Owned by the Gagudju Association, the traditional owners of Kakadu, its huge grey shape scars the surrounding landscape.

As we sat in the 'head' of the ugly beast drinking tea, I complained bitterly about this horrible marriage of ancient and modern.

Rita disagreed. She said that the Ancestral Beings were probably laughing their heads off.

My sister Rita spent all her life working in the field of education. Although she had been principal of three very old and distinguished Anglican girls' schools in countries as far apart as Zimbabwe, New Zealand and Australia, posts she took when as a young widow she was left alone to support two small children under five, her real love lay in teaching the indigenous peoples in whatever country she happened to be living at the time.

She had started schools in Papua, New Guinea, taught illiterates in Zimbabwe, and once her children were independent, she went as a teacher and administrator to Elcho Island in the Gulf of Carpentaria in the Arafura Sea, above Arnhem Land.

A mission station had been formed there in 1944, but Rita rarely saw eye-to-eye with the missionaries, although she was a devout Christian, a deacon of the Anglican Church and had a degree in theology from London University. She found them incredibly 'narrow' and 'bigoted', refusing to attempt any understanding of Aboriginal traditions, cosmology or spiritual beliefs.

She once told me that some of the missionaries, in an attempt to wean the local people away from alcohol – alcoholism is a major problem on the island – were importing *kava*, a homemade alcoholic brew from Fiji, which was less potent than Scotch or brandy.

Understandably, there was no love lost between my sister and the missionaries, but the Aboriginals loved and respected her. She was 'adopted' by the local clan and given a totem animal, a whale, symbol of Mother-Father Dreaming, not only because of her imposing size and expansive manner, but because the whale is a very sacred animal to the local tribes – the highest animal in the sea.

To give her the whale totem was a symbolic gesture of the great respect they had for her. The great black thunderheads which mass overhead before the coming of the rainy season are symbolic of the great black whales which dive and play in the oceans beneath, and represent the great whale ancestor.

It was this ancestor who created the clouds by spraying

them with the mist from his blowhole, so revealing an intricate pattern of triangles which is still used in ceremonies today.

Whale Dreaming sites are found all over Arnhem Land; Rita even showed me one on a reef at Southport, just outside Darwin.

After four years Rita returned to Darwin where she took up the post as principal of a large primary school. Her pioneering work in the field of primary education made national headlines.

One October evening, during *Gunumeleng*, the pre-monsoon season of hot, humid, almost unbearable weather, Rita sat at home working on a tapestry. She heard a tap on the screen door. When she opened it she saw an elderly black man standing there. It was Alfred, the tribal Custodian from Kakadu. Rita's family had been made part of the tribe and now Alfred was visiting her as part of his custodial duty to the family.

Alfred had brought Rita a message. She was to 'go home' to her mother across the sea.

Rita took this message very seriously indeed. She phoned me in Johannesburg to tell me that she would not be visiting us that Christmas. I was disappointed and asked her why.

I knew of the special relationship that existed between Rita and her Aboriginal friends so I accepted what she told me. But I was convinced that my mother, who lived alone in England, was going to die. That was the reason for the message.

I was wrong.

Rita went back to England just before Christmas. She told me how glad she was to be going back to the country of her birth with all the happy memories of childhood and young womanhood that it held for her. It was wonderful to be with her mother.

Late on Christmas Eve she woke up, called out to my mother in the next room, and died in my mother's arms.

She had 'gone home'.

NINE

Blood Red Moon On The Amazon

After our unforgettable night alone in the ruins of Machu Picchu, the next day our group is to take the tourist train back to Cusco (what luxury after the crowded, noisy local train that had brought us here!), whence our flight to the Amazon.

But there is time for one more trip into the Sacred City before the train is due. Rómulo tells us that the Machu Picchu ruins were originally known by his people as *Picchu Wanakauri*, 'the Mountain of Origin'.

It is still early, with the morning sun just coming up over the rim of the mountains and a heavy dew everywhere underfoot, when Alan and I, Gordon and Wilma, Joy, Sue and Big Carol follow Mark, Carol and Rómulo over to the far side of the ruins below 'Young Mountain', Waynapicchu, to visit the Pachamama stone.

A few bored-looking llamas stare down their noses at us as we pass through the central grassy flat plain towards the rock. They don't look very happy. And apparently they're not. Llamas usually live at much higher altitudes, above 3350 metres, and don't take well to the warmer climate of Machu Picchu. They are always dying off, explains Rómulo laconically.

'They're only here for the tourists.'

Obviously the locals aren't strong on llama animal rights movements in this part of the world.

The Pachamama rock is a huge, upright flat stone whose surface has been smoothed and polished by the passage of time. We sit down on the wet grass and contemplate it.

'Pachamama is the source of so much good,' Carol reminds us. 'She provides us with everything we need and yet, particularly in the West, we abuse and destroy her.'

Not so the Quechua, who praise and thank her on a daily basis, a practice as time-worn as the mighty mountains around us. Although they worship and respect the *apukuna,* the divine lords of the mountains who are responsible for the well-being of humans, animals and plants, it is Pachamama, Mother Earth, whom they love.

'Sit quietly, think your own thoughts, and then go up to the Pachamama rock and respond to it in whatever way seems appropriate,' advises Carol.

When it is my turn, I approach the rock and spread my arms out against the flat surface which has been warmed by the sun. I lay my cheek against it and say a silent 'Thank You' to Mother Earth, whom we all take so much for granted. It is the nearest thing to a hug possible.

It may sound now that it was a sentimental, even mawkish thing to do, but at the time my gesture seems absolutely appropriate and quite natural.

When we have all finished making our own obeisance, because in a way a gesture of reverence is what each one of us has made, we return to our semicircle in front of the rock.

It is at this point that Joy finally breaks down. Up to now, she has coped pretty well with her intense grief at losing her husband of forty years. She has often remained aloof from the rest of us and we have interpreted this aloofness as her attempt to come to terms with her great sadness. She now sobs her heart out, great wrenching sobs that rack her small frame and fill the empty morning air around us.

There is no one else about. I go and put my arms around her, as does Wilma, and the three of us sit rocking and swaying with the motion of Joy's grief-stricken body, for all the world like a Greek chorus in a Greek tragedy.

Later, Joy tells us that this was her final moment of catharsis. Her cynicism, unhappiness and frustration, along with the emotional baggage of many years, have now been washed away in the torrent of tears, and she feels 'healed'.

Since returning from Peru, Joy has written her first novel, in which she works out many of the themes of her own life. It was the magical journey to Peru, she told me, that not only inspired her to write it, but also gave her the creative energy.

We pick up our luggage from the hotel in Cusco – we had only been allowed one small hand bag for our trip to Rómulo's farm and Machu Picchu – and fly to Puerto Maldonado on the banks of the mighty Amazon. We fly east, over the snow-covered peaks standing sentinel to the mountain-ringed town of Cusco, over the great, green jungles to the point where Peru borders Colombia and Brazil.

On arrival at the tin-roofed airport, we climb into a large open-sided truck with wooden seats and gaily painted sides, where the young driver sits on the floor to manoeuvre the pedals and gears, and rattle off along a road lined with tropical vegetation to the tiny riverside town of Puerto Maldonado.

At the end of our short journey, we climb down the high steps of the truck and, carrying our overnight bags, make our way in the noonday heat through the tiny town down to the river where we are to board the large motorised canoe which will take us to our jungle camp.

Puerto Maldonado could have been lifted directly from a Graham Greene novel or a Luis Buñuel movie.

Bicycle taxis clatter by with beautiful, if grubby, young girls perched behind the driver clutching him tightly round the waist; mangy dogs lope purposefully along muddy alleyways; staring, sloe-eyed children watch us from where they sit in the dirt; slim men with black pencil moustaches in open-throated, once-white shirts lean lazily against interesting-looking doorways; scruffy chickens run hither and thither in the way of all brainless fowls; and the narrow streets are lined with small shops selling everything from washing powder and flour to herbal remedies, caramel-coated Brazil nuts, carved wooden spoons and stuffed piranhas.

I have to confess I do an 'Erma Bombeck' here. One of the late American humorist's funniest books is called *When You Begin to Look Like Your Passport Photo, It's Time to Go Home*, and one of its funniest chapters recounts her misadventures with tourist souvenirs, the kind of trash you buy thinking at the time that it will be perfect for the TV room or Auntie Flo but which, when you get home, you realise is truly awful kitsch.

I buy a stuffed, mounted piranha for my son who is a lawyer. I think if he puts it on his desk it will serve as (a) a talking point for nervous clients, and (b) a symbol. He laughs when he give it to him on my return, but to this day I don't know whether it sits on his desk or not.

Our camp is two hours upstream from Puerto Maldonado. On the canoe, its thatched roof fringed with palm fronds to keep off the midday sun, we meet Manuel, our young guide. He is impossibly beautiful, slim, raven-haired and dark-eyed, and speaks very good English. He is an engineering student from Cusco, and works at the camp to pay for his studies.

As we chug slowly upstream the river broadens until both banks are lost to sight. Occasionally we see another canoe, or some fishermen pulling up their nets, otherwise the river is empty. Finally, our canoe noses its way towards a high bank, where steps carved out of the mud and edged with wooden poles lead up to a simple camp consisting of a few wooden huts on stilts, roofed with plaited palm leaves. Hundreds of small green parrots are nesting in holes in the high river bank and as our canoe approaches, they rise up in a great, green chattering flock, wheel out over the surface of the river, and then fly towards the camp, where they perch in the tall trees and scold us noisily and excitedly.

We climb up the steep steps, still carrying our bags, and are welcomed into the thatched dining-room area by our two young Indian hosts who offer us a drink made of delicious unfamiliar tropical fruit. Each glass is decorated with green leaves and a bright tropical blossom which I stick behind my ear in jaunty, South Seas fashion.

It's like stepping straight from one world into another. From an altitude of 3 350 metres, from a bustling, quaint Spanish colonial town with cobbled streets and gracious centuries-old buildings with heavy carved wooden doors and wrought-iron balconies, we have stepped into a simple lodge by the side of the Amazon in the heart of the jungle. The huts are of wood and straw, there is no electricity and very few people – only our hosts, our guide, and the nine of us. (Rómulo has stayed at home with the rest of his family in Cusco.)

There is a wealth of tropical flowers, plants and trees, hundreds of different kinds of butterflies and a multitude of birds. The liquid, flute-like calls of several different kinds of orioles fill the air, sounding like our familiar African Black-headed Oriole, but denser, louder, more grand in every way.

As darkness falls and the moon rises, it becomes much cooler. A light wind ruffles the muddy brown tide of the great river.

We have eaten thick flakes of aromatic fish steamed in hollow bamboo rods and boiled manioc roots. Now we sit on some cleared grass outside the wooden huts of the lodge.

It is nearly time. The last entirely visible eclipse of the moon in the twentieth century is about to begin. We are nine travellers from three continents who are no longer strangers, but a bonded group, friends. We sit in silence waiting for the natural phenomenon to take its course.

Carol tells us that the shamans believe that at a moment of natural wonder such as this, Peru is the focal centre of the spiritual energies of the world. I have felt those spiritual energies and believe that they have been part of the process of my growing spiritual awareness.

An owl calls repeatedly, its strange but somehow familiar sound punctuating the steady chorus of millions of insects. The wind rustles in the huge trees and the fabled river pulses inexorably along.

As we sit silently on the banks of the mighty Amazon, the words of the Dalai Lama that had made such an impression on me a few short weeks ago in Johannesburg resonate in my mind. I can hear again his deep, clear voice:

We must always acknowledge the interconnectedness of all things. Recognise the profound mutual interdependence of everything – it's part of the natural world.

I have been making connections – hitherto unrecognised – ever since I left home and have been travelling in Peru. I have opened those dusty memory files and have accessed my past, and in so doing have come to discover the milestones in an also previously unrecognised spiritual journey: my childhood and schooldays, my time spent in the Itu Leper Colony, the landscapes with no boundaries in Australia. Tonight I'm going to make a connection of another kind but one, none the less, which will also heighten my spiritual awareness.

We sit quietly. At eight twenty, exactly as predicted, the shadow of the sun trembles on the edge of the pale buttermilk moon. The few wisps of cloud that have been scudding across the myriads of stars have vanished. It seems as if both we and the world are holding our breath.

I look at the moon through my binoculars. Her craters, mountains and valleys are sharply etched. As the shadow of the earth moves up over the surface of the moon, the moon turns blood red. Not a fiery glowing hue, but a soft, somehow comforting colour. Even when the eclipse is at its fullest, a glow of rosy light imbues the moon and the surrounding heavens. There is beneficence all around us.

It is now time to connect with our 'Power Animals'. Carol reminds us of the ancient lore of Peruvian cosmology, which goes back thousands of years, of its three great power animals among many lesser ones – the condor, the puma and the snake.

The condor, the heaviest flying bird in the world, creature

of the high Andes, connects man to *Hanakpacha*, the upper world of superior energy. Here, not only the spirits of the ancestors live, but also Christian saints, prophets, and those who today we might describe as having attained a higher state of consciousness.

The puma, the beautiful and elusive jaguar, symbolises *Kaypacha*, the world of the here and now, where animals, plants, people and the natural forces of nature live together in harmony with Pachamama, the beloved Earth Mother.

Ukhupacha, represented by the snake, is the inner world where good and bad spirits reside. Entry to this underworld is through the rivers that unite and divide our planet. It is also our inner world.

And over all, visible and invisible, known and unknown, magic and reality, rules *Uywakke*, the supreme creator of all life.

On our travels we have seen temples, sacred springs and holy places carved to commemorate these three very different, but always interconnecting worlds.

'Sit quietly,' Carol advises. 'Meditate if you can. See if you can connect with your own power animal. Greet it if it comes and be prepared to learn from its ways. The tortoise will teach you patience and wisdom. The dolphin, intelligence and the meaning of freedom. The dog will show you loyalty and bravery.'

'So, do these animals just happen along into one's mind or consciousness?' I'm trying to suspend my disbelief.

'Usually you will pass through some door or entrance to meet your power animal. Be willing and receptive. Let's see what happens.'

My mind is telling me that all this is hocus-pocus. New Age gobbledegook. Except there is a simplicity and sincerity in Carol's words that touches some long-forgotten innocence in me.

She continues in her soft voice. 'Empty your minds of everything, but remember that the cosmic event you have just witnessed is made even more powerful by the unique forces of energy that are here with us in Peru. Strange things may happen.'

I close my eyes and try to shut out the Amazon night. Power Animals, I think – all very well for spiritual beings, hardly the thing for me, even if I have been becoming more aware that there is more to life than surface as the trip has progressed. But this is taking things a bit too far!

But I persist in my efforts to clear my mind of all its cynical baggage.

Suddenly, I am standing ankle-deep in a sunlit forest pool. There is total silence. Before me is a thin, high waterfall. I wade across to its fine falling spray and push my way through the curtain of water. I am now in another pool, similar to the first, also surrounded by trees and plants, equally still and quiet. A shallow, sloping white sandy beach is at the far side of the pool. I wade over to the white beach and take a few steps up it. The silence seems to intensify. The stillness is almost tangible.

Then – there is movement in the bushes. I turn my head towards the sound. The leaves part and, as I watch, a lioness comes towards me, golden and glowing in the sunshine. She comes up to me and looks at me with great golden-green eyes. We both stand still. Then as if by some pre-arranged signal, some remembered behaviour on my part, I put my arms around her and lay my face along her flanks. She is soft and warm.

A feeling of utter peace and joy comes over me. I do not want the moment to end. We hold this position for a moment or two, and then she gently moves away. She pads softly down to the pool, crouches and laps the clear, bright water. When she has finished drinking, she gets up and walks back the way she has come towards the undergrowth. As she goes past me, she pauses and wraps her long tail around me, almost like an embrace. Then she vanishes into the bushes as silently as she has come.

The silence is absolute.

I stand for a moment, then wade back through the water-fall, the way that I have come.

I open my eyes and find myself on the banks of the Amazon.

Our pilgrim band shares its experiences. We have all, incredibly, made a connection with an animal. Alan has 'seen' an elephant, Joy has heard whales singing, Wilma has made contact with a white cat with blue eyes. As we sit and talk about our individual experiences the moon becomes golden, like a harvest moon. I tell the others about my lioness.

*

Some weeks later, I shared this remarkable experience with Gareth Patterson, the 'Lion Man' of Africa, who has spent his life amongst lions. It was Gareth who brought back to Botswana from Kenya the three orphaned lion cubs – the male Batian, and his sisters Furaha and Rafiki – after George Adamson, of *Born Free* fame, who was rehabilitating them into the wild, was brutally murdered by poachers.

I have known Gareth for fifteen years. We first met him when Alan and I and our two youngest daughters, Tara and

Tiffany, who were thirteen and ten years old, had been invited to a game lodge in Botswana, on the banks of the Zambezi River. Gareth, a tall, tanned young man with sun-bleached blond hair and intense dark-brown eyes was our ranger. He was then nineteen.

As the years went by, we all grew closer and closer, and we were able to visit him at least once a year. He taught us about the birds, animals and ecology of the bush as we drove with him in an open-sided vehicle or trekked with him through the bush.

On one occasion, early in our friendship, before Gareth had made lions his life's work and study, we were walking along a dry river bed when we literally stumbled across two huge male lions lying in the gravelly sand.

'Stand still!' Gareth instructed.

It's very hard to stand still when you're nose to nose with Africa's biggest and most powerful cats. But we did. Had we moved the lions would have seen us as prey and attacked us. After a few moments, which seemed like years, Gareth told us to slowly back off. Hardly daring to breathe, we walked slowly backwards along the river bed, until at last we rounded a bend and the lions were out of sight. Although Gareth was still very young and relatively inexperienced, he had shown no fear, and had known instinctively how to behave with the beautiful creatures who were to dominate his life.

My youngest daughter Tiffany has been terrified of elephants ever since, as a small girl of seven, she was charged whilst on foot by a rogue male in the Sabie Sands area of South Africa. Over the years, Gareth used all his skills and patience to cure her of her phobia, walking with her up to feeding herds, showing her elephants playing and swimming in the rivers, marvelling at the tiny, newborn babies who look like grey marshmallows. But to no avail.

And it's as if the elephants know they have a willing target. I have hardly ever been in the bush with my daughter when there hasn't been an 'elephant episode' of some kind. We have been charged many, many times; have been sitting quietly birdwatching by a dam in the Kruger Park when an elephant has taken exception to our being there and chased us off; have rounded a corner in the same park and startled a browsing elephant who has then pounded after our vehicle with flapping ears and trumpeting loudly, for what seemed like an eternity.

Many of these incidents happened with Gareth. Once in Botswana's Tuli Block, our open Land Rover was surrounded by a small breeding herd. The elephants roared and trumpeted, making mock charges towards the vehicle, and appearing so dangerous that Fish, the Botswana ranger, and Tiffany were both on the floor hiding under the back seat of the vehicle. We shouted and yelled, banging the Land Rover's sides with as much force as we could muster, and finally Gareth was able to turn the wheels, rev up and get us out of a very frightening situation.

But although Gareth admired and respected elephants, as all of us do who have had dealings with them, Gareth's love was for lions, and his many books relating his life with lions are now known all over the world.

Like my son Simon, Gareth was born in Nigeria. I don't know if it was this fact that first bonded Gareth and me together, but we became more than just friends, and although we didn't see all that much of each other, he became my 'adopted' son. I would find myself thinking of Gareth, for no particular reason, when suddenly the telephone would ring – it would be Gareth. Similarly, he could be thinking of me, and his telephone would ring.

We have always been instinctively on the same wavelength, often know what the other is thinking, and share many of the same sensitivities. I like to believe we are soulmates in some way – two people who are intuitively in tune and in touch with each other's minds. Those of you who have special friends or soulmates of your own will know what I am talking about.

Not long after I returned from Peru, I was sitting on my stoep at home in Johannesburg, taking a coffee break from correcting galley proofs for a magazine I edit, when I heard the dogs barking at a vehicle at the gate.

I knew it was Gareth. I hadn't seen him for some months, and he had not known of my visit to Peru.

We hugged, and I commented on how thin he had become. As always, we talked about Batian, Furaha and Rafiki, the three lions whom Gareth unselfconsciously and with passion and utter conviction, calls his 'children'.

In a cruel ironic twist of fate, two of the lions that Gareth had 'inherited' from George Adamson after his murder – Batian the male, and his sister Furaha – had also been, in Gareth's terms, 'murdered' themselves. Batian, then three years old, had been lured over the Botswana border to South Africa and ruthlessly and senselessly shot, whilst Furaha and her cubs had been unjustly accused of killing a Botswana game ranger and had also been mercilessly shot.

For three long years Gareth had lived alone in an isolated corner of Botswana bordering South Africa, and had successfully rehabilitated these animals, his 'children', to the wild. He had slept with them, hunted with them, and had given them a fierce, unconditional love. In turn, the lions loved him back. Sometimes this could cause difficulties. Because the lions totally accepted Gareth as the dominant male member of their small pride, they treated him unequivocally as such. When Rafiki came into oestrus, she would present herself to Gareth, push her hindquarters against his legs, and jet copious amounts of urine on to his chest, all the while growling ominously with flattened ears.

Brian Jackman, well-known and highly respected British author and wildlife journalist, writer of the hugely successful TV series *Big Cats Diary,* told me when we met at a game lodge in Botswana that the most remarkable sight in his thirty-year career as a wildlife writer was Gareth with Batian, Furaha and Rafiki. He had been privileged, as one of the very few people whom Gareth allowed into his remote bush camp, to see Gareth 'call' his lions.

Brian described to me how, as the first light of the African dawn broke, Gareth walked outside his tent and called, 'Come on, Batian. Come on, Furaha. Look! Come on, Rafiki!' His calls echoed among the stony hills in the early morning air. There was the answering roar of a lion from a kilometre away.

Gareth called out in joy, 'They're coming! They're coming!'

Suddenly, there were grunts, moans and soft roars, as one by one, Batian, Rafiki and Furaha, now fully grown lions, hurtled out of the bush and hurled themselves at Gareth, placing their huge paws on his bare shoulders and greeting him with unbelievable love and affection whilst he stroked their tawny flanks.

'I had tears in my eyes as I watched,' Brian told me as we sat one evening at a lodge in the heart of the Okavango Delta.

Gareth has never got over the death of his 'children', deaths which broke his heart, but is comforted by his firm belief and subsequent experiences that, after their untimely and cruel deaths, the 'spirits' of Batian and Furaha often visited him as he grieved for them in his remote and solitary camp.

I told Gareth about my experience in the Amazon jungle. About meeting my power animal.

'Describe the lioness,' said Gareth gravely.

I did so.

'What was the last thing she did before she left you?'

She had curled her tail around me like a loving embrace.

Before Gareth spoke again, the hairs on the back of my neck had begun to stand up and my eyes filled with unexpected tears. I knew what he was going to say.

'That was Furaha,' Gareth said.

TEN

The Golden Cats

Gareth's own spiritual journey has been associated with the natural world, and with lions in particular, for as long as he can remember.

It was a grey, overcast, depressing day. A cold drizzle was seeping through the heavy clouds as a small seven-year-old boy stood with his hand tightly clutched in his father's before a tiny cage in a pathetic little zoo in Margate, a holiday town on England's southern coast. He shivered as he watched the poor old lion standing forlornly in front of a faded mural of the African plains. He couldn't explain what he felt to his Dad, but he intuitively knew that something was very wrong with this situation. It didn't feel 'right'.

A few months before the same small boy had been with his parents in the vivid brightness of the Jankari National Park in northern Nigeria. He had seen a golden glowing shape pass in front of his eyes. It was the tawny flash of a wild lion moving away into the bush. When he shouted, 'Look, there's a lion,' the adults had dismissed his claim as childish fantasy. But minutes later the rangers also glimpsed the animal as it padded off, and the parents captured the moment on their video camera.

It was whilst watching the moth-eaten old animal in its zoo cage and almost subliminally comparing it to the magnificent creature that he had seen in the wilds, that the young Gareth Patterson knew his life's work was to be with lions.

Over twenty-five years on, he has lived alone with them in the African bush as a human member of a wild lion pride, he has written about them, has filmed them, has shared their joys, their triumphs and their heart-rending sadnesses.

One of Gareth's earliest and most enduring influences was the work of George and Joy Adamson in Kenya. They had first came to the attention of the world in the mid 1950s when Joy's book *Born Free* captured public imagination in a way previously unheard of. In *Born Free* Joy told the story of how she and George, who were living and working at what is now Kora National Reserve in Kenya, had reared and cared for Elsa, a tiny orphaned lion cub, before finally successfully rehabilitating her back into the wild as a fully grown, 'free' lioness.

Born Free was made into an immensely popular movie, still a classic of its kind, and its theme song went to the top of the hit parade in many countries around the world. With Elsa, the *Born Free* era began. *Born Free* is perhaps the most well-known and loved story of an animal that shared its life in the wilds not only with its own kind, but also with man.

Since that time, over a period of almost thirty years, George 'returned' twenty-five lions back into the wilds and today their descendants roam Kenya's Kora and Meru game reserves.

Joy Adamson went on to write *Living Free* and *Forever Free*, stories that touched the hearts of millions and in turn created an attitude of compassion and concern for Africa's wildlife. Her compelling and moving accounts of returning orphaned cubs to the wild opened up public awareness to much wider environmental concerns, an awareness that had been sparked off by American environmentalist Rachel Carson in her landmark book *Silent Spring*.

Gareth Patterson had been entranced by Elsa's story and was an ardent follower of the Adamsons' work from the time he was a youngster growing up in Nigeria and Malawi. He believes their first meeting was ordained by fate. He first met George just weeks after three newly orphaned cubs whose mother had been shot were brought to George's camp *Kampi ya Simba* in Kora. Gareth was researching material for his second book *Where the Lion Walked* and from their first moment of meeting, the legendary white-maned old man and his young disciple forged inseparable bonds. Later, when George was brutally murdered by poachers, Gareth brought the year-old cubs to the Tuli Block in Botswana and took over George's role of rehabilitating them.

Over the next two-and-a-half years Gareth achieved the almost impossible by successfully returning the three lions to the wild and giving them back their freedom. It was a time of great happiness but also of heart-break, a time of laughter and a time of tears. George had named Batian, the young male lion who was to become Gareth's 'son', after 'Mbatian', Mount Kenya's highest peak and the name of a celebrated Masai *laibon* – a chieftain, clairvoyant and master of religious ceremonies. Batian's sisters he named Rafiki – 'friend' in Swahili – and Furaha – 'joy'.

The Tuli Block is a ruggedly beautiful corner of north-eastern Botswana where huge, striking red rock formations mingle with acacia woodland, riverine forest, hills, wooded valleys and open grassy plains. Ancient baobab trees stand sentinel over Stone Age ruins that have existed here for more than 30 000 years as majestic Black Eagles soar overhead. The area is home to huge elephant herds, the eland – Africa's largest and highest jumping antelope – zebra, wildebeest, leopard. And lions.

For more than three years, Gareth lived in this wilderness with his three lions. He has always called them 'my' lions, a term he felt could be misinterpreted. But once, on a rare visit down to Johannesburg from Botswana to purchase supplies, when he was telling me about the great progress the three lions were making, he tried to explain what he meant when he called them 'my' lions.

'The "my" is a term of affection and love and not one indicating ownership. I've never felt the lions "belonged" to me – the thought has never crossed my mind, because, I suppose, our relationship is, in part, based on respect. Those of wild hearts cannot be owned if we heed natural law. The definition of human ownership applied to the wilds baffles me. I cannot grasp the notion. I cannot see how a single grain of sand from a riverbed or a fallen leaf upon the ground, or a hill, or a Fish Eagle high in the sky can be "owned" – be the possession of man.'

Finally, after two more years, two years in which Gareth walked, ran, hunted and slept with his lions as a human member of the pride, the rehabilitation begun by George Adamson was complete.

And then the first tragedy struck.

Batian, Gareth's lion 'son' was cruelly lured across the

border into South Africa and shot. Gareth, Furaha and Rafiki, Batian's sisters and Gareth's 'daughters', were joined in an agony of grief. Often in those first few months after Batian's death, Gareth and the lionesses would be acutely aware of an invisible presence as they went about their daily lion lives. Gareth is convinced that Batian's spirit was often with them and told me how the lionesses would stop and silently acknowledge its nearness, gazing with a piercing, fixed stare at the unseen presence.

On one occasion, he had been tracking Furaha and her three cubs. He followed her to an aardvark hole, where she had placed her cubs for safety, then quietly continued to follow her until, after about a kilometre, in quite thick mopane scrub, he found her resting alone upon the banks of the stream bed. Her head was to one side, her cheek resting upon her paws.

Gareth had felt a strange sense of sadness because although she was so much a part of the wilderness canvas, she seemed at the same time to be so alone. He softly called her name – 'Furaha!' – and she came forward to greet him. She nuzzled him but then walked past him and suddenly stopped short, gazing ahead with a fixed stare on her face. After a few seconds she slowly turned, looked at Gareth and came up to him. They had both, man and lion, felt the presence of 'another'. Gareth believes it was the spirit of Batian.

Not long after this incident, tragedy struck yet again. Furaha, her sub-adult cub Tana, and Rafiki's cub Sala, were falsely accused of killing Isaac, an African game scout, and were mercilessly and swiftly shot before any facts could be established. Rafiki and Gareth mourned yet another loss.

Soon after Furaha's death Rafiki visited the killing site late one night accompanied by her mate Nelion, and then moved on to visit Gareth who was alone in his camp. He hadn't seen Rafiki since the senseless killing of the lions and did not know if she was aware of what had happened.

But according to Gareth, it soon became apparent that she *did* know. She came up to him, pressed her head against him, and uttered loud tortured moans. As Gareth tried to comfort her, he felt her raw anguish and angry pain. He has often told me that her grieving at the realisation of her family's deaths will haunt him for ever.

Today, Rafiki still survives, the founder member of one of the Tuli Block's largest prides. Gareth does not visit her. There is much unfinished business in the area. Isaac's murderer has still not been found. Gareth believes his death was related to poaching activities, and he was told by a local landowner to 'get out' of the Tuli.

A few months before I went to Peru, Gareth returned to the Tuli Block. He asked me to go with him.

We stayed at Tuli Safari Lodge, a good distance from where Gareth lived with his lions. The visit was a private one and was very painful for Gareth. He forced himself to stay away from his previous haunts. In the light of what happened to Batian and Furaha he still fears for Rafiki's safety.

I walked with him through the sandstone rocks surrounding the lodge and listened as he relived many of his memories. The time Furaha saved him from a leopard. How she led him to her first cubs. How he and his pride would doze in the heat of the noonday sun under a shepherd bush, the tree whose thick shade the lions always preferred to any other. How the lions behaved when they experienced their first rain. How they grew, became mature and successful. How he loved them.

He relived yet again how Furaha and Rafiki grieved when

Batian was killed and how he shared their anguish with them.

As we walked through the African bush he pointed out a flycatcher's nest clinging in the bark of a giant baobab tree, the spoor of a porcupine, a pair of klipspringer antelope watching us closely from a 'balancing' rock, the fresh tracks of a big male leopard, and any number of voluble cuckoos flying overhead.

Gareth knows that his work in the Tuli Block has come to an end. There is a strong possibility that the Botswana Tuli bushlands will become the heart of a symbolic Peace Park, linking up with large portions of the wilderness in Zimbabwe and South Africa. Initiatives are being taken for the ecologically debilitating agricultural border farms and game farms south of the bushlands to be developed into a South African game park.

Gareth believes that the Peace Park initiative will allow wildlife from the Botswana bushlands and the Zimbabwe Tuli safari area free movement, as in the historical past, into a former portion of its natural range. Lions would be able to move south into the northern part of South Africa with no fear of being shot. There would be no more cross-border poaching and habitat would be reclaimed for the original fauna and flora.

✳

I had 'met' Furaha for the first time on the banks of the Amazon River in Peru on the night of the last full eclipse of the moon this century.

Just before finishing *There's More To Life Than Surface* I returned to the Tuli Block alone. I was compiling a chapter on Botswana for *Fodor's Guide to Southern Africa* and was staying in a tiny tented camp belonging to Mashatu Game Lodge.

One evening I went out with Richard, the brother of a former ranger whom I had known years ago when Gareth was a young game ranger in the area. I asked Richard about the Tuli lions.

'When I was growing up in this area there were plenty of lions. But poachers and professional hunters who lure the lions over the border to South Africa have destroyed so many.'

Like most of the local people who live and work in the Tuli, Richard has great affection and respect for Gareth. He asked me about him, because Gareth no longer visits the Tuli Block for fear of reprisals against Rafiki.

I told Richard that Gareth continued to work to save Africa's lions. He and his partner, Merafe Ramono, have established SEKAI, an environmental working group whose motive is to expand the public's knowledge of the traditional African beliefs, rituals and codes that historically have governed the relationship between the peoples of southern Africa and the animal world.

Gareth and Merafe believe that by highlighting these age-old environmental ways they can promote the reverence and respect for wild animals that has been lost or forgotten by, for example, the promotion of the foreign culture of trophy hunting, the killing of wild animals purely for sport. SEKAI is a Tswana word meaning 'symbol' or 'omen'.

'We rarely see lions now,' said Richard quietly, as we watched shooting stars fall down the velvety African sky.

'And Rafiki?' I asked.

He sighed, whistled softly under his breath and shook his head. 'I don't know.'

As we drove back to camp our headlights caught

movement. A pride of seven lions was moving softly through the bush. As we stopped, they stopped.

The small mature lioness leading the pride stood still and stared at me. She looked well, although scarred. As our eyes met I felt our connection to Gareth, to her sister on the banks of the Amazon. I said her name softly – 'Rafiki' – as the pride moved off softly into the darkness.

Richard was amazed. It was more than a year since he had seen lions.

'How do you know that's Rafiki?' he asked me wonderingly.

I was unable to answer him.

I just knew, that's all.

*

Over the years Gareth and I have often discussed the question of spirituality. He is totally unequivocal – his spiritual path is inextricably linked with the lions. It was never a conscious, deliberate decision on his part to follow that particular spiritual path but, rather, he believes that he has been 'led' along that path. He firmly believes that he was destined to do what he does.

When he puts his arms around one of his lions, he feels that it is the nearest thing to being next to God. He feels completely whole, in his rightful place, where he belongs. He believes in a religion based on nature where everybody is equal. He castigates Christianity for promoting man as ascendant to the animals, whereas in many African religions man is not seen that way at all. Animals and humankind are inter-dependent and co-dependent.

'Look at the Native Americans,' he would argue passionately during our discussions. 'They understand that there is no discrimination in nature. They regard themselves as the two-footed ones and the animals as four-footed – it's as simple as that.'

Gareth believes wholeheartedly that animals have souls and that many people implicitly recognise this from the relationships they have had with their own animals.

He often told me the story of how, on the second anniversary of Batian's death, he had gone down to the cairn of stones that he had built in Batian's memory. He had walked a short way past the cairn to a nearby tree where he and Batian had often sat together. He was thinking about what an impressive, beautiful animal Batian would have been, and was wishing for some 'sign' from him, something tangible.

He got up and walked back to the pile of stones, along the way he had come a short while before. To his amazement, he saw the spoor of a young male lion, exactly the same size as Batian's had been at the time of his death. A few moments before there had been nothing.

Then an even stranger thing happened. After Batian's death Gareth had taken the lion's identification collar and put it in a hole in the tree which he had just been sitting under. It had disappeared not long after he put it there – he assumed elephants had got hold of it – and he hadn't seen it for two years. As Gareth followed the spoor of the young lion on the anniversary of Batian's death, he found his collar in the middle of the path. When he'd last seen it, it was buckled up like a belt. On this day, as it lay on the path in front of him, he saw that it had been cut through the middle as if with a sharp instrument.

Gareth had got the 'sign' he had so fervently been wishing for.

Many times after the death of Batian and Furaha, as he sat alone in his camp, Gareth would hear the lions roaring. He would rush to greet them as he had always done in the old days, but there would be nothing there. It was winter and the ground was dry and hard and yet there was never any sign of spoor. Gareth believed that it was the spirits of Batian and Furaha that had visited him.

✳

I'm not sure about ghosts, animal or otherwise, although I had a personal experience with a ghost many years before I met Gareth.

Four years after we lived in Itu, Malcolm and I were transferred to the old slaving port of Calabar, a colourful town of wooden houses, mud streets, a crowded market and steep river banks where the ferry plied its way to and from Itu on a daily basis.

I was teaching Shakespeare's *Julius Caesar* and Thor Heyerdahl's *The Kontiki Expedition* – the set books for the Cambridge School Certificate English Literature examination – to Nigerian children at a Scots Mission School. My pupils loved Shakespeare, but totally debunked Heyerdahl's tales of sea monsters, a straw boat that sailed for weeks before sighting land, and an ancient human migratory route. None of my explanations could convince them that Thor and his little band were telling the truth. They appreciated his book as fiction, and volubly pitied me for believing in such outrageous fantasy.

After school closed at one o'clock, I would sometimes take Simon, then four years old, and his sister Sarah, aged two and a half, down to the quayside to watch the ferry – for all the world like an old riverboat steamer from America's Deep South – arriving and departing.

We lived in a very old, tall wooden house built on stilts with a flight of wooden stairs leading up to a wide wooden veranda which went right round the house. Wooden slatted doors led into the dark, hot interior where ceiling fans circled lazily. The house was built on a bluff overlooking the river, with views of the mangrove swamps upriver, and the port of Calabar downstream.

The house was reputed to be haunted by the ghost of Sir Roger Casement, who had lived there for a period of time in the early years of the twentieth century as a young Assistant District Officer for the British colonial government. I vaguely knew that Roger Casement, who was a hero to the Irish and a traitor to the British, had been hanged for treason by the British for his part in the Irish Republican Easter Rising of 1916.

Giles, the previous UAC station manager whom Malcolm had taken over from, warned us that Casement's ghost haunted the house. He had heard strange noises and sometimes felt an icy 'presence' in the house, but Malcolm and I suspected that these happenings only took place after one too many brandies at the Calabar Club. No, Giles did not know *why* Roger Casement should have chosen to haunt this particular house, and I for one didn't believe in ghosts anyway.

With the certainty and assurance that only a twenty-six-year-old colonial wife and mother could muster, I had the haunted wing – wing being a euphemism for two dusty rooms – swept and polished and moved my two small children into it as a nursery.

A photograph of Roger Casement at the time – a

photograph I found years later in the British Museum – shows a young bearded man with a thin, ascetic, somewhat ravaged face, staring intently at the camera from beneath his heavy pith helmet.

But at this stage I knew nothing. I briskly put any idea of a ghost out of my mind.

Six weeks later, after I had sung lullabies to my children and kissed them goodnight, Simon called out to me as I left the bedroom.

'Mummy, why does the man with the long black beard never say goodnight to us?'

Needless to say, I re-closed the 'haunted wing' and moved my children to the other end of the house.

There was a corollary to the story. Malcolm and I told no one of the incident because we felt rather foolish about our behaviour. Can you imagine what they would make of this at the Club, we asked ourselves. So we kept silent. We knew that no one could have told the children about our resident spirit – the servants spoke no English, and the story of the ghost was not widely known amongst the expatriate population.

Some months later Malcolm and I were playing one of our regular weekly games of bridge with Bishop Moynahan, the eighty-year-old Roman Catholic Bishop of Calabar and Father Oliver, one of his parish priests.

Malcolm and Father Oliver were playing together, and the Bishop and I were partners. I was playing a hand of Three No Trumps (it's strange how one's memory recalls such trivial details) when we heard loud footsteps circling round and round the outside veranda. We thought it must be the old night watchman from whom we had got Polly, our African Grey Parrot.

Malcolm called out to him to go away. There was no response, but the footsteps continued.

Bishop Moynahan, who was dummy, got up from his chair muttering that he would take care of the situation. The Bishop was a very tall, well-built man of infinite compassion and wisdom, who had spent forty years of his life as a missionary in Nigeria. He was down-to-earth, extremely practical, and took no nonsense from anyone.

Meanwhile, the three of us continued playing. I had just successfully made my contract when the Bishop came back into the room. He collapsed into his chair, pale and shaking. He had gone out to the veranda and found no one there. But he could clearly hear footsteps. He had walked to a corner of the house and, as he stood there, the footsteps rounded the corner and went past him. At the same moment he felt an icy wind blowing past him.

None of us knew anything about ghosts, although I know now that what the Bishop experienced that night was a 'classic' description of a ghostly visitation. The four of us sat in silence, not quite believing what we had heard and what the Bishop had experienced. The footsteps had now disappeared.

Years afterwards, when I was living in Northern Ireland, I was hospitalised with some difficult-to-detect virus. I was alone in a small room – the virus could have been contagious – when there was a knock at the door. It was Father Oliver. Somehow he had located my whereabouts and had taken a train up from Dublin, where he was on leave from Nigeria, especially to visit me.

We talked about Sir Roger Casement. While in the British consular service he had exposed the ruthless exploitation of the people of the Belgian Congo. Much of Joseph Conrad's *eart of Darkness* – a signed copy of which I had read at my randfather's urging as a youngster – is based on Casement's ontemporary reports to his superiors. Maybe he had been appy at the Calabar house, Father Oliver suggested to me a that small isolation ward in Newtownards Hospital, and hat was why he haunted it – to relive happier days.

But I subsequently found out something to my mind even nore bizarre, something which suggested to me another ersonal spiritual link to my time in eastern Nigeria as a oung woman. When I was researching this book, I found ut to my utter amazement that Roger Casement had also ved in Peru, and whilst there had similarly exposed the avage exploitation of the Quechua people by the Spanish olonisers.

The Dalai Lama's words, 'the interconnectedness of all hings', seemed once again to have found meaning with me. t was for Roger Casement's exposé of the brutal situations n the Belgian Congo and Peru that he was knighted by the British Government in 1911, only to be stripped of his nighthood after his 'treason'.

I don't know if the spirit of Roger Casement could be nterpreted as a milestone on my spiritual journey but, ooking back, the events at Calabar certainly opened my mind o possibilities that I had previously scorned.

To this day, I don't know whether or not I believe in ghosts, ut I wanted to share this experience with you.

Something else I have learned over the years, is not to eek and expect a rational answer for all the things that happen o you in life.

I had spent so much of my life being a professional cademic, a dyed-in-the-wool intellectual, that I almost nissed out on developing the awareness that there are things that defy explanation, things that are there to be *experienced* rather than known or understood.

*

Gareth Patterson has often talked to me about the necessity for *feeling* with animals. By feeling with them, he believes that you can enjoy deep spiritual experiences as he has done.

One of his deepest experiences of this kind occurred one early African dawn. Although Batian was not quite a fully mature male lion, Gareth felt that the time for him to roar was imminent. Apparently the first roaring of a lion is a major milestone in its life.

Early one morning, as Gareth and Batian were standing on top of a large sandstone rock watching the sun come up, Batian threw back his head and roared. Gareth described the experience as amazing – standing with his hand on the lion's shoulder, just where his mane ended, and hearing and watching him roar at the dawn. He found it an incredible spiritual experience.

'I felt every breath of that roar,' he told me, 'and everything – the trees, the birds, everything within the radius of the sound of that roar – was connected by it. I was at the centre of so much.'

Gareth is 'connected', as the Dalai Lama said on that cold Johannesburg day shortly before I left for Peru, to the natural world. He is firmly walking along his destined – for he believes it is destined, not chosen – spiritual path.

But for many people the road is less clear. We live in a world of spiritual confusion where there is much conflict.

Many of the organised religions – major faiths such as

Christianity, Hinduism, Judaism, Islam – claim that their numbers are increasing. And why not? In a world that often seems more and more confusing, there are many people who feel the need for the fastnesses, security fences and clear parameters of faiths that prescribe, define and determine what their spiritual paths should be. These spiritual maps are readily available and show you which road to take and what signposts to follow.

However, there is a growing number of people who look for a road less travelled. Not for them the comfort zones or security of dogma or organised devotion. These people are determined to find their own path. Sure, there is plenty of millennial *angst* about, but there's also a feeling of spiritual revival and renaissance – a hunger to find the meaning of life.

'These are the days of miracle and wonder,' Paul Simon sang and, as never before, people are seeking those miracles and wonders in the hope that with them they can transform their own lives and so bring meaning and purpose to them. Regulated religion is all very well, but what if we can make and define our own regulations, make our own map of where we want to go spiritually?

Scholars are arguing that Gnosticism is on the rise. Gnosticism is a synthesis of Christianity, Greek philosophy, Hinduism, Buddhism and the mystery cults of the Mediterranean which flourished during the second and third centuries after Christ. It was a rival to, and an influence on, early Christianity.

Gnostics believed, and believe, that each individual can make his or her own spiritual way, and in so doing achieve individual salvation. Cynics and non-believers castigate the Christianity that followed as taking away this individual responsibility and assuming the mantle of power for itself. Rules and regulations, sins and penance, baptism and salvation, were simply priestly power plays to keep a ruling religious hierarchy firmly in place. Non-believers – in the traditional sense – were classed as pagans, infidels, and savages. If you didn't conform, you might be burnt as a witch or, hundreds of years down the line, dismissed with the sneer 'New Age'. If you want a life get a religion. But a regular one.

But now a modern form of Gnosticism is returning. It may not be known by that name, but there is a widely held belief that we can choose a spiritual path of our own, and be the instruments of our own salvation.

Heresy or Hope? It depends on your point of view.

ELEVEN

Walking In Two Worlds

People at the end of the twentieth century may be struggling to find a spiritual path, but it seems that ancient people who had strong connections to the earth, to Pachamama, to whatever particular name they gave their natural universe, have always taken a strong spirituality for granted, just as their life has always been inextricably bound up with the other world, or another world.

Amongst the Quechua of the high mountains of Peru, for example, I saw how people, the earth, all natural things, the Christian God, the *apukuna*, other sacred beings and sacred animals, were all part of the cycle that made up everyday life. Man and spirit, men and the spirits, were all part of the same existence. In Australia's Outback and Top End, I had seen how the Aboriginals, arguably the oldest people on earth, in their landscape which knows no physical nor spiritual boundaries, also have an unquestioning acceptance, an unchallengeable certainty that mind and body, spirit and physical form are one.

My own association with these people and their time-honoured beliefs had dispersed some of the darkness and confusion about my own spiritual path. My Peruvian experience had been the axis; for the first time I was able to look backwards and forwards in time and begin to pull the threads of a lifetime's experience and study into a clearly discernible pattern.

❋

About five years before I climbed Ayers Rock, I had visited America's Southwest for the first time and explored some of its sacred sites, in particular the Anasazi sites. (Say that word out loud – *Anasazi* – it's like a whisper resonating with memories and ways long gone – *Anasazi*.) They were the prehistoric peoples of the Four Corners region of the American Southwest, where the states of Arizona, Utah, Colorado and New Mexico touch, known for their pueblos and cliff dwellings, and the pottery, tools and decorative items they produced.

These ancient Pueblo people, the ancestors of today's Pueblo peoples, can be traced back in the Southwest to the year AD 1. I saw the ruins of their civilisations at Montezuma Valley in southwestern Colorado, and in the Tuyasan village which is one of thousands of ancient habitation sites in the Grand Canyon National Park. The evocative remains of Anasazi dwellings – the masonry patterns, the sturdy walls, practical fireplaces and food stores – are easy to empathise with.

However, in many ways they are a mystery people. We still don't know what happened to them. They disappeared about eight hundred years ago. Just like that. It all stopped.

There were settlements everywhere – and then nothing. We also know very little about their beliefs. How did they interpret drought? Was it caused by unknown spiritual powers? To whom did they pray? *Did* they pray? Why did a child die? What happened after death? What did the stars mean? Was there any significance in the fall of a leaf?

And do we ourselves know any better now?

What we do know is that unlike the modern Pueblo tribes, each band of Anasazi built an underground *kiva*, the sacred pit-house forbidden to women where the men worshipped. Who and how and why they worshipped remains a mystery. But if you stand in the impressive ruins of Pueblo Bonito, the largest 'Great House' in Chaco Canyon in New Mexico, built in the ninth century AD and the largest of all prehistoric Southwestern pueblos, you will get a feel not only of a busy and purposeful past culture, but also of something beyond the everyday life of that time. Yes, it was a busy trade and distribution centre, whose valley floor had hummed with noise. But as the dry desert air blows around you, the warm colours of the old dwellings complementing the dusty blues and greys of the vegetation, there's a feeling of power, of mystery, of ancestral voices that speak unequivocally of forces beyond and above the natural ones.

What we know today is that for all the Native American tribes, religion and culture were inextricably entwined. Everything has spirit, everything is part of the Great Mystery. You didn't ask questions about the Great Mystery. It was part of your thinking from the moment you began to think – maybe even before, when you listened to the stories told by your mother and the wise ones as you slumbered half-knowing, half-awake around a smoky fire in the tipi.

You understood from birth that you were put on earth to

follow a life path, your Earth Walk. This was the Great Mystery. You understood that spirits are present in everything – in mountains and trees, stones and birds, male and female, sea, sky, land and water.

You knew that you, as a human being, fit naturally into your surroundings. There was no division, no conflict, no 'us' and 'them' in nature.

Luther Standing Bear, Oglala Sioux Chief (1868-1939), reiterated the premise central to all Native American life and thought:

> The American Indian is of the soil, whether it be the region of forests, plains, pueblos, or mesas. He fits into the landscape, for the hand that fashioned the continent also fashioned the man for his surroundings. He once grew as naturally as the wild sunflowers; he belongs just as the buffalo belonged . . .

Standing Bear also said:

> I am going to venture that the man who sat on the ground in his tipi meditating on life and its meaning, accepting the kinship of all creatures, and acknowledging unity with the universe of things was infusing into his being the true essence of civilisation.

Native American shamans from the north and south of the Americas are central to their culture. In Africa a shaman is called a *sangoma*, an *inyanga*, a *sanusi* – in the old colonial days he or she was known pejoratively as a witchdoctor. A true shaman is a holistic healer, treating his patients' physical, psychological and spiritual needs and symptoms. Gifted individuals, often inspired, they can uncover the cause of ill health or poor hunting.

In the Central Kalahari deep in Southern Africa, a San shaman will put himself into a trance state, the better to communicate with the Divine.

In a moment I'm going to tell you the story of Indio, the North American shaman I met when I returned to the Southwest nine months after my journey to Peru.

But first let me tell you about the Sun Dance. There are many different versions of this important Native American ceremony but the central features remain the same. Its name is said to derive from the Sioux, who called it the 'gazing-at-the-sun' dance, but its significance perhaps comes from the Cheyenne, who called the structure in which the ceremony was held 'new life lodge'.

The idea behind the dance is to re-create the world – to make it over again as fresh, new, joyous and innocent. The ceremony was held over a period of several days during late summer or early autumn when Mother Earth is at her most bountiful.

The dance takes place in a large east-facing open-air lodge, especially built for the purpose, with a forked pole erected in the middle. Dancers face this pole as they dance, often for long periods, often going into a trance state.

The most dramatic feature of the Sun Dance is its self-mortification aspect. Remember Richard Harris in the movie *A Man Called Horse*? Initially, the dancers, usually young warriors, would go without food and water for many days, dance to exhaustion, and in the process set themselves and the earth free.

Occasionally thongs were threaded through a dancer's nipples and fastened to the top of the central pole. These the dancer would strain to break as he wove, turned, jumped and twisted. If he was unable to break away, the medicine man would cut him free.

After the ceremony the participants and the tribe knew that they could expect health, fertility and food. The world was restored to its primal innocence and harmony, the well-being of the tribe was ensured, and man and spirit could once again walk together in peace.

Now let me tell you Indio's story. Indio is of the Yaqui Pasqual Nation, an independent tribe which is found all over the Southwest and in Mexico.

Imagine the scene.

It was the end of May and Tucson, Arizona, the 'lightning capital of the world', was hotting up. Indio and I were sitting under the palm-thatched roof of one of the shelters that encircles the Sun Dance arena in his reservation just outside Tucson.

We had been brought together by strange circumstances. A few weeks earlier in Flagstaff, Arizona, I had made a live crossing to my radio station in Johannesburg. A listener to the broadcast called her son Michael, a healer who lives in Tucson. He called the radio station, who in turn had called me (I was then in the high mountains of New Mexico above Taos) and, as a member of the Peyote Church, he had arranged for me to see Indio. Not an easy task because Indio shuns publicity so as better to concentrate on his life's mission – to heal and restore the self-esteem of the young people of his tribe. But he was interested in Africa and had never met anybody from Africa before.

Indio was young-looking, late fortyish I would guess, with a serene unlined brown face, a long pigtail, and calm, wise eyes. He was wearing old, torn jeans and a faded T-shirt. As we talked, a couple of children from the reservation circled around him, occasionally stopping to listen before running back to play in the dusty arena.

He told me his story.

Concerned for the children of the tribe – 'our children' – Indio was determined to try and make a difference. One way he thought he might be able to restore hope and self-esteem in the youth of his community was to resurrect the Sun Dance ceremony – one of the oldest and most meaningful of all native American rituals. It takes place once a year over a period of four years (the number four is of paramount importance in native American cosmology), in late summer. It's a celebration, said Indio, of life and the Great Spirit.

Participants go without water for eight days and without food for four and dance all day and all night for several days. They experience many things during and after the ceremony – a spiritual awakening or reawakening, a release of emotion and the letting go of emotional baggage, pain, grief, anger, resentment, hatred.

Indio had seen some people unable to cope with what they had undergone, who denied both the experiences and themselves. Others moved on spiritually and in human terms.

A large cottonwood tree stood in the middle of the dancing space in front of us. This space was big, half the size of a football field, and round. A sandy track surrounded it, being itself surrounded by a covered walkway roofed with fronds of bamboo. The cottonwood tree was in the shape of a Y and covered with brightly coloured garlands and pieces of cloth. A small carved buffalo – symbolic of the importance and wealth the animal once represented – was placed carefully in the tree.

'We can't afford a real buffalo now,' laughed Indio.

The two arms of the Y represent the male and female and where the trunk joined was their union. The roots represented the ancestors who hold everything together.

When Indio started the Sun Dance three years ago (1998 will be the fourth and possibly last ceremony), he was regarded as a rebel, a threat to the status quo of the tribe who earn big revenues from their casino operation and are not interested in the 'old ways'.

He was philosophical about its future.

'It's in the hands of the Creator now. If he wants it to continue, it will continue.'

Three years before he was ridiculed and threatened when he told the tribe that he wanted to have a Sun Dance Ceremony. The tribe said no. But he was so persistent that finally they had to let him go ahead. They offered him a patch of land way off in the desert. But he refused this. He wanted the ceremony in the reservation where everyone – especially the children – could see it.

'So they offered me this place,' he said.

'This place' three years ago was the reservation trash dump, full of old cars, old fridges, waste stuff and garbage – plenty of it.

'They thought I would turn it down.'

But Indio didn't turn it down; he said 'yes', and every day for a year he loaded a piece of the trash by hand on to his old pick-up truck and carted it off. Then he began levelling the land and planted some grass. A few people from the reservation came to help him, and finally members of his family – who previously had been ashamed or amused or just hadn't known how to handle the situation – also came and helped.

'That first year, I thought maybe six or seven people would

come to the Sun Dance. But there were plenty. Many more than I thought came, and this year, our third year, hundreds and hundreds came. They camped in the desert. But now I feel it's become an "event" – it's too big. I hate big events and big crowds.'

In 1997, the year I met Indio, tribes came from all over the United States, including three tribes from Alaska who didn't know they were neighbours until they 'discovered' one another at the Tucson Sun Dance.

'Do the children come?' I asked him.

'Some, but not enough.'

Indio speaks with great sorrow of the futility of the young ones' lives. Of how they can't get jobs if they are male. Of how they cut their hair, change their names and pretend to be Mexicans in order to get a job. The women marry outside the Nation and are happy to have money and a TV.

'Now there are gang wars, alcoholism and drugs every-where. Look at our graveyard.'

He points to the big cemetery lying ironically alongside the Sun Dance arena. Tawdry plastic flowers gleam and dazzle in the midday sun as it bounces off the mounds and mounds of dusty red soil – many of them fresh. A few gravestones and small monuments dot the graveyard in between the myriad mounds.

'Any time of the day or night there will be our people in that graveyard. It's like a cult of the dead. They even bring candles – our people never had candles. These graves are of drug lords and victims of gang warfare. And suicides. Sometimes as many as three of our young people a week commit suicide because there is no hope for them. In the old days we had a ceremony when a child was born called the Water Ceremony. We bathed a new baby with water to symbolise the grief and tears ahead of it in life. But when someone died, we called it "Going Home". We buried the body in the ground with no stone and no markers and were happy for them – because they were "Going Home". Now it's all reversed. We worship the dead.'

Indio travels the country as one of the best-known and most respected of all Native American healers and wise men. His grandfather, White Feather, was a famous shaman and medicine man.

Indio's knowledge of healing plants is formidable. He's often called out in the early hours of the morning by hospitals all over the state to make diagnoses of patients. He uses an egg, which he first passes over the patient's body, then breaks to read the signs it offers. Mumbo-jumbo? It may sound like it, but Indio's diagnoses have become respected by patients and the medical profession alike.

He offers some of his time-honoured remedies – 'the desert is my pharmacy' – willow bark for headaches; orange blossom as a tranquilliser, used traditionally for mental illnesses, anxiety and tension; peyote for pain; bamboo ash mixed with water, the resulting fine powder rubbed beneath the eyes, for cataracts and blindness brought on by diabetes.

The day after I sat with Indio in the Sun Dance arena, he was going to California to consult with two tribes who live among the giant redwoods who wished to know how to 'legalise' their tribe. If a tribe is not registered by law as a Native American tribe, it has no rights. Indio had been asked to share his wisdom and experience as, in his words, 'an objective outsider'.

He told me he was going to northern California by bus. He has never flown, because he does not want to sever his physical connection with the earth.

'Maybe one day I will have to take a plane. When that day comes, I will fly.'

Indio spoke to me with total frankness and humility. He is poor, but his true power lies in the fact that he doesn't need anything.

'True power doesn't need to be used, it needs to be experienced,' he remarked. 'I want nothing for myself. I have nothing. I don't own anything. The tribe fears me and my strength because I threaten their big cars and their jobs. They make so much money from the casino, but nothing comes back to the people of the reservation. They give me this house in the worst part of the reservation – where the gangs and the alcohol are – and where they think I can do least harm. That's why I built the Sun Dance area here – everybody can see it and it can't be ignored.'

I asked him what he wanted to achieve.

'Hope. It's for our children. They must have hope.'

Apparently only three children a year from Indio's reservation complete their education. There's no education on the reservation itself so the children are bused to school. They're discriminated against, made fun of, forced into fights and then labelled as 'troublemakers' and expelled.

The shadows were lengthening across the sandy arena as I listened to him.

I was reminded of the time, at the end of the Eighties, when I had been setting up a joint co-operative TV series in Juneau, Alaska. Some of the Inuit Elders had told me the same kind of stories as Indio had been telling me. Of dispossessed and almost broken people, of cultural imperialism, and of their battle to regain self-esteem, and to reinstate the traditional values of a culture that had survived in the world's harshest environment for well over ten thousand years. Values such as co-operation, respect for nature, family values, sharing and humility.

Indio spoke to me about how he had been imprisoned for more than nine years for conducting Native American ceremonies at a time when it was illegal to do so.

'I went to a prison which had a big Native American population. They had nothing of their own. When I left they were conducting pow-wows, sweat lodges and were remembering and celebrating their own traditions. The prison governor told me he was pleased I was leaving. Because I had accomplished too much.'

Indio has a sweat lodge of skins in his own backyard. Shabby and small but much used. It's been trashed by the tribe and is frowned upon by the administrators, 'educated' Indians who have been brought into the reservation from the towns.

Indio is wise, calm and full of pain for the children, but stoical and philosophical about the future.

'It's in the hands of the Creator – not mine.'

Was he passing on his knowledge and wisdom to the children?

'I try. I take them out into the desert to help me collect medicinal plants and herbs. I don't try to "teach" them, of course. I make it all a game, so that they say, "Can I cut that?" "Can I collect those?" '

There were tears in my eyes as I sat under the bamboo thatch and listened to and watched this lovely man. There was a holiness in his spirit which tangibly manifested itself like a cloak around him. There was purity, goodness and truth surrounding him. And an ineffable aura of sadness.

The purple mountains glimmered in the sun, fading and disappearing as the shadows of clouds passed over them. The plastic flowers wilted and drooped in the heat of the grave-yard. The detritus of the reservation lay in the yards about us. Music and dishonest laughter blared from a nearby television set. Indio sat amidst it all. A shining beacon of true light and faith.

A Salish woman, Mourning Dove, wrote over a hundred and fifty years ago that

> *Everything on the earth has a purpose, every disease an herb to cure it, every person a mission. This is the Indian theory of existence.*

Indio's very existence is his reason for being; his life an attempt to restore balance and equilibrium to a people who once knew no other way.

But what about those people who are perhaps still looking for a mission or a reason for being?

Indio was tired now. He had been talking for hours.

I put one last question to him. What would he say to someone who was looking for a spiritual path?

'Stop right here,' he said pointing to his heart. 'You don't have to travel the world or be always looking. It's right here inside all of us. Listen to your heart. Stop, take time to listen, and follow what you hear.'

✳

On that post-Peru journey to America's Southwest I met bestselling author, Barbara Kingsolver. She lives with her ornithologist husband, Steven, and two young daughters on a small rambling ranch, a few miles outside Tucson. Barbara was trained as a biologist before becoming a writer of poetry, three critically acclaimed award-winning novels, *The Bean Trees*, *Animal Dreams*, *Pigs in Heaven* and her most recent novel *The Poisonwood Bible*. Over and over again in her writing she returns to her favourite themes of family, community and the natural world. When I asked her if we could talk about the theme of spirituality, she was surprised and pleased.

'In all the interviews I've ever given, no one has ever mentioned spirituality before.'

She was clearly delighted with the opportunity.

It was the middle of May and very hot. We sat in her air-conditioned study and as we talked her chubby baby girl toddled and crawled about our feet. Alan and Steven sat outside in the shade of the casuarina trees talking birds.

Barbara has the eye of a scientist but the vision of a poet.

'It's hard to talk about religion or spirituality because those two words are loaded with millions of connotations, horribly appealing and horribly awful – everything from the Crusades to sweat lodges or New Age things. My writing is an extension of everything I believe in. I'm not one of those writers who finish a book and then figure out what it was about. I decide what it is I need to say and then say it. In writing there's always pain and it's always a matter of being quite pedestrian – a matter of social welfare, social change, social responsibilities. It's my way of trying to make the world better.'

She remarked again that nobody had ever before asked her about spirituality or religion.

'It took me by surprise and I wonder if it's because you're not from the United States, because here in the States we have such an aggressively secular culture. It seems as if we're almost embarrassed to admit that we're driven by a sense of morality, a sense of what's right and wrong in the world, and how to do good and how to make things right. We don't talk about that. It's a peculiar thing about our culture.

'I wonder what it is that people are looking for so desperately. Part of our secularisation is to believe only in those things which we can grasp hold of. There's a huge gap in many people's lives, a nothingness, no faith, nothing in our life that we can take on faith. So people are looking for something they need but they don't know what it is.'

Could it be called a simple-minded spirituality? I ask.

'In a way, yes, and it's not necessarily bad. The whole business of picking and choosing a culture is one of the few things that we can really call American culture. We have so little that's ours because we came here from everywhere and have very few long-term traditions that hold us together. So we have to construct the concept of an American culture and some of it is good, and some awful. But this business of working around the different cultures and taking pieces that work, like Santa Claus from the Dutch, and the Christmas Tree from the Germans, and whatever, and constructing something that's meaningful, that's fine. It's a wonderful melting pot with all these different flavours and spices simmering away, but nobody's melting. In the same way you can construct your own spirituality.

'I find that a lot of what I do is exploring the spaces between – the inner spaces where people can look at the world, the same world, but with entirely different eyes. That's why I've written several books that include characters who are Native American, Guatemalan, Mexican – from here or there – so the same world can be seen in quite different ways with different perspectives.

207

'When I moved to Tucson nobody was writing about Indians, nobody was writing about the Southwest, nobody had ever heard of the Southwest. Now people in Manhattan and all over the world know about it. And just as the icons of religion are very loaded, now the icons of the Southwest have become very loaded too.'

That's why Barbara Kingsolver moved from the terrain that made her famous to writing about Africa in *The Poisonwood Bible*.

'Obviously I won't move on permanently and I'm sure I'll write about the Southwest as long as I live here, but I guess after seeing the hundredth version of the jacket of a translation of one of my books with a saguaro cactus on the cover, I thought I need a little break. I need to write a book that nobody can put a saguaro cactus on the cover.'

(Saguaro cacti are those huge prickly green natural columns which rise up out of the desert and which seem to be stretching their arms up to the sky – the stereotypical Southwestern symbol.)

We talk about the modern quest for spirituality. How can someone find his or her own spiritual way?

'Look at your community. A character in *Animal Dreams* said, "It's what you do that makes your soul, not the other way around." If you want to have peace in your soul do things with your hands that will generate a sense of goodness in yourself, not the other way around. Don't try to design goodness out of thin air and think that's going to make you a good person. You become a good person by doing good things, and wherever you live there's a need. It might be over the wall, it might be on the other side of the fence, it might have to do with the existence of the fence, it might be an emptiness that needs to be filled concretely, or hunger, homelessness or injustice. That's where I think peace comes from.'

I asked her if she'd ever met a really evil person.

'Oh yes,' came the swift reply. 'Half of them are running the country. But I think a truly evil person is rare. I've certainly encountered them, but probably their mothers loved them. If you spend enough time with them you will understand them. I think that what we call evil in a person is something we think of as a wicked behaviour without motivation. I think we're most frightened of the people who seem possessed by some vile magic that makes them do unpredictable, bad things. And when you look at the most vilified criminals in our culture, they sometimes even talk that way, saying "Well, the Devil made me kill all those people." Ultimately I think we're terrified of the things we can't explain. An evil person is one whom we inadequately understand.'

I remarked that her books were always positive. That when you got to the end of one of her compulsive stories, firstly, you couldn't bear for it to end; and secondly, you felt uplifted.

'I think action is the antidote to helplessness – that seems to be all I ever talk about. People say "How do you remain hopeful?" and I always answer, "I don't have a choice. I have kids, you have kids." Hopelessness is an immoral choice. The minute you say I can't do anything about this, it's hopeless, then you are giving yourself permission to just lie down and weep and never do anything again. If you do that you're turning your back on the kids and the only way to sort of trick yourself in thinking that tomorrow will be better than today is to spend the whole day doing something, to sort of figure out what you hope for and then live inside that. It's a vastly unpopular outlook and has been for quite a while.

'Today there's a style of writing that's morally empty, it strives for moral emptiness, it strives to have no sort of judgement, no value judgement. It simply observes the world and refrains from comment. And that scares the pants off of me, because that's where gang rape comes from. I'm not saying that a person who writes like that is capable of gang rape. I'm saying that the culture that accepts no judgement of any sort – that accepts a hollow core, an amoral point of view – as acceptable and even desirable, is in big trouble. I tell you that having a moral vision is essential for a culture.

'Poverty is not a moral failing. Making your living from selling drugs is probably a solution rather than a problem. What *is* the problem? I think Dr Laura would say drugs are the problem. I would say drugs are the solution and let's look at the problem. I suppose that's what I have in common with Jane Austen and Dr Laura, we all have a strong moral vision. But it's a question of your point of origin. How far back in the chain of events are you willing to look for origins of problems and solutions?'

For Barbara Kingsolver, the path is plain. Have a clear moral vision, do something useful and needed in your community, avoid hopelessness. Your spiritual way will then unfold before you as you go.

A few months before I had heard the Dalai Lama say

> *If you contribute to other people's happiness, you will find the true goal, the true meaning of life.*

*

In *The Celestine Prophecy*, James Redfield describes how he visited Sedona in Arizona, recognised worldwide for the presence of its powerful energy areas known as vortices.

At one of these spiritual places, Boynton Canyon, he experienced a miraculous healing.

If you go to the red rocks of Sedona today, you will see the sick and the crippled, the walking wounded, winding their way up the short path to the lip of that canyon. Local guides describe it as America's Lourdes – to my mind an overly extravagant, if not false claim.

Visit the place by all means, but go as well to a Medicine Wheel elsewhere in the red rocks of Sedona and learn about yourself in the way the Plains Indians have traditionally done since the beginnings of time. Find out how the medicine wheel symbol reflects an understanding and reverence for life and how the ancient earth wisdom of Native Americans is relevant today to all of us – how it can teach us wisdom, no matter what our backgrounds or creeds.

Boynton Canyon is a flat-topped ridge overlooking the mesas, mountains and plains of Sedona's majestic red rock scenery. The rocks are red because of the large amounts of iron oxide in the soil which is believed to transmit electro-magnetic energy – hence the spirals of natural energy known as vortices. Red earth has been used in sacred rituals and early burial rites in places as far apart as Australia, southern Europe, Africa and the Americas. And long before *The Celestine Prophecy* popularised this beautiful part of America's Southwest, Sedona had always been known as a special and sacred place by the original people of the area.

But what is a Medicine Wheel other than a trendy symbol of New Age spirituality?

Since returning from Arizona I have even seen a Medicine

Wheel used as the central motif in a cigarette commercial. In Arizona, nine months after I returned from Peru, I found out its truths and how it teaches.

Imagine three rings of stones, one inside the other, the rings growing smaller as they reach the centre of the wheel.

The outer circle is the Sacred Hoop, the container of all life, the earth, sun, moon and stars.

The circle inside this represents the four corners of the world – east, south, north and west – as well as the four races of man: red, white, yellow and black.

The innermost and smallest circle is made up of seven sacred stones. Seven is a mystical number to the Plains Indians who talk about seven tribes, seven worlds and seven directions. But the number seven is also a powerful number in many cultures. Think about the seven days of creation, the seven colours of the rainbow, the seven chakra, seven musical notes, the Seven Wonders of the World in ancient times, seven deadly sins. We even talk about a state of bliss as being in a seventh heaven.

Native Americans say that this inner circle symbolises the centre of the universe and the centre of your own body. It's a very important part of the wheel. All things come from the centre, interconnecting all living things into one giant hoop of life. Native American peoples say we all come from one Great Spirit. That's why we are all interdependent – if we upset the Sacred Hoop of Life, or spider web as it's sometimes called, we upset and destroy the delicate balance of all things.

Four lines radiate from the centre of the wheel, each going to one of the four cardinal directions. One points east, another west, another south, and the final one points north. It's in these directions that most of the teachings occur, and although the teachings vary from tribe to tribe, the key messages are the same.

Deborah is part Cherokee. She has studied Native American cultures for many years and shares her knowledge and expertise with visitors to Sedona. She's a small, slim, dark-haired, thirty-something young woman who wears a long 'Western' skirt, a long-sleeved blouse tightly buttoned up at wrist and throat to keep off the hot Arizona sun, and a Stetson.

Alan and I and our youngest daughter Tiffany were her only clients on that particular day. Tiffany was the reason we were in the Southwest. She had just graduated with a Master's degree in Fine Arts, majoring in Design, from the University of Arizona at Tucson. We had come to be at her graduation in the way of all proud Mums and Dads.

We met Deborah at the office of Sedona Red Rock Jeep Tours in Sedona's charming, if very touristy, main street. As we rattled off out of town in an open jeep on our way to the Medicine Wheel, she told us that most of her knowledge of the Medicine Wheel was learned from the Dakota people.

She described the basic philosophy of the wheel.

'Native Americans say we are all born into the Sacred Hoop of Life. From birth we all begin to move round the wheel in a clockwise direction, starting in the east, and as we move on into the different parts of the wheel – south, west, north – we receive the lessons, the teachings and the blessings of life. The more you move around the wheel, the more empowered you become spiritually. If you jump around the wheel from one place to another, with no ongoing sense of direction, then you will create problems for yourself and those around you. Native Americans believe that it is crucially important to move in a clockwise direction, to follow the natural flow of things. That's how you become wise and empowered. When your body dies, your spirit lives on. The body is just a vehicle for your spirit which is eternal. It merges back to the one creator, restores itself, and if it so chooses, re-enters the Hoop of Life. Reincarnation is very valid for most Native American peoples. Some people are born very wise. Why? Because they have been on earth many times before and have learned their lessons.'

By the time she had finished talking we were high up in the red rocks surrounding the little town. It was like being in the middle of one of those old John Wayne cowboy movies where the stage-coach hurtles through the steep-sided ravine pursued by whooping Indian braves wearing war-paint and riding spotted ponies. I thought ironically to myself how times had changed. Now it was the White Man who was the Bad Guy, and the Indian who was the Good Guy.

Deborah parked the jeep and we walked along a rocky path to a ridge overlooking the endless valleys below. A Redtailed Hawk soared high above us – a good omen, according to Deborah.

The Medicine Wheel, old and grey, was at the edge of the ridge but we may only enter it after we have been 'cleansed' in a smudging ceremony.

Deborah lit a smudging stick, a small, tightly rolled cylinder of sweet grass, and as it began to smoulder she passed it over us, over our heads, behind our backs, up and down our legs, over our whole bodies. The smoke was fragrant and tickled the nostrils.

One by one she took us to the edge of the ridge and passed her hands over us in a healing ceremony. She is a well-known and practised healer. I felt heat emanating from her hands as she passed them over me.

'You must relax more. You're too busy, you do too much. It's not necessary to prove yourself any more,' she whispered to me. 'Try to become a walking meditation.'

Once we'd been cleansed we could enter the Wheel, but first Deborah told us how the Wheel 'works'.

There are four areas – east, south, west and north. One's spiritual journey begins in the east – the 'doorway' into the Medicine Wheel, the Doorway of Illumination. This is where light is brought in from the darkness and represents a new day, fresh beginnings. Springtime is the season honoured, and the element honoured is that of air. The animal symbol is the eagle, Medicine of the Creator. The eagle flies so high that he is in communion with the Creator and represents alliance with him. That is why eagles are especially important to the Native Americans who wear eagle feathers in their bonnets.

'What does it mean if you are in the east of the Wheel?' asked Tiffany.

'As an adult, if you are in the east of the Wheel, then you are probably experiencing something new – optimism, excitement, a new faith – it's all part of the "newness" of life.'

'And the south?' asked Alan.

'I knew you would ask that,' Deborah said laughingly, 'because Coyote is the guardian here, and you certainly belong to Coyote Medicine.'

Alan didn't know whether to be flattered or offended.

'What's Coyote Medicine?'

Deborah related that in Native American lore Coyotes could be deceptive. They have a façade of intelligence, honesty and seriousness, but really they are full of fun and tricky.

Tiffany and I hooted with laughter at Alan's crestfallen face. He cheered up when Deborah went on to say that Coyote, sometimes called the Trickster and the Sacred Fool, was also playful, curious, tenacious and loved to test boundaries. Native Americans believe that Coyote Medicine also represents lateral thinking, creativity and flexibility.

Alan was now willing to admit that he might fall into the Coyote Medicine category. 'What happens to you in this part of the Wheel?'

'Well, the south is aligned with high noon. The season is summer and the element honoured is fire. Here you'll learn new ways of thinking and to find humour in all sorts of situations. Spend as much metaphorical time as you like in this part of the Wheel, until you find yourself moving naturally into the west.'

The west, explained Deborah, is associated with maturity, the season of Fall and the element of water. Here is Bear Medicine, which represents strength and introspection.

'This is where you go inside yourself – like a bear into a cave – and seek your own truth and your own strength. This is the part of the Wheel that demands we grow up and stop depending solely on others. It's the place of the adult, of responsibility, of making commitments, taking action and getting your head together.'

'What does that mean in practical terms?' I asked.

'Next time you have a problem, the next time you're scared, instead of bolting or regressing, stop. Go inside yourself. Go into your cave like the bear does. Disconnect the phone, turn off the television, don't call your best friend, don't call your therapist. Stop, go inside yourself and meditate. Seek the truth and then act on it.'

'What happens if you don't act on it?' This question from

Tiffany.

'Then nothing will happen. You can talk about it all you want, dream about it all you want, but unless you roll up your sleeves and take action, your dreams will die.'

'What happens once you are through the west?' Alan wanted to know.

'Once you are through the west you will have a solid foundation. This is self-empowerment. If you regress, that is disempowerment.'

The last part of the Wheel is the north, associated with winter, early evening, wisdom, and with earth as the element.

'Without earth you have nothing, so the Native American peoples call this place the Prince of the Earth. It's also the place of White Buffalo Medicine because White Buffalo is the animal here and White Buffalo is all about prayers and abundance. White Buffalo Woman is the most sacred of beings to the Plains tribes, because it is the buffalo who saved them from extinction several hundreds of years ago. On August 20, 1994, a female white buffalo calf with brown eyes was born in Minnesota, in the year that marked the end of a five-hundred-year cycle of Native American prophecy. Many people equate this event with the Second Coming of Jesus because indigenous myth and legend tell that when White Buffalo returns to the people of the plains, they will once again be saved.'

Connections, I thought to myself, yet again. I had interviewed White Buffalo, a Cherokee Chief, on my radio programme by telephone just after this calf was born in August 1994. I had forgotten about it until this moment high above Sedona.

As we sat on the old wooden benches outside the Wheel, Deborah told us more about the north of the Wheel, how it is the place of the Elders, the place of wisdom. How Elders will always sit in the north at Council fires. How they are full of wisdom because they have walked the wheel many, many times. They have the last word in any decision.

'The United States has no wisdom in its culture,' said Deborah sadly. 'There's no wisdom, no one thinks ahead. All we do is to develop everything. America – everybody tries to emulate America, but in terms of the Wheel we are babies. We live somewhere between the east and the west.'

'Do you have to be old to be in the north?' asked Tiffany.

'Often, yes. But not necessarily so,' replied Deborah. 'People come into the north who are completing a cycle of some kind, analogous to the ending of a day. It could be the end of a project, maybe.'

'So that could be me, I've just come to the end of my studies.'

'Right. The north is the place not to do anything – a time for reflection, of integrating what you've just been through. So learn from your experiences, extract wisdom out of them. If you don't take time to reflect and integrate this wisdom, then you'll hop out of the north and back into the east again. You won't have learned anything because you didn't stop to take time.'

Her words reminded me of Dan's theories of incarnation. How he believed that being reincarnated over and over again was no guarantee of wisdom, that repeating reincarnations did not necessarily make anybody an 'Old Soul', because it may be that nothing new had been learned in those repeating incarnations and you could still be at the same stage of spiritual evolution as when you started.

'The Native Americans also believe,' continued Deborah, offering us all some iced water from the cold box she had carried with her, 'that the north is the place to stop, slow down, learn and let go time, and also to let go of that which you no longer need. The Elders teach that you must be careful, however, not to get stuck in the north of the wheel. It's easy to get stuck because wisdom can be very heavy. They teach that it is important not to think that you know it all. Don't always try to hang on to the old. Learn to trust that life can always teach you more and maybe bring you something better.'

'So the north of the Wheel is the final stop?' asked Alan.

'It's the gateway to the spirits, yes. When it is time for you to "Go Home", your spirit will exit through the north. But your journey does not necessarily end here if your time has not yet come. It can also be a temporary resting place, where we shed all that no longer serves us, then be free to enter the east once again – a time for renewal and new beginnings.'

One by one we entered the wheel and took our time moving round it. Something drew me to the north of the Wheel where I sat with my head in my hands and did some thinking. We had learned a lot and absorbed a lot. What sense the teachings of the Medicine Wheel make, I thought to myself.

> *Everything an Indian does is in a circle, and that is because the Power of the World always works in circles, and everything tries to be round . . .*
>
> *The sky is round, and I have heard that the earth is round like a ball, and so are all the stars. The wind, in its greatest power, whirls. Birds make their nests in circles, for theirs is the same religion as ours . . .*
>
> *Even the seasons form a great circle in their changing, and*

*always come back again to where they were. The life of a man
is a circle from childhood to childhood, and so it is in everything
where power moves.*

Black Elk, Oglala Sioux holy man (1863-1950)

We continued to sit, grown quiet at what we'd learned: me
in the north, Alan in the south, and Tiffany in the east. I had
no idea that the Medicine Wheel of the Plains Indians was
such an effective teaching tool, not only for the members of
the tribes, but a tool that we can also use for personal and
spiritual insights.

Deborah had one final word for us.

'The Wheel is not only the physical expression of the
Native American belief that all life is sacred, but also a symbol
of the Wheel of Life, forever moving, forever evolving,
bringing us the teachings and truths of walking the path.'

TWELVE

Paths Are Made By Walking

Michael wasn't cured of his incurable disease at Boynton Canyon in Sedona. He cured himself with Peyote Medicine.

Michael, tall, slim, good-looking, was a producer, editor and musician in South Africa's vibrant pop music industry. A roadie for many years, he toured Southern Africa with local and international stars. Like many people in the industry he tried drugs, sex, rock 'n roll, but there came a day when he started to think about more than just ordinary things. He had a major spiritual awakening and came across Eastern mysticism. He became initiated and had a guru. But this phase of his spiritual journey passed and he felt ungrounded.

Then about ten years ago he became the victim of an incurable disease – no cure, no cause – called Horton's Syndrome. This disease manifests itself in acute neuralgia in the head, face and neck which Michael was told was one of the worst pains that a human can suffer. He would have up to eight attacks of blinding, unbearable pain each day, rolling over on the floor, screaming, beside himself with the agony. His wife, Sarah, an American citizen who was working as a staff photographer on a well-known paper in Johannesburg, took photographs whilst Michael was in this state, producing an award-winning photographic essay. The photographs are shocking to look at – a record of a human being in uncontrollable pain.

After Michael and I had returned from our day with Indio at the reservation outside Tucson, Arizona, we sat with Sarah in their tiny garden that is full of herbs, medicinal plants and the couple's nine cats. Michael had introduced me to his 'angel' and, indeed, Sarah looks exactly like a modern version of one of Dante Gabriel Rossetti's pre-Raphaelite angels – long, golden tight curls, big blue eyes and an expression of utter sweetness.

I commented that she looked like an angel, and Michael said simply, 'She is.'

After his long road to self-realisation and recovery, Michael is today a respected and successful healer.

As we drank decaffeinated coffee in the peaceful garden he told me about his illness. How all the nerves in the side of his face, his ears, eyes and nose, starting in the back of the neck, would go into spasm. The pain was excruciating. He said words couldn't really describe it.

But, ironically, the disease had started to steer his life in a particular direction. He couldn't drink, it was hard for him to watch TV, but he still somehow managed to continue in the music industry. But the attacks ruled his life. He tried everything and everyone to find a cure, from conventional medicine to way-out and off-the-wall stuff. He was desperate.

'Then I met Sarah. She was on a journalism fellowship to the *Mail & Guardian*, one of South Africa's best newspapers.

I decided to let go of the life I'd been living, even though I was well known and very successful. So we came to the States and settled in San Francisco. I became a house painter, spending most of my time high up on scaffolding, just thinking – thinking about what it was I wanted to do. And still having the pain. Then two years ago, on New Year's Eve, I made the decision that I would never again go to somebody else for help, because no one had ever been able to help me. I made the decision that I would try to heal myself.'

Then things began to happen pretty fast. Sarah had a massage voucher that she was supposed to give as a Christmas gift, but she had secretly kept it so that she could use it herself. It was sitting on the breakfast table between them one morning and Michael asked her if he could use it. Perhaps a massage would make him feel better.

He had the massage but wasn't really happy with it. He realised that if he had the knowledge he could do a much better job. The next day he told Sarah that he was going to Massage School.

'That was the start of my new life as a healer. It's been a long and continuing road. I went to the San Francisco School of Massage and became a certified massage therapist. I became more and more interested in healing, especially self-healing. Then I discovered the energy, the emotion of human energy, and found I had the power to work with human energy. This led me to Reiki and I became a Reiki master.'

'What's Reiki?' I asked. It was a word I had come across in esoteric magazines, but I had no notion of what it was or what it was supposed to do.

'Reiki is Universal Life Energy. A Reiki practitioner guides this Universal Life Force in a person's body by means of massage and manipulating the pressure points and creates a perfect balance of mind and body.'

'Sounds very New Agey to me.'

'All I can tell you,' said Michael gravely, 'is that it works. And far from being "New Agey" as you call it, it's a very ancient healing process of spiritually guiding the Universal Life Force in your body. It helps you to move through blockages on every level of body, mind, emotion and spirit.'

'How?'

'Reiki accelerates the body's ability to heal itself and opens the mind and heart to the cause of pain and disease.'

But I wasn't really convinced until Michael told me that he works with a Reiki team at the Cancer Care Centre at the Tucson Medical Centre, one of the first hospitals in the world where a Reiki team works alongside doctors and nurses doing energy work with cancer patients.

'Then I realised that the patients, even though they were getting this wonderful therapeutic energy treatment, were still in the wards, still confronted by that environment. So I began training all the Reiki volunteers to use Sound Therapy.'

'What's that?'

I was learning a lot of new expressions as I sat with Michael and Sarah in their restful garden.

'Sound Therapy cures by using all sorts of different sounds to detract attention away from your body. As the body relaxes so it will automatically start to heal itself. Whilst I was doing massage, I became interested in sound and Sound Therapy. My background as a musician helped enormously. Then when Sarah got this work offer here in Tucson we decided to move here and I opened a healing practice.'

I asked him to explain a bit more about Sound Therapy.

'Part of it is learning how to pick a particular piece of

music for particular types of people, for what they are needing. We put headphones on the patients and get them to close their eyes, so that during the treatment they are not in the ward, but are taken elsewhere by the music.'

'What's all this got to do with your healing yourself?' I asked.

'Whilst I was doing the Reiki and Sound Therapy I was also exploring other methods of self-healing. I wanted to teach other people about self-healing so that they wouldn't be reliant on me. For example, with Reiki, I can give you a treatment, send you on your way and then you can do it yourself. Similarly, with Sound Therapy I can show you what music to use and send you away. So I became more and more interested in finding out about self-healing techniques and then sharing them with others. Then I became aware of a medicine path – a spiritual path that incorporates plants with power – the use of plants to alter one's consciousness. And then the fate that had brought me to Tucson manifested itself.'

A colleague of Sarah's had been involved in a photographic project with the Peyote Foundation. Through him, Michael met the head of the Foundation, who introduced him to the medicine, to taking peyote, and showed him how to do it. He also introduced him to ceremonies.

'At that point another whole world opened up to me – the world of Native American philosophy and its belief systems. I realised that this was what I had always been searching for. I became involved in doing sweat lodge ceremonies, in taking the peyote, finding out what it does to me, and how it opens me up. In the process of finding the peyote and using it and doing these ceremonies I was completely healed of my disease and my ten years of pain had gone. It doesn't exist any more.'

To the uninitiated and thrill-seeker, peyote is a hallucinogenic drug prepared from the Mexican cactus, genus *Lophophora*. But peyote is also used sacramentally in the Native North American religion of Peyoteism.

Michael is now an Elder in the Peyote Foundation and conducts many ceremonies for them.

'I've seen alcoholics cured overnight, I've seen other diseases cured. The medicine shows us the things we are doing wrong. The Native Americans say that it shows us a good way to go. "Go in a good way", they will say to you. That way involves respect, compassion and tolerance.

'The Native American Church uses peyote as a sacrament for holy communion, a means whereby they commune with God. That's the way I view it too. To me it's a very holy plant and when I take it and have it in my body it's almost like certain things that have been sleeping in my brain are awakened, and from that moment on stay awake. You might never have to take peyote again or might never want to. But any shaman will tell you – if you have a problem, eat the medicine.'

Michael sees his path of self-healing as very much a path of self-empowerment. He used to want to change the world around. In the apartheid days in South Africa he was a political activist. At another stage he became very eco-active. He recorded music 'Save the fynbos' (the fragile, rare vegetation unique to South Africa's Cape), but came to realise that the fynbos wasn't dying *outside* of him, as he put it, but was dying *inside* him.

'What I'm discovering in my path is that we are not here to rearrange what is happening with creation, we are here to take from within ourselves and place whatever that is in creation. When you met Indio, what you saw surrounding him, that whole thing around him, it's what he's taken from inside of himself and placed in creation.

'I don't belong to any religion. I don't regard peyote as a religion. But I do see it as a faith and source of faith. The spiritual path of realisation that I'm on now is understanding that I have to draw on my own strengths. The only way that anybody learns anything is by himself.'

Not long after I returned to South Africa, I had an excited e-mail from Michael. Although Sarah had always empathised and been sympathetic and understanding of Michael's 'path', she had never taken any active part in it. Her journalist's instincts for a grittier truth, reality and the here and now had kept her apart from what Michael was actually doing. His e-mail told me that Sarah had agreed to go with him to visit a little-known tribe of Native American Indians in Mexico, where he had been asked to be an observer at some of their peyote ceremonies. Sarah accompanied him and when she got back to Tucson she e-mailed me some amazing drawings and paintings that the tribe had done for her. Bright, intricate, impossibly vivid, these artworks are pinned to my notice-board and I glance up at them as I write.

Sarah and Michael are very, very happy and at peace.

∗

Let's go north again. Not to Alaska, but to Canada.

Nearly half a century ago, a band of Dineh Indians on a tribal revenge mission wiped out a whole family. But not quite. Lying silently in a corner of the tipi in a cradle made of skins, a tiny baby was overlooked and so spared. Called the 'Miracle Child' by his tribe, he survived to become not a shaman – Tim dislikes that word – but a 'helper'.

In spite of an intensely spiritual experience as a teenager, when he stood alone on the edge of a high cliff in his native land and heard divine music, the music of the spheres, Tim went on to become a rebel, a drifter, and finally ended up in prison. His vocation as a healer and helper only caught up with him in later life. Today he lives in Germany, where The Great Spirit has sent him, conducting ceremonies, helping people to 'go in a good way', counselling and telling stories about his Dineh culture.

In my quest for finding out about the spiritual paths that people are following today I kept coming across the Native American sweat lodge ceremony. From LA to London, from Nuremberg to New Jersey, ordinary people are flocking to sweat lodges. To some critics, this is cultural hijacking of the worst kind. To others, it is a genuine attempt to see if the time-honoured ways of a people whose culture had meaning, moral values, grace and dignity, have any relevance for others today.

I met Tim when he was a guest on another host's talk show on my radio station. I had been asked to go and talk about my experiences in Peru, and Tim was a fellow guest.

We took an instant dislike to each other when he told me he never read books.

'What do you need books for? Life is the best teacher,' he remarked churlishly as we made our way into the small studio.

Afterwards, when we got to know each other better, he told me that he had immediately mistrusted me as an 'intellectual', a bad word in his vocabulary. In turn, I had thought him sullen and rude, not understanding where he was coming from in terms of what he did, thought or believed.

He was a handsome, dark man with black piercing eyes and a hooked nose. A long plait of black hair hung down his back. He looked the stereotypical Indian brave who had raced across the screen in my childhood visits to the movies.

That evening on Clive's show, Tim asked me to take part in a sweat lodge ceremony that he was holding the following weekend in the Maluti Mountains on South Africa's eastern border with the tiny mountain kingdom of Lesotho. Alan and I had already planned a visit to Rorke's Drift in Natal, where we were to explore the historic British/Zulu battlefields.

But when I got home that night and told Alan of our invitation, his immediate reaction was: 'Cancel the battlefields. Let's go!'

So we did. I am quite sure, however, that if the invitation had come prior to our visit to Peru, we would have dismissed the whole idea as so much New Age gobbledegook. But Peru had opened our eyes to many possibilities, to other options outside our former spiritual comfort zone – a zone that had said 'Maybe there's something out there, but who knows and who cares?'

I, for one, had accessed that 'something' in a slatted wooden hut on the banks of the Amazon. That experience I will share with you later, because it was the culmination of a long journey, a journey that was only revealed to me in Peru, and one that is ongoing.

Our journey from Johannesburg to Rustlers' Valley in the mountains of the eastern Free State took us about three hours. After unpacking our things in a small stone rondavel decorated with murals of unicorns and other fantastical animals, people and signs, Alan and I made our way to a circle of about twenty people sitting on the grass. Tim was part of the circle. We knew nobody except Clive, my colleague at the radio station, and were certainly the oldest people there amongst men and women who seemed to be from all walks of life. Later we were introduced to a teacher, a butcher, a publisher, a motor mechanic and a psychologist, amongst others.

Mountains ringed the valley, the sun was fiercely hot, and ducks, geese and friendly dogs wandered in and out of our circle as Tim told us about the sweat lodge.

'The sweat lodge is based on the central idea of purification. You're there to purify yourself. My people have been doing it for so long that there's no record of when it all began. It uses the four basic elements – fire, earth, water and air.'

A middle-aged German man with a ponytail asked Tim what we could expect to experience in the sweat lodge. Would it be a spiritual experience? Would people see visions?

Tim answered that it was impossible to foretell.

'It's really difficult to give you a direct answer because the experience is an individual one. But if you get really involved in there and your heart is open, you will work some of your problems out. It works, that's all I know. It just works.'

The lodge Tim and his helpers had built at Rustlers' Valley was a turtle lodge. And it looked exactly like the back of a turtle. It was a low, round-domed structure made of willows covered with layers of thick blankets, so low that you could not stand up in it. In Canada, amongst his own people, such a lodge would have been covered with animal skins and furs. There were two low doors that you had to crawl through – an entrance at the front and an exit at the back. After the ceremony starts these doors are closed and covered over with blankets so no light enters.

Tim explained to us that there were four stages to the ceremony, four 'doors' during which he sings and prays. At the end of each session the doors would be opened to let in some cool air. The ceremony used the four basic elements. The sacred heated rocks represent earth – the physical aspect of the human being which has to be cleansed. The fire represents the emotional self – also to be cleansed. The water represents the mental state which has to be cleansed and purified, and the air represents the spirits which we cannot see.

'It's really a ceremony where people come to pray and purify themselves. Our lodge, like an upturned saucer, sits on the robe of Mother Earth, or the ground. We like to emphasise that word *robe* because when we go into the sweat lodge, we go in through this robe, into the earth, back into her womb again. We are praying there and asking to be cleansed so that we can come out as reborn people. You must go in with an open heart. That's crucial. Once the doors are closed it's dark, the only light comes from the red hot rocks. Then it's total darkness.'

Tim told the group that menstruating women were not allowed to take part in the ceremony, much to the disappointment of one young woman who had come many miles to participate.

As we walked back to our rondavel, after Tim had finished his explanations and answered many of our questions, I remarked to Alan that it was a good thing neither of us was claustrophobic. After hearing Tim's description of the lodge and the ceremony, I could well understand that it was an exercise in mental and physical purification but that it would be a claustrophobic's nightmare.

Just before sunset we made our way down to the sweat

lodge which had been built away from the rondavels and other buildings of Rustlers' Valley. We had been told to wear shorts or swimsuits, but to bring warm clothes to put on after the ceremony had finished.

We sat on the grass with the others and made prayer strings which we were to tie into the bent willow branches of the roof of the lodge after we'd gone in. As the sun went down we busily knotted ribbons into pieces of string as if we always did this kind of thing at sunset on a Friday evening. It was oddly relaxing.

Then, one by one, thirty of us – because now more people had arrived – we crawled on our hands and knees into the sweat lodge. The women went first. Previously heated sacred rocks had been placed in the centre of the lodge by the 'Keeper of the Sacred Fire', a young man in a skin loincloth and with a feather in his hair, who had been assiduously tending the fire in a pit outside the entrance to the lodge whilst we were making our prayer strings. The rocks were red hot and gave off great heat. Even before all thirty of us had crammed into the lodge I had begun to perspire profusely – hence the term 'sweat lodge'.

After the doors were closed we were literally packed in together – knees pulled up under our chins, shoulders, hips and thighs pressed firmly against one another. But, amazingly, when I closed my eyes there was a sensation of space, of being in one's own space. It was very dark. Tim had crawled in last and sat at the very centre of the lodge beside the glowing stones which were the only source of light. He was also wearing a skin loin cloth, and an eagle feather in his hair – the eagle is his totem animal – and his dark skin glistened in the dim light. He asked us to pray in our own language. If we did not wish to pray then we should speak what was in

232

our hearts.

'It doesn't matter what religion you believe in, the Creator is not partisan, only people are.'

As we all began to pray or say things in our own languages – Hindu, English, Xhosa, Afrikaans, German – Tim started to sing in his own language, a strong, melodic ritualistic rising and falling of the voice that spoke of ancient mysteries, ancient ways, universal truths.

After the first 'door', when Tim had finished his first round of prayers and exaltations, the blankets were pushed aside from the doors. As the oldest woman in the group I had been told to crawl in first. I had crawled in a circular movement from left to right round the wall of the lodge so ended up sitting on the right hand side of the entrance. As the blankets were pushed aside I gratefully gulped in great breaths of the cool night air. Two people got up and left the lodge at this stage. They were unable to stand the heat – or maybe their own thoughts . . . who knows?

During the second 'door' one young man broke down in racking sobs. He told us afterwards that he had been mourning the death of his mother for some weeks, but had been unable to shed tears. The sweat lodge was his emotional catharsis. I was reminded of Joy at the Pachamama rock in Machu Picchu, and of how she had undergone her own emotional and spiritual catharsis there.

As the ceremony continued the atmosphere became intense and electric. People were murmuring, shouting, one was weeping; others were keeping their own counsel or singing softly to themselves.

It was an unforgettable experience.

After the third 'door' Tim was so exhausted by his songs and prayers, that he lay silent and prone for several minutes.

By the end of the fourth 'door' we had all joined in last ritual prayers and songs, our voices rising and falling with Tim's. There was a feeling of exultation.

When we finally crawled out into the cool night air, with the constellation of the Southern Cross blazing above us, we were exhausted, spent, and totally at peace. We put on our warm clothes and stood around the dying embers of the sacred fire holding hands. We hugged one another.

I can't claim for myself that the sweat lodge ceremony was a spiritual experience that could in any way be compared to my 'Everlasting Moment' on the banks of the Amazon; I felt no link to a divinity or a cosmic consciousness. What I *did* feel was that I was in touch with something much older and wiser than myself; there was a race memory of a harmony with the earth, with other people, of being at peace with myself and in balance.

Alan had thoroughly 'enjoyed' the ceremony, and couldn't wait for the next lodge the following day. He felt good, and also at peace with himself.

Tim also performs other Native American traditional ceremonies. Every summer he goes sundancing, a ceremony he learned from the Sioux people, the Lakota. He has also sundanced in the southern part of Colorado with the Ute Indians.

'In Germany, I dance the Earth Dance. We often don't realise just how much the earth gives us. Our food comes from her, our materials for the clothes we wear, the energy we use, everything comes from Mother Earth. We just take from her and don't give back. So we have an Earth Dance and we ask that the earth be healed. Those who take part in the dance make a commitment to go on a vision quest or on a heal first, before the dance starts.

'The ceremony begins on the fifteenth of June. Before we go in to dance there are a lot of activities – such as preparing the land. Participants don't eat or drink for four days before the ceremony, and rise before sunrise and undergo a two-door sweat. They dance all day during the sunlight time, and each evening they quit and sweat again. When everything is ready we light a sacred fire which will burn day and night for seven days. If it's cloudy we use flint to light the fire. If it's not then we ask the sun to light it.

'During the dance we plant trees. There's one tree in the centre, an oak, and around this oak tree we plant seven rose bushes to represent the woman – Mother Earth. On the outer circle we plant two times twenty-eight white birch trees. These will grow with the people each year the ceremony continues. We pray for the earth, we pray for the people who are polluting the earth.'

Tim is beginning his ninth year of the Earth Dance in Germany.

'The European people have become very strong at it now. But I'm nearing the end of my time there. The spirits say that I only have so much time left there and then I must move on somewhere else. I don't know where. The spirits will tell me.'

Tim's totem animal is an eagle. The very first time he constructed a turtle sweat lodge in Southern Africa was also in the foothills of the Maluti Mountains. After the work was done the workers rested and waited for the sun to go down before the ceremony could start. As the tired little group sat there, a huge eagle soared over the mountain peaks and slowly circled around the place where they were sitting. Tim knows the eagle was sent as a sign of the Great Spirit's blessing and approval – as confirmation that his work in Africa was important.

Tim talked about his own quest for spirituality.

'When I was back in my country, Canada, when I went back to the village where I was born, everybody said, "He's back!" The whole village was tense. They call me the Miracle Child or the Wonder Child because I didn't get killed as the rest of my family did. But I don't want to live in that kind of environment because there are a lot of factions and families who might think I've come back for revenge. I'm not interested in those kind of things.'

The day after the sweat lodge I sat alone with Tim and asked him how and where his spiritual journey had begun.

'It's very difficult for me to tell you how it all began, because it's something that's in you. You have sequences of experiences in life which are very difficult to talk about, very difficult. It's hard to express in words what really happens. Because it's an emotional feeling when you are in contact with the Divine Light and communing with God – you know everything, you know the universe, you know how everything came to be, but there aren't words to really describe it. It just is. It's love, maybe. That's why I bring people together in the Theatre of Ceremony and hope that one of them may be touched by it. Maybe all will.'

I thought again of my own Everlasting Moment in the hut on the Amazon, of my own precious communion with something beyond our present reality.

What would Tim say to someone who wants to start a spiritual quest?

'Every person is different. I can't say you must do this or do that. I just say, well, what's holding you? Why can't you let go? What is it that you want to know? I've noticed that a lot of people in the Caucasian world who start a spiritual quest are interested in the power it could give them. The power over other people. That's wrong. It's the power that they will find in and for themselves that's important.

'I've observed that many people who come into this area of a spiritual quest are people who need help. They've lost touch with their emotions, their family values, and they need to find some sense of themselves – they need to be grounded, to identify with this world. So often they are lost and caught up in the rat race and realise there's no meaning to that. Everybody's running after the illusion.

'So if you're looking for a spiritual way it often means that you've come to the last point in your life where you really want to believe in something so you can feel good about yourself, so you can make some form of contribution to the human race, to Mother Earth, to whatever it is you believe in. And it's important that you find somebody, the Dalai Lama, a *sangoma*, a shaman, a regular priest – whoever – who will let you communicate your thoughts and feelings and then say to you, "Why don't you try this?" or "Why don't you try that?" Don't talk to somebody who says you *have* to do this and you *have* to do that. I don't like anybody who instils fear in people. To me that's working on the dark side. I don't like fear. I believe that people who use fear to draw people into their belief system, or hold out Heaven and Hell as promises or threats, are dangerous and life-destroying.

'The person you choose to listen to or to be your mentor should have enough life and spirit experience so they can understand where you're coming from. Then that experience can be used to nurture you and to heal you. Maybe a sweat lodge, or a smudging ceremony, or even just talking will be the beginning of your quest. But first you've got to actively seek that spiritual way.'

We talked for a long time about the way we live our lives today. How we're all scurrying and hurrying and rushing about and don't take time out to assess, to think, to wonder, to take advantage of what we have. Buddhists would say go into yourself, find emptiness, and in that way find peace. The Dalai Lama would suggest that being aware of the inter-connectedness of all things is the starting point. Tim says that most people have lost their identity in this strange world we live in.

'Because we live in a world of illusions, we have lost contact with what's real,' said Tim. 'So many people want to feel some kind of emotion or have some kind of contact. Because everybody is running around making money, they've often lost physical, emotional contact with their kids. So family values have deteriorated. So we end up with all these crazy kids on the street who are looking for love, and they don't get it, so they get into drugs or prostitution or whatever. We're really in a big mess today. And we're all responsible. Everybody's responsible. We've created this society. Now we have to clean it up.

'Don't forget, whoever you are, that there's a part of you that's continuously in contact with the universe. The problem is we think, think, think. We think too much. What we need to do is to listen. There's a special sound your body makes when you're meditating – it's called a hum – almost like the hum of an electrical transformer. Listen for it.

'We're all connected to the Universe all the time but we don't always hear that sound, because we're preoccupied. But be quiet, go to a quiet place, try to meditate and you will hear that hum. Then you will know that you are connected to the Universe.'

When Tim finishes his work in Europe he hopes to return to the Canadian mountains where he had his first mystical experience.

'I was in communion with God, I knew everything, I understood everything. But because nobody had told me about such experiences I didn't even begin to understand them. I didn't know what was going on, what it all meant.'

It's not easy to know 'What is going on', 'What it all means', as we live our lives. Tim was finally shown his spiritual way because he searched for it. I believe that there's a lesson to be learned from Tim if we can heed some of his advice. The essence of his message and his experience was this:

Purify yourself in whatever way seems most appropriate for you. Listen to the Universe and realise that there is a continuous connection. Listen also to your heart. Find a mentor or guide who will help you seek your way – not one who will be judgemental and prescriptive, but one who will counsel you to seek your own way.

> *Caminante, no hay camino,*
> *Se hace camino al andar.*

> *Traveller, there is no path,*
> *Paths are made by walking.*

THIRTEEN

Marching to a Different Drum

There's More To Life Than Surface – what does that mean? Alan asks Kate.

'What do you think it means?'

'Don't know. Don't even know what the surface is. Would you like a chapter from me?'

'Only if I have the right of refusal after I've read it.'

'The problem is that I don't have any dramatic tales to tell. No mind-bending, earth-shattering spiritual revelations. No deep convictions even.'

'So you're just Joe Soap – the ordinary man?'

'That's me.'

'But you've always had ready explanations for everything, from birth to death, and everything in between.'

'It isn't so much that I've got explanations, it's that I don't accept the usual off-the-shelf explanations all that easily.'

Alan continues his story.

And that's true enough. I'm not impressed by the flood

of books that bring us ever more sensational revelations about the Bible, about the Meaning of Life, about Life after Death, about amazing codes, numbers and ciphers that will enable us to reinterpret earlier sacred documents, about experiences in previous existences . . .

I'm not convinced there is a life after death. Joe Soap and Doubting Thomas all rolled into one.

*

I'm five years old. It's winter. In Newcastle, Northern Ireland, perched on a strip between the sea and the Mountains of Mourne, the winter winds shriek and howl down from the mountains, churn the ocean into an uncontained fury, buffet the trees until they jig in a frenzied dance.

I lie in my bed, listening to the wind, and grappling with the difficult concepts of space, time, death and infinity. I dare say almost every child has this experience. When my mind starts to crack under the impossibility of the task, I wrench away, terrified, and probably never again have such a profoundly philosophical few moments in the entire rest of my life. Certainly never come any nearer to an understanding.

Now I'm eight years old. I'm walking down the narrow cement path that bisects our backyard. It's summer time. The path is veined with rocks and fissures – my father is no more of a handyman than I turn out to be. An ant scurries out of one of these cracks, at that frantic pace common to all ants. My foot is committed, in mid-air, and I cannot arrest it in time to save the ant's life. Suddenly, the world comes to an end for that ant. Everything else goes on as before, the grass keeps on growing, the distant call of a cuckoo still pulses in the warm air, but that ant is no more. Now here's what was, just a moment ago, a sentient creature, impelled by its genes to scurry around as the very personification of the work ethic – I won't say that it had hopes, fears and ambitions – but it was certainly holding its place in the great scheme of things, if there is a Great Scheme of Things. Now, suddenly, that's all changed.

I experience a dazzling moment of comprehension. For ant, read man. Something in our nature, some basic arrogance, finds it difficult – impossible for many of us – to accept that we can be snuffed out, as finally and as inconsequentially as that ant. If we have no difficulty in comprehending the ant's fate, why should it be so hard to see ourselves in the same way? When that immense foot falls on us, there is only darkness.

Not even darkness, but nothingness.

So is there an overall plan, or is it all totally random? At the detailed level, it seems random. If that ant had paused to investigate something before coming out of the crack, if I had stumbled a few paces before my fateful step, or a million other 'ifs', that ant would have met a different end. If John's secretary hadn't bungled his flight booking, he wouldn't have been on that plane . . . If Susan had come round that corner a fraction of a second later . . .

Half a century after ending that ant's life, I recount the episode to my friend Mark. We're sitting in the Kusi Runa Hotel in Cusco, Peru. Cusco is a very spiritual place, as is all of Peru.

What does that mean, 'a very spiritual place'? It means lay lines, spiritual concentrations, vortices of energy, a resonance of history and great antiquity. It also means standing on the edge of a vast amphitheatre high up in the mountains and watching credulous tourists holding metal rods that apparently move of their own volition. I would need a much more convincing demonstration of the presence of spirits, but it's true that there is an 'atmosphere' to Peru.

But would I have felt that atmosphere if I didn't know anything about Peru's history, or the Quechua religion or gods? Did the conquistadores feel it as they raped and pillaged their way towards a place in the history of colonialism? Would I still be unable to travel without a shudder through Glencoe in Scotland's highlands, without the hairs prickling on the back of my neck, if I had never heard of the massacre of the Macdonalds by the Campbells?

Yes to all of the above, because I certainly do believe that 'atmospheres' exist and that you can sense them without knowing the reasons for their existence. And I believe that many happenings and circumstances cast a long shadow, often *before* they occur as well as after.

But I do not know why.

I do not know why, when my grandmother kissed her sons goodbye as one by one they departed for service in the First World War, she cried only when the youngest one left. Not because he was the youngest, but because she knew she would not see him again.

But to get back to Cusco and Mark. When I recount the saga of the ant, and use it to expound my idea that it isn't so difficult to conceive of life in the here and now, and only the here and now, with no hereafter, Mark stares at me in astonishment.

'But surely you don't deny that you have a soul?' he asks.

And in this time, in this place of Cusco, no, I don't deny the existence of my soul.

But neither do I confirm it.

A number of things bother me about the idea of a master

plan and a master planner. One of them is that I accept that a master plan does not have to be understandable to us, and that the planner may have designs and objectives we cannot even dream of, but notwithstanding this, I have a real problem.

This problem is, why should it be necessary to torment mankind with the unknown? Why should there be any doubt about miracles or angels, about heaven and hell, about life hereafter, about good and evil? Why riddles and parables and mysteries and maybes? Think of the torment suffered by millions upon millions of people because of this lack of certainty. Think of the appalling cruelty of countless unending religious wars.

I have put this question to a number of ministers of various religious persuasions (interesting that we use the word 'persuasion' in this context), and I believe I have always received the same answer. It runs along the lines of 'Your faith has to be tested. It is a crucial test of your faith that you should believe in the master planner without concrete evidence, and that's what "faith" means.'

This is one huge cop-out of an answer. No one can refute it, any more than anyone can prove it. It totally begs the question of 'Why?' Wouldn't a god of infinite compassion and love *show* some compassion, and not make the state of believing so very difficult to attain?

Reincarnation? The only comment I'll make is that there are no convincing first-hand accounts of remembering a previous life. Some cranks lay claims, and quite a few charlatans, I've met some of them on Kate's radio programme *Believe It Or Not*, but the world still awaits proof. So, if you cannot remember an earlier life, what difference does it make whether you ever had one or not?

I develop as a solitary and introspective child. I have little in common with children of my own age. I become so reclusive and anti-social that it's practically a disease. But you have to have something, and in the absence of friends I turn to nature. I get to know every tree and rock in the Mourne Mountains. Winter and summer, in fine weather or storms, I roam the mountains. My conversation is with the soughing of the trees and the babble of the streams. I come to feel a full oneness with the grasses, trees and rocks. I reach out and clasp the trunk of a tree and feel the life surging within it. A granite rock breathes to me.

There is nothing unique in this, many children have a strong affinity with nature. Wordsworth had a theory about it, claiming that as babies we come 'trailing clouds of glory, from God who is our home', but that as we grow older we lose this ability to commune with the natural universe. Be that as it may, it's clear that there exists a dimension of understanding, of love and comprehension, that transcends our mundane patterns. 'Less sophisticated' societies are often so close to nature that their spiritual world and their everyday world are indistinguishable from one another. They are not only indistinguishable, they are one and the same. The Native Americans, the Quechua in Peru, the San in the Kalahari, their spiritual worlds, and the spiritual worlds of so many other cultures and societies, are every bit as real as any other world.

So, yes, I'm cynical. I don't believe in ghosts, however well documented, and I won't until I have a personal encounter with one. And if that should ever happen, I'd look for some scientific explanation, some method of transmuting those vibes that I know exist, that give us 'atmospheres', those shadows that are thrown by events and happenings, some scientific explanation akin to radio waves or television pictures.

The idea of reincarnation is ludicrous to me. The concept of life after death is something that I cannot handle intellectually.

Look at it this way, is it really likely that I will meet up with loved ones, my parents, my brothers and sisters, my wife, my children, my friends? Even dogs and horses I have known? (Isn't it significant that practically all the major religions, with the exception of the Hindu, keep pretty quiet on the subject of animals in the life hereafter?) I also cannot accept that as we ascend into a state of grace – if we deserve to – then we'll all be unrecognisable. Without flaws and foibles and imperfections, what would we be? Unrecognisable even to ourselves. And if the rapists and perverts and murderers are going to have their acts cleaned up, be forgiven, and in due course be accepted into the Elysian Fields, then I don't want to know them in their new state any more than in their terrestrial one.

There's a thing called the 'Right to Life' that has been taken up like a mantra. It is quoted as if it's an obvious, God-given law. Why should this be assumed, what evidence is there of such a law? The same rapists and perverts and murderers will go along happily with the concept of such a law, for obvious reasons. I see no reason to give them the protection of such a law in the next world, any more than in this one.

I've got just as many problems with the more prescriptive religions, such as Catholicism and Islam, which say that we have to earn our places in the hereafter. The better we behave in this world, the better off we'll be in the next. Just look at all those believers stashing away their Green Shield Stamps, storing up for the Big Prize. And one of the problems with this is that good and bad are comparative terms – it would be ironic to find that we struggle to comply with all the tenets of our faith only to find that we've got it all wrong and miss the cut-off anyway.

If I suggest that little of religious theory or dogma is really for the thinking person, this doesn't, however, mean that life itself is nothing but a vale of tears. There is joy to be found in nature, and in human relationships – joy which is no more explicable in scientific terms than is religion. My heart *does* dance with the daffodils, whether I will it to or not.

And this simple fact links in with that issue I was side-stepping earlier. At a detailed level, all events seem happenstance and unplanned. But is there another level? Is the macro picture any different to the micro? If there is, for me, an acceptance that I am moved by influences that are not understandable at the level my mind is able to operate on, is it possible that there is a whole dimension of life that I understand only very dimly, if at all?

The answer is an unequivocal 'yes'. It isn't only possible, it's certain. And in this other dimension, maybe patterns can be discerned. I hesitate to ascribe them to a master plan, but on rare occasions we can tune in to a different wavelength and hear the beat of a different drum, one that is enormously mysterious and exciting.

I'm a few years older. I'm standing with another boy in a clearing in the woods. I'm holding a long stick which I repeatedly raise and lower.

'I wonder,' I muse, 'if I did this for a thousand years, and then I stopped doing it, would this stick then remain still, or would it keep on rising and falling?'

'Are you mad?' asks my down-to-earth companion. 'Of course that stick won't move when you stop causing it to move. How could it?'

It's now half a century since I stood idly waving that stick, and I still don't know the answer. I suppose I've learned that there are more things in heaven and earth, never mind anywhere else, than I have dreamed of in my philosophy.

I'm twenty-five years old. I'm a serving officer in the British Army. I'm seconded to the Royal Nigerian Army, stationed in the humid tropical Nigerian jungle, and in 1960 the battalion is ordered to move to the Cameroons where there is a 'political' problem. I'm a platoon commander in a rifle company commanded by a no-nonsense Scot. We're in the midst of preparations for the move which will be several hundred miles by truck on poor roads.

The company barber requests an interview with the company commander. The barber says he doesn't want to go to the Cameroons. The company commander is unsympathetic, pointing out that none of the soldiers wants to interrupt a fairly comfortable lifestyle to journey to the unknown and dangerous Cameroons. But the barber, an old Nigerian, is a civilian, and cannot be ordered to come with us. However, he needs his job, so a lot of pressure can be brought to bear. The conversation is conducted through an interpreter, and I'm an interested spectator. Basically it boils down to no Cameroons, no job.

The barber is really distressed, explaining that he knows if he goes to the Cameroons he won't return to Nigeria.

'Nonsense,' says the company commander, running out

of patience. So the barber comes with us, unwillingly and unhappy.

The first day on the road, one of the three-ton trucks fails to negotiate a bad bend, overturns and rolls over and over down a slope. There are about thirty soldiers in the truck, plus the barber. Only one man is killed. The barber, of course.

Now you can say it's coincidence, but it didn't seem like that at the time. The old barber, pleading piteously, had been adamant. There were no two ways about it, he would not return to Nigeria if he went to the Cameroons.

Coincidence? For barber, read ant? Or an instance of an event casting its shadow before it occurs? How can this happen? Can there be a scientific explanation? So far there isn't one, but that old barber didn't need one.

It's a year or so later. I'm sent to the Congo, subsequently called Zaire, and now the Republic of Congo. Formerly a Belgian colony, the Belgian military have pulled out with unseemly haste when the Belgian government detected a ground swell of nationalistic fervour. The Congolese soldiers, leaderless without their Belgian officers, mutiny and splinter into various uncoordinated small power factions.

Most of the few remaining Belgian officers are killed, as are many Belgian and Congolese soldiers. Belgium sends in a punitive force of paratroopers, and the situation rapidly deteriorates. The mutineers run amok. Belgian civilians who haven't got out in time are often murdered, rape is an everyday horror, even being a nun is no protection, and the badly disciplined remnants of what had constituted the national army wage bloody war against one another. A hideous reign of terror seizes one of Africa's most beautiful countries. A United Nations peace force is sent into this confused and confusing situation. Nigeria sends a contingent to this peace-keeping force.

In such an unstable setting, we do not know friend from foe, as the balance is continually shifting. We don't know who we're supposed to be protecting, against whom. Which makes for a highly flammable state of affairs.

One example of how dangerous it is takes place in a town called Kindu. The UN force at Kindu is supplied by planes flown by a contingent of Italians. The Italian pilots stay with their clearly distinguishable blue and white planes at the airstrip, some several miles from the nearest UN army personnel. One night the crew are attacked by nearby mutineers. The Italians are hacked to death with pangas. There are many cannibals among the local population and for a few days human fingers are on sale in the market, priced at the rough equivalent of one shilling each.

The UN Security Council, meeting in New York, issues an ultimatum. The murderers are to be identified and delivered to the UN forces by a certain date and time. Failure to do so will result in the bombing of Kindu by UN planes.

On the day that the ultimatum expires, the UN planes, 'bombed-up', are on the runway at a major town called Luluaburg, where our Nigerian brigade is headquartered. The pilots are waiting for the order to take off. Local mutineers from the Armée Nationale du Congo have got wind of this, and some hundreds of them arrive and surround the airfield, threatening to open fire on the planes if they should attempt to take off. Our battalion has already thrown a cordon around the airfield, so now we've got the planes at the centre, a circle of UN troops around them at the airfield perimeter, and a wider circle of mutineers around us. It's a bizarre version of the Mexican stand-off. Tense moments. The order to fly comes over the radio. The planes take off. The Congolese do not open fire, apparently weighing up the pros and cons and deciding that discretion is the better part of valour. As it happens, the Security Council recalls the planes when they are half way to Kindu and no further action is taken.

I tell you about this incident to give you an idea of just how tricky the whole set-up is. Nothing can be taken at face value, here where yesterday's ally can be shooting at you today, where danger can lurk in any innocuous setting, where the most appalling violence can explode spontaneously, where there is no cause and effect.

I quickly come to rely on what we like to call a sixth sense. Time after time I find myself in a situation which is supposed to be delicate and dangerous, but I feel no danger. At other times, say on a routine patrol to a peaceful village, a place where there has never been any trouble and where there is no reason to expect any, I'll sense danger. It feels like hackles rising on the back of my neck. And sure enough, it always turns out that this sense of danger is justified.

I come to trust this sense implicitly, and it's never wrong. It saves my life more than once. What is it? Can it be explained as some sort of logical interpretation of my physical surroundings, a heightened awareness of everything going on around me? Maybe there's a silence when birds should be calling? Or something out of the ordinary in a pattern of light and shade? If so, it isn't a conscious examination of my surroundings that gives me the answer. Can it then be explained by simply saying that there is such a thing as a sense of danger, so palpable a sense that you actually sniff the air to try to detect it?

I don't know, but what I do know, as I scan a jungle track and monitor input from unknown sources, is that here again I am listening to the beat of a different drum. Something other than deductive powers is at work here. I am not for any moment suggesting any kind of divine intervention, all I'm saying is that something is going on that I do not fully understand.

Now it's the 1970s and I'm living with my wife and children in South Africa. We're in a school lift club. Three fathers each do a week's duty in turn, taking the children to school in the mornings whilst the mothers collect them again in the afternoons.

Early one winter's morning I suddenly shoot upright in my bed, waking my wife.

'What's the matter?' she asks.

I explain that I've had a very vivid and upsetting dream. I'm shaking and sweating from this dream. I've dreamed that Reggie, a friend who is in the lift club, has died.

This week it's Reggie's stint with the early morning lift. It's a bitterly cold morning and when Reggie arrives at the gate, with his daughter in the car, I put on my dressing-gown and slippers and track through the heavy frost. While our two girls are getting into the car, I go round to Reggie's window to speak to him.

'How are you keeping, Reggie? Haven't seen you for a long time.'

'Too long, Alan. We must make a plan, get together soon.'

Reggie takes the girls to school, then goes on to his office and blows his brains out.

There's no doubt about the phenomenon of telepathy, we've all experienced it. So maybe Reggie was sending out some sort of signal of his intentions, or at least of his distress? If so, I, and only I, picked it up. And I'm not an imaginative or 'fey' kind of person.

Not long after this I dream that two big dogs belonging to a friend are shot. I haven't even seen these dogs very often. I tell my family about this dream, but I don't tell the woman who owns the dogs. A week or so later, the dogs are shot and killed by a farmer. This dream is a little harder to explain away, because who would be sending any telepathic messages?

Our youngest daughter Tiffany contracts a serious illness when she is seven years old. It is eventually correctly diagnosed as Steven-Johnson syndrome. This condition is consequent to an extreme allergic reaction. In Tiffany's case it is a reaction to any form of sulphur drugs. Before it is diagnosed it reaches life-threatening proportions and she is hospitalised. One of the symptoms is acute itching all over the body. We try everything, bathing her with cold compresses, holding her arms and legs tightly to stop her scratching herself, applying all kinds of lotions and unguents. Nothing works, the itching becomes worse and worse.

Eventually I clasp one of her wrists in one of my hands, one ankle in the other, and what I do is – and I can only describe it in this way – I *transmit love* to her. I can feel my strength flowing into her, like a transfer of something physical. She stops scratching and trying to tear herself to pieces.

I have heard of the Laying on of Hands, but never experienced it, never practised it. When Tiffany is in her twenties, I mention this episode to her, not for one moment expecting that she will remember it because, for one thing, she was gravely ill at the time. To my surprise, she remembers it with total clarity. I do not set out to be any sort of faith healer, nor do I have any idea why I could alleviate her distress. I am certainly not at all conscious of any 'religious' content to the situation.

Now I'm in my sixties. I don't feel any different physically to how I felt in my twenties or thirties. Age is, after all, a state of mind. But now something occurs that brings me up short, that causes me to ask myself where I'm coming from and where I'm going. I ask myself if I've learned anything in the course of my life. I'm forced to admit that the answer is 'no'. I've stumbled across many questions but have found few answers. There is very little I can be certain of. And it's only because my life is now threatened that these questions surface.

What happens is that my wife and I go on a four-day walking trail in the Kruger Park. We have always got away into the wilderness as often as possible. It's a restorative process, visiting the 'bush', better than any potions or pills. Except that this time it isn't. I contract malaria which fast deteriorates to the dreaded cerebral malaria state. Suddenly my life is at risk.

Doctors and nurses battle for my life. I am so doped up and spaced out that most of the time I don't know where I am or what is going on. I experience bouts of relative sanity, separated by hallucinatory raving. During one of these critical phases of the illness I become quite sure that I am dying. This is tough on my family, and particularly on my wife, who for a period of five weeks doesn't know if she's going to find me alive when she arrives at the hospital.

One morning my daughter Tara comes to visit me, accompanied by a friend. This is at a time when often I don't recognise even close members of my family, but this morning, I do recognise Tara. I tell her of a dream I've just dreamed. Such a clear dream. I've dreamed that I'm walking through a most beautiful garden, lush and exotic, with the beautiful music of many songbirds. The further I walk into this garden, the more beautiful and enticing it becomes.

I believe that this is in many ways a classic Near-Death experience. But the end of the dream is that I turn around and retrace my steps, out of the garden. Not of my own volition, I tell Tara, it's as if I'm externally programmed.

Now we come to something of an anti-climax. When my wife visits me at midday, she at once mentions the dream I've described to Tara and her friend.

'What dream?' I ask.

I have no recollection of it. To this day, I can remember telling Tara about the dream, but I cannot remember the dream itself. Another inconclusive conclusion.

In hospital, during the more rational interludes, I try to sort out my mind on a number of matters. When it becomes clear that, against the odds, I am not going to die, I ask the question 'Why not?' I still don't know the answer to that one. Some of the nurses inform me sagely that I must have unfinished business, but if so I don't know what it is. When I think I'm dying, I regret many things, but that hardly fits into the category of unfinished business. I regret that I won't again see Tiffany, our youngest daughter, who is studying in America. I would have liked to say goodbye. But otherwise, I can't really think of a lot of unfinished business.

There are regrets, certainly. I regret the times when I've

hurt people's sensitivities, by being insensitive myself. I regret things I've done, things I've said and, particularly, things I've thought. I regret many lost opportunities to show compassion and understanding. I do regret hurts I've caused, sometimes unintentionally, sometimes intentionally. And I very much regret that I didn't keep in closer touch with my parents when they were alive, or with my brothers and sisters. Now two of them are dead and I never told them how much I loved them.

I'm discharged from hospital and gradually regain my health. I keep running over the years of my life in my mind, and realise that running through the whole fabric is a strong thread of personal and family relationships. And these relationships are what it's really all about.

I receive a letter from one sister. She has found a few old photographs, taken in Ireland, and has had them restored and enlarged. I look at the faces of half a century ago. I see young and carefree faces. I see a sunny day that I remember, the corner of a shed, an ancient lawnmower. And in those faces I see the inheritance that is mine, and will be my children's, and my children's children.

I see the same thing on my wife's side. I see the continuity of generations. I look backwards at mothers, fathers, parents, grandparents, great-grandparents, and back into the depths of time. My mind fast-forwards to the present. My youngest great-niece is just over a year old and she is so like her dead grandmother – my sister – that I cannot take my eyes off her. Not alike only in looks, but also in expressions, gestures and vibrations. When I'm in the company of youngsters, family members, I'll see a forehead that reminds me of a grandfather. I'll hear a certain laugh and I'm catapulted back to a different place, a different time, a different country, but the same laugh.

And an idea begins to form of what life is really all about.

Any earlier effort on my part to detect a pattern or a purpose has failed. I am no closer to the meaning of it all than I was when I was a child of five struggling with the concepts of time, space and infinity. I do not know if there is a life after death, if I have a soul, or if there is a heaven.

No, I don't have any dramatic tales to tell. The only conclusion I have reached is not original. William Shakespeare expressed it very well some four hundred years ago:

> And nothing 'gainst Time's scythe can make defence
> Save breed, to brave him when he takes thee hence.

We're all going to die. But all of our forebears live through us, and each of us will have what amounts to eternal life through our children and our descendants. And that, somewhat strangely, can be as comforting as any religion or belief. It gives purpose to our existence. It makes us immortal.

A few months before I contract cerebral malaria, Kate and I go to Peru.

My personal experiences in Peru are interesting, surprising, confusing, frightening, even comical. But not spiritual.

Take our time spent in the Amazon, for example.

Here we are on the banks of the Amazon, a mixed bag of travellers. Myself, Kate, and seven others.

The night before our rendezvous with the shaman Felipe, our group leader Carol has introduced us to the concept of 'Power Animals'. We sit on the banks of the river. It's an environment conducive to strange happenings, I must say.

After a full eclipse of the moon there's now bright moonlight once again, not a breath of wind, the timeless Amazon flowing silently past.

Carol asks us to commune with our power animals. Sure enough, as I sit there concentrating on nothing, my animal appears. An African elephant. He is old, wise and benign. I have walked along a path to meet him, having first seen him at a distance. Nothing else happens. It's a clear case of self-hypnosis, auto-suggestion.

The following night we meet with a shaman in a little wooden hut at the back of the camp. Felipe is an *ayahuascero*, a shaman who conducts indigenous healing ceremonies using ayahuasca, a sacred plant that has been used for healing in the Amazon for thousands to years.

I'm talking about only my own experience. I'm not going to describe the others in the group, or their experiences or behaviour; Kate will do that when she writes of her own experiences in the little wooden hut.

Suffice to say, I march off with the others to the little hut in the bright moonlight and I suppose I'm the only one of us who is motivated by nothing more than curiosity. I don't have any questions to be answered, any spiritual troubles to be eased, any great mysteries clamouring for explanations, not even a headache or a backache or any health problems that I'm aware of. Jaunty, I suppose, is the word I would use to describe my attitude.

We sit around in the hut and it's all very quiet so there's immediately an atmosphere, a sense of expectancy. This sense is heightened by the shaman's presence. He is ageless, serious, wise and benign, and the strength of his personality is immediately stamped on the evening.

I toss back my first cup of ayahuasca. It doesn't taste too

bad and as I don't feel any immediate effects I waste no time in downing another. Now I sit back and make myself receptive to whatever is to come.

After a few moments I find myself standing to one side of a large field. A long straight row of yellow sunflowers faces me from the opposite side of the field. All the sunflowers are bobbing and dancing in the sunlight. Then the sunflowers change into sheep, all standing up on their hind legs, forelegs linked, all weaving and dancing and laughing. It's a kind of Disney's *Fantasia* scenario.

I'm enjoying this, but it starts to change. The sheep metamorphose into different creatures. Not animals as we know animals, just creatures. They become menacing, they approach me, they swarm around me. I back into a room but the creatures are there, crawling out of cracks, fluttering against windows. I can only describe them as demons because they resemble those demons you used sometimes to see in children's books – horns, pointed ears, cloven hoofs and so on. And very, very menacing. They give me a hard time, until I'm able to force myself back into the 'real' world. Now when I look around, the demons have gone – except for one or two squeaking in a corner – but my companions have changed. Some have enormously long noses or chins, some have great tall pointed heads, and they've all got claws instead of hands.

All except my wife Kate, who looks kind, serene and very beautiful.

Now the shaman spends a lot of time on me. He sings, a most soothing sort of crooning, he blows pipe smoke on to my head, he massages my scalp. Eventually, through an interpreter, he explains that my head is too full of complex thoughts and that is why I'm having such a difficult time.

In a few hours I'm more or less back to normal, although my vision remains distorted for quite a while, with people's faces only gradually losing their grotesque features. When I describe this experience afterwards to a friend, he tells me it sounds like being high on LSD, when he has seen cars flying through the air and so on.

The experience is highly unpleasant. Startling. Frightening even. But not spiritual. It is unlike any other experience I have ever had, but I don't feel anything spiritual about it.

I find the entire Peru experience absolutely enthralling. I love the mountains, the high plains, the Amazon and its jungles.

I admit to a feeling of something which I call 'atmosphere' in many places. In Machu Picchu, certainly, a place where the presence of people who have been there before is tangible. At the great temple of Ollantaytambo also, with its hundreds of steps, where you wonder how it can all have been achieved. Did they have a technology, thousands of years ago, that the world has since lost? Almost certainly, because no other explanation has been found as to how such building was achieved. The immense silence that pervades so many of these places certainly adds to the atmosphere.

Another day, high up in the mountains, we walk down hundreds of feet into a vast amphitheatre. It is allegedly one of those vortices of energy that have been identified in many places in Peru. I look at the others in our group, earnestly taking turns to hold divining rods and practically dancing to the vibrations given off by the rods. I see nothing that I feel is not driven by the holder's imagination.

But atmosphere, yes. And I'll go as far as to believe it's possible that events of long ago, and personalities of people who are dead, can leave an imprint on the atmosphere of a place.

I would not believe it *impossible* that future events could do the same, because chronological time and space seem to present certain attributes which so far have eluded scientific explanation. But I think that most – and probably all – of what we cannot explain today will be explicable in purely natural, physical terms as our knowledge of the natural universe becomes more and more developed.

Like everyone else, I suppose, I have faced life's enigmas and recognised only my own lack of knowledge and experience.

But even if we haven't got explanations, we've got life itself. Tragic and sad sometimes, but often stimulating, challenging, exciting. Joyous.

FOURTEEN

The Everlasting Moment

It is on the banks of the Amazon, under a blood red moon, that I meet my golden lioness. I later find out from Gareth that the lioness was Furaha. It was her spirit that had returned to me.

The day after the eclipse, Manuel the young engineering student who is our guide at the Amazon camp, takes us on a walk through the jungle.

We climb back into the long wooden canoe that brought us here from Puerto Maldonado, and chug off upstream to where the trail begins. On the way we make detours into narrow backwaters of the great river to look for birds.

Manuel clutches an old, tattered, illustrated bird book and tells us how he has taught himself the different species and their calls. In South Africa we have a brightly coloured red and green bird called the Narina Trogon which is on every birdwatcher's 'wish-list'. In the forest today we hear the calls of five different trogons. Manuel tells us there are seventeen different kinds of trogons in Peru.

As we glide along a creek bordered by huge trees and overhanging vines, a small, handsome, chestnut-coloured bird swims along beside us. It is the Sun Grebe. On my return to South Africa, I tell one of my friends, a top ornithologist, about the grebe. He splutters his disbelief. He led a birding expedition from Africa to the South American jungles especially to see this bird, among others. They never saw it.

The canoe finally comes to a stop at a bank where the beginnings of a trail lead off into the jungle. A constant, vibrant hum surrounds us – creatures calling, insects thrumming, things growing. We walk for about an hour, marvelling at the mighty trees, the exotic plants, the insects, flowers, and perhaps most of all, the butterflies. There are huge turquoise blue ones, others of pink, white, orange and brown, and fluttering crowds of tiny yellow ones which rise and fall about the muddy puddles along the way. Sue counts twenty different species in the first hour.

At the end of the trail is a small village of palm-thatched huts at the edge of a big fresh water lake – the only such lake in this part of the Amazon. It is some sort of public holiday and a party of about fifty excited, chattering schoolchildren are also here to swim in the lake. Heaven knows where they have come from. We change into our swimsuits behind some trees, climb into a small canoe, and set out for the middle of the lake. A very small crocodile basking on the muddy bank eyes us unblinkingly. Once in the middle of the lake, we climb over the sides of the canoe and have a swim. The water is cool and refreshing after our sweaty walk through the steaming jungle.

Joy, who is terrified of crocodiles and is nervous about any kind of physical danger, romps in the water like one of the schoolchildren. Later, as we chug along the river on the journey back to our camp, she suddenly remarks, almost as if she was thinking out loud: 'You know, I've always been scared – scared of snakes, scared of heights, scared of criticism, scared of all sorts of things. But on this trip I haven't been scared of anything. Like today, my fears seem to have left me. Gone completely.'

Back in camp after a meal of fresh fish and rough-textured root vegetables, we walk back along the wooden walkways to our cabins on stilts. On each veranda is a woven grass hammock, swinging invitingly in the breeze coming off the river.

I pick up my book, climb into the hammock and begin to read. I'm reading an adventure story. In the middle of the nineteenth century, Jules Crevaux, a French naval surgeon, explored part of the Amazon and Orinoco basins. In 1880, the French magazine *Le Tour du Monde* published his adventures in a series of lithographs, one of which I was now reading.

> *A rushed journey is a waste of time; you can see nothing. I am here by the grace of God; I must take advantage of it and examine nature carefully, for I shall never return to these waters again. Instinct tells me to let myself drift with the swift current. Reason stops me; for an explorer, hurrying through an unknown land is like running away from the enemy.*

I put down the book. Questions race through my mind. I stare through the great trees towards the river. The flock of small green parrots which we had disturbed on our arrival is flying in and out of their nesting holes in the muddy riverbank. They are focused, intent on their purpose.

Have I been hurrying through an unknown land? Not

only here in Peru, but during my life's journey?

In a way, yes.

Has my reason, like that of the French explorer, stopped me from assimilating and absorbing what I have seen with my eyes, felt in my soul? Is perhaps my old reality being superseded by a newer reality – a reality that is now telling me to put aside cynicism, to open my mind completely, to recover and recognise the milestones in my spiritual journey, and as Wordsworth suggested in his *Preface to the Lyrical Ballads* to make 'a willing suspension of disbelief'?

But a lifetime of intellectual study, academic discipline, reasoned argument and a kind of sheer bloody-mindedness still stand in my way.

That night we meet the shaman Felipe, the *ayahuascero*. He is to conduct an indigenous healing ceremony with us, using ayahuasca, the sacred healing plant that has been used by the Amazon shamans for thousands of years. No one in our group knows anything about the ceremony nor the plant to be used. We are totally ignorant of any procedures, have done no reading on the subject, have met no one who has been involved in such a ceremony. You might say that we were in a state of perfect innocence.

However, we've already taken part in another shamanic ceremony – on our first night in Peru in the cold, candle-lit cave above Cusco – have soaked up the spiritual energies of the Temples of the Sun at the holy places of Pisaq and Ollantaytambo, have meditated in the great stone circles of Moray and corresponded, each in our own way – Christian, Jewish, Buddhist, agnostic, New Ager, Old Soul, disbeliever and unbeliever – with our own religious beliefs at the *Intiwatana*, the Hitching Post of the Sun at Machu Picchu.

We are ready for anything.

At the back of this jungle camp, set apart from the other buildings is an old wooden hut. As darkness falls, our small group – once strangers, now friends – makes its way to the hut. Inside the bare room are two wooden beds, each with a hard mattress covered by a threadbare blanket. There is no other furniture of any kind.

Carol has told us that the ceremony may take hours, so I choose to sit on one of the beds. Next to me sits Big Carol. Sue and Wilma sit on the bed opposite. Alan, Gordon, Mark, and Carol, who is to act as interpreter, sit on the wooden floor. Joy, whose newfound courage seems to have deserted her and who now appears to be in an anxious state, sits at the foot of my bed.

The only light comes from the moonlight shining through the ill-fitting planks of the cabin walls. The mighty river booms softly outside. There are night noises – birds, insects, small jungle creatures.

Carol tells us to use the ayahuasca ceremony as an opportunity – an opportunity to ask the spirits, the divinity, whomsoever, for something we think we need; to be cured; to learn something about our lives, their meaning and purpose. Whatever.

'Ask whatever you need to know.'

A short, lean man in jeans and T-shirt comes quietly through the door. In the dim light it's difficult to guess his age, but he's not an old man, nor a young one. He puts his bits and pieces of ceremonial regalia on the floor and sits down beside it. Before a word is spoken, as his eyes are becoming accustomed to the faint light, he points to my husband Alan, and says something in Spanish to Carol.

'Felipe says you have something wrong in your chest. There's a sickness there.'

A couple of months ago, Alan, who had never been ill in his life, had suffered a bad bout of pneumonia.

Carol tells Felipe our names, but nothing else. After studying us closely, Felipe gives us each in turn a small glass of a thick, viscous-looking, red liquid which he pours out of a large Coke bottle. He measures each tot with the precision of a pharmacist preparing a prescription. One by one we drink, handing back the empty glass to be refilled for the next person. When my turn comes, I reach out for the glass, but at the last moment, Felipe takes it back, looks at me intently, and adds a little more of the liquid to the glass. When we have all drunk, Felipe speaks to us through Carol.

'You will remember every detail of this experience. If you keep your eyes closed you will stay in the other world. When you open them you will be back in the hut. You may open and close your eyes at will.'

At this point, Joy, who has taken only a tiny sip of the sacred medicine, gives a little strangled cry, gets to her feet and leaves us. She does not come back.

Felipe tells us that for his people there is no gap between the real world and the world of dreams, day and night, the seen and the unseen. I think of the Aboriginal Elders, Barney and Alfred, and recall their almost exact philosophy of life. Everything is equally real and has equal validity. I think of Alice, who found it quite natural to step through the looking-glass of surface reality to the other reality beyond.

For the next hour or so we sit silently listening to Felipe as he sings, prays and blows smoke over us. He calls upon the Christian god, the spirits, the *apukuna*, Pachamama, a whole pantheon of gods and goddesses to help and direct us. He is no longer Felipe from the Amazon jungle, but the shaman, the guide of souls, who can take leave of his body and cross over from the visible world to the invisible world.

As Carol suggested, I make a personal request. No, I'm not going to share with you what I asked for from the spirits, the divinity, the whomsoever or whatever. Maybe later you may guess. But I *will* share with you what happened to me.

It's dark because my eyes are closed. I feel very peaceful sitting here. I wonder what the others are doing?

I open my eyes and have a quick look. Everybody is sitting quietly with tightly closed eyes. Mark and Sue are sitting in the lotus position of yoga. I close my eyes again. After what seems quite a long time my darkness begins to light up.

I can see bright, bright colours. Colours of an impossibly unnatural brightness. Psychedelic colours. Glowing purples, dazzling pinks, iridescent greens, glowing oranges, bright golds. Images are beginning to form. Look, there's a mosaic floor of beaten gold – a bit like Yeats' Byzantium – and here's the face of a Byzantine Madonna, long, lugubrious, dark. Here's the face of a Christian saint. There's a bejewelled Russian icon.

Suddenly thousands upon thousands of images rush into my sight at an uncontrollable, indescribable speed. They become subliminal. Many of them are traditional religious images but seem alien and unfamiliar because of their artificially bright, psychedelic colours.

Strange that all these shapes and forms have a religious look. I wonder if I'm seeing these images because of all I've learned through the four years of *Believe It or Not*? I suppose I've been immersed in this kind of thing for a long time. Mmm, probably. Well, let's see what happens. Problem is I'm not really enjoying these colours. They're sort of phoney.

A word comes into my head that I haven't seen or used

for years – *meretricious*, meaning showy, falsely attractive, unreal.

This is all very well, but I wish I could get outside these colours and visions. I much prefer the natural world. This all seems a bit claustrophobic.

The images continue in split second sequence to fill up my vision. Time no longer has any meaning. I continue to experience colours, dots, lines of dazzling lightning all interspersed with religious images – candles, saints, golden icons, statues.

Suddenly an owl appears at the top of the frame. I give a sigh of relief. I have always had a special place in my heart for owls. Many people see them as omens of death and doom, but from the time I was a small child, I have loved owls – loved to hear them calling, loved to watch their soft, silent flight, always felt comforted by their presence.

'Hello, owl. I'm glad to see you.' He is sitting with his wings slightly held out from his body and is looking straight at me. I look back at him. Then he disappears. The shapes, forms, images and brilliant colours continue at a frenetic pace. This same owl will appear three times during this stage of my experience, and each time I take comfort and think, 'Thank goodness for something natural in the midst of all this psychedelic stuff.'

Quite suddenly the images and colours vanish. I feel as if I've been given an electric shock. I can see nothing. I sit quite still. At once I am enveloped in a moment of perfect mental lucidity, total clarity. The feeling is so sharp, so crisp, so critical, so unutterably clear, that it's like being back in Antarctica where everything is so pure, so pristine it's as if the world has just been made. I genuinely feel the scales fall from my eyes. I see who I am, my strengths, my weaknesses, my role in life. I see the strengths and weaknesses of my family and friends too, and the part that I play in their lives.

I think, 'Yes, this is it, this is my life's purpose.'

I experience a total acceptance of who and what I am. I feel a great surge of self-respect, respect for life, respect for others. I sit frozen in time and space, all-seeing, all-knowing, very wise.

Then I am engulfed in a feeling of perfect love. I feel love all around me as a physical presence – the love of my family, my friends, everybody I know. And a divine love, a love over and beyond all that I know. I bask in this love, my soul stretches in this all-encompassing love and I am aware, for the first time in my life of how lucky I am.

Then a feeling of such total peace enfolds me that I silently acknowledge, 'Yes, there is a Peace that passeth all under-standing, and this is it.'

I am in touch with the divine.

There are no questions left, no cynicism, no doubt.

I am in a state of perfect happiness, acceptance and peace.

I am sublime.

My whole life has been leading up to this – this is my Everlasting Moment.

I have reached a point in my spiritual journey where I have recognised it for what it is, for what it has been – a series of milestones reached when I was an evacuee, a convent schoolgirl, at Itu Leper Colony, on top of Ayers Rock, with Blind Dan, in the words of the Dalai Lama, and in the holy places of Peru.

My experience lasts for several hours. I have not been in any trance-like state; on the contrary, every now and then I open my eyes to see how the others are doing. Sue sits immobile, in a deep alpha state. Felipe's powerful energies have drawn her into another dimension. Wilma has joined Gordon on the floor. He has had a bad experience. She puts her arms around him and rocks him like a baby. Sobbing quietly, they comfort each other. The next day Wilma tells us that what she had learned during her ayahuasca experience was that she must use her healing touch, which she had used only occasionally in the past, much more often. A gift to be treasured, in the future she should spread her gift much more widely.

The others have all been very quiet, lost in their own experiences.

Suddenly Alan begins to see terrifying visions. Earlier on, he had asked the shaman for another glass of ayahuasca because he said that his first glass had produced no effect.

I now begin to realise that there is also a darker side to the spiritual dimension that I had accessed so positively. Felipe's expertise, acquired during a very long and sometimes perilous apprenticeship, has enabled him to guide me towards a spiritual ecstasy.

But he is unable to banish the demons that now pursue, torment, and threaten Alan. Alan's body is rigid with terror. I watch Felipe enter Alan's mind and suffer with him. At first, the more he prays and chants, the worse Alan's experiences become. Finally he calls Alan over to him and motions him to sit on the floor. For a very long time, he cradles Alan's head in his hands, blows smoke over him, metaphorically caresses him with his prayers and songs, and eventually quiets him.

'I felt as if he was right inside my head, comforting me, reassuring me, healing me.'

Many hours later, as Alan and I walk back to our own hut in the early dawn light, he describes to me what he has gone through.

'When I first saw the demons – they were like something out of a Hieronymus Bosch nightmare – I thought, no problem, I don't believe in demons anyway. I'll just open my eyes, return to reality, and they'll go away. But they didn't. Not only that, but everyone in the room became demons too, ears became sharp and elongated, snapping teeth menaced, fingernails grew into long talons.

'Except for you, Kate. Your face was beautiful. You had an aura of total peace around you like a shining light.'

I have not yet mentioned my own sublime experience to Alan.

Just before we leave the hut, Felipe asks, through Carol, if he can say a few words to me. He wants to give me a message. He looks at me with a piercing gaze.

'You are a very strong woman. You have a very strong spirit. I do not know what you do in your life, but I can see that you do too much. Your life is overfull, preoccupied.'

The soft, Spanish phrases rise and fall.

'But tell her,' he continues through Carol, 'that there is something in her life, something she does, that reaches thousands of people. I don't know what this something is, but tell her that God is blessing her work and will bless her all the days of her life.'

*

Some months after we returned home from Peru, Alan contracted cerebral malaria, which is usually fatal. The malarial parasites attacked his lungs and produced ARDS,

Acute Respiratory Distress Syndrome. For almost four weeks he lay in a cubicle in an intensive care ward, hooked up to life support machines, hovering between life and death. His doctor and the Zulu nurses who cared for him said that his subsequent recovery was a 'miracle'. Many of these nurses were devout Christians and attributed his miraculous recovery to the power of prayer.

I had mentioned Alan's critical state during one of my radio programmes and people all over South Africa had been praying for his recovery – not only Christians, but Muslims, Jews, Buddhists, Hindus – people of every religious persuasion, as well as those who belonged not to an organised religion, but had their own personal faith. Sometimes we forget just how much goodness there is in the world.

Some of the other nurses believed that Alan had only pulled through because of his indomitable spirit. They had seen many patients in a similar condition die.

But there was another, sharply different point of view. A friend of mine, a clinical psychologist who had herself visited Peru some years previously and whilst there had undergone a very deep and unusual spiritual experience, believed that when Felipe 'healed' Alan in the moonlit hut by the Amazon he had foreseen Alan's critical illness and 'cured' it in advance, using the same multi-dimensional powers of perception that enabled Felipe to pick up Alan's earlier pneumonia when he had first come into the hut.

One night during Alan's illness, when it seemed as if he wasn't going to pull through, I drove home from the hospital hardly able to see because of the tears streaming down my face. As I pulled into the driveway of our thatched house, I saw an owl sitting on top of the garage roof, with his wings slightly held out from his body and looking straight at me.

It was 'my' owl from Peru, the one I had seen that night in the hut by the Amazon. When I got out of my car he didn't fly away but stared at me. His huge yellow eyes transmitted a clear message. I knew then that my husband was not going to die.

Felipe also 'cured' Gordon's psoriasis. Gordon had told us of his hideous skin disease not long after we first met as a group. But it was not until we bathed in the medicinal hot springs of Agua Calientes that we had seen the full extent of his painful and disfiguring illness. His hands and face – all the visible parts of his body – were unscathed but the rest of his body was a mass of sores and scabs.

After Felipe had soothed Alan, he called Gordon over to him and said through Carol that he wished to heal him. He had not been told anything about any of us and Gordon's psoriasis was not evident. Nevertheless, Felipe knew instinctively that Gordon needed to be healed. He made Gordon take off his shirt and trousers and lie down on the floor in front of him. He whistled softly through his teeth when he saw the bare, ravaged body, and then prayed, sang, blew smoke and passed his hands softly over Gordon for a long time.

The next day Felipe came back with us on the canoe to Puerto Maldonado. He visited many of the small shops lining the dusty streets, disappeared into back alleys and collected all kinds of herbal ingredients to mix with the plants he had gathered in the jungle earlier that day. In the bus back to Puerto Maldonado airport, Felipe concocted, with much praying, smoke-blowing, shaking and stirring, a foul-smelling healing potion for Gordon to take back to California. He was not to use it before he got home.

I had an e-mail from Gordon on his return.

'I can't believe it! After twelve years of misery, my itching has stopped!'

I'm told that psoriasis can be caused as the result of a traumatic life event. Twelve years ago Gordon and Wilma had experienced just such an event.

'That night in the hut the shaman exorcised me,' wrote Gordon.

Gordon and Wilma, devout and committed Christians, are today convinced that Felipe rid them of their personal demons. Gordon has retired now, and together he and Wilma continue their ministry to the sick, terminally ill and grieving. And are two of the best 'hospital clowns' going!

Shamans have always known that ayahuasca is something sublime, divine, something special. A visionary plant that allows one to see and hear spirits, to access another dimension of consciousness, to clarify our lives and offer some meaning to them, ayahuasca is not to be taken lightly – literally or metaphorically. If it is taken out of context, for the wrong reasons, without the crucial concomitant chants, prayers and rituals, without the spiritual knowledge, power and experience of a true shaman, then it is nothing. The streets of Peru are filled with spiritual hustlers who hawk their suspect brews to anyone gullible enough to believe them.

I believe that my ayahuasca experience was the culmination of a spiritual journey that has been very many years in the making. That it was the culmination of a quest that I had hardly ever voiced, and had certainly not given any overt credence to. I believe now that I was guided to that moment, by what or whom I do not know. It doesn't matter.

I also believe that we all have a number of transcendent

experiences given to us, but that we overlook them, misinterpret them, deny them, because we live in a world that has lost its connection to the sacred.

But if you allow yourself to become aware that such an experience is possible, even if you do not go out actively searching for it, then I believe such an Everlasting Moment will come to you.

Maybe it already has.

If not, be aware, look for milestones and meanings, seek what is truth for you. Make your own spiritual connections.

I don't think it's an easy process. Sometimes the precious moment of revelation takes a lifetime to achieve – it took me over sixty years.

Gareth's Everlasting Moment occurred when, with his hand on Batian's shoulder, he heard his lion 'son' roar at the dawn for the first time. Dan, the Veiled Prophet, had to lose his sight before he could 'see', while Carol's moment came with the building of Willka T'ika, her place of sanctuary and harmony. For Indio it was the Sun Dance; for Michael, peyote. For Alan it was the realisation that the Everlasting Moment is family and generation, and for Will it was when he saw the old Aboriginal elder rise from the sea, 'reborn' into youth.

I wish you well on your spiritual journey and with *your* Everlasting Moment.

Postscript

Some months after I returned home from Peru, when the business of daily life had taken over and blunted the edge of my spiritual perceptions; when my children were blithely telling their friends that Dad and Mum went on a 'trip' in Peru; when I had recounted my spiritual experiences on my radio programme; when people believed me, sneered at me, listened thoughtfully or decided I had gone flaky; when I had been accused of going 'New Age', heretical, off-the-wall, satanic or slightly senile, something happened which reinforced everything that I had learned not only in Peru, but had also learned unknowingly during my entire life. That there is an extra dimension, a divinity, a cosmic consciousness – call it who or what you will – that can be accessed by those who actively seek it or keep an open mind.

Early one summer morning, when the doves were murmuring in the thatch and the grass was still wet with dew, I went out into my garden on the most mundane and unspiritual of all journeys – to hang out the washing.

I had just finished pegging all the wet clothes on to the clothesline when I suddenly had an overpowering feeling – so overpowering that I stopped dead in my tracks, stood still, and let the feeling engulf me. I felt enveloped in a warmth and beauty that I cannot now describe. I shouted out loud with joy as I stood in the midst of a tangible presence of peace, harmony and goodness.

Somebody or Something had just given me a cosmic hug.

If you would like more information on our special
journeys to Peru described by Kate Turkington in
There's More To Life Than Surface,
Please contact us at:

USA Fax/Tel: 415 665 4645
South Africa Fax/Tel: 021 685 7095
Peru Fax: 51 84 201181
Visit our web site www.travelperu.com
e-mail: info@travelperu.com